ANCIENT CHRISTIANITIES

ALSO BY PAULA FREDRIKSEN

*Augustine on Romans: Propositions from the Epistle to the Romans,
Unfinished Commentary on the Epistle to the Romans* (1982)

From Jesus to Christ: The Origins of the New Testament Images of Jesus
(1988; second edition, 2000)

*Jesus of Nazareth, King of the Jews: A Jewish Life and the Emergence of
Christianity* (1999)

Augustine and the Jews: A Christian Defense of Jews and Judaism (2010)

Sin: The Early History of an Idea (2012)

Paul: The Pagans' Apostle (2017)

When Christians Were Jews: The First Generation (2018)

ANCIENT CHRISTIANITIES

THE FIRST
FIVE HUNDRED YEARS

PAULA FREDRIKSEN

PRINCETON UNIVERSITY PRESS

PRINCETON & OXFORD

Published by Princeton University Press
41 William Street, Princeton, New Jersey 08540
99 Banbury Road, Oxford OX2 6JX

press.princeton.edu

All Rights Reserved

Library of Congress Cataloging-in-Publication Data

Names: Fredriksen, Paula, author.
Title: Ancient Christianities : the first five hundred years / Paula Fredriksen.
Description: 1. | Princeton : Princeton University Press, [2024] | Includes
    bibliographical references and index.
Identifiers: LCCN 2024012622 (print) | LCCN 2024012623 (ebook) | ISBN
    9780691157696 (hardback) | ISBN 9780691264974 (ebook)
Subjects: LCSH: Church history—Primitive and early church, ca. 30–600. |
    BISAC: RELIGION / Christianity / History | RELIGION / Ancient
Classification: LCC BR165 .F745 2024 (print) | LCC BR165 (ebook) | DDC
    270.1—dc23/eng/20240402
LC record available at https://lccn.loc.gov/2024012622
LC ebook record available at https://lccn.loc.gov/2024012623

British Library Cataloging-in-Publication Data is available

Editorial: Fred Appel and James Collier
Production Editorial: Nathan Carr
Text Design: Karl Spurzem
Jacket/Cover Design: Karl Spurzem
Production: Erin Suydam
Publicity: Kate Hensley and Charlotte Coyne

Jacket/Cover Credit: Mark Dunn / Alamy Stock Photo

This book has been composed in Arno Pro

Printed in the United States of America

10 9 8 7 6 5 4 3 2 1

For Oded Irshai, colleague *praeclarissimus*, in friendship.

The patina of the obvious that encrusts human actions:
this is the first and last enemy of the historian.

PETER BROWN, *RELIGION AND SOCIETY
IN THE AGE OF SAINT AUGUSTINE*

CONTENTS

PREFACE

This book tells the story of the origins and development of ancient Mediterranean Christianity up to the fifth century in the post-Roman West. It is easier to see when this story ends than when it begins.

How odd, the reader might think. The story obviously begins with Jesus and then passes to the apostles, thence to Paul. That is the implication of the order of the books in the modern New Testament: first the four Gospels, then the Acts of the Apostles, and then Paul's letters.

The New Testament, however, as a closed and stable collection of texts, is the product of the fourth century. Its twenty-seven writings represent but a small selection of the many gospels, letters, acts of apostles, and books of revelations that circulated in the years between the mid-first century (from which we have our earliest evidence, the letters of Paul) and the establishment of an imperial church in the course of the fourth. The impression of the origins and development of Christianity given in the New Testament is the construction of these later, fourth-century initiatives, a story retrospectively generated. If we use our peripheral vision, if we look to other noncanonical and paracanonical texts, if we consider the materials available through archaeology, and if we trace the lively interactions of all these data with the wider Mediterranean world in which they were embedded, a different, richer, and much less linear story emerges.

My goal is to introduce the reader to the complexities and ambiguities, the ironies and surprises, the twists and turns of this richer story. Rather than follow a temporal arc from Jesus to the late empire—a tale first told by Eusebius and repeated, with variations, by many modern textbooks on Christian origins—it is organized thematically. Each chapter surveys materials from these five centuries. This thematic presentation avoids the impression of linear development that a single temporal arc can convey.

The story of the evolution of Christianity—really, of Christianities—involves a large cast of characters, superhuman as well as human: not only theologians, bishops, and emperors, but also gods and demons, angels and magicians, astrologers and charismatic wonder-workers, idiosyncratic ascetics and aristocratic patrons and millenarian enthusiasts. All these played their part in the development of what began as and would always remain a vigorously variegated form of biblical religion.

This is a story of many different peoples, and many different gods. Ancient empire had accommodated many different gods as a matter of course. Gods and humans were conceived as forming family groups: peoples were linked by tradition and history to the gods that they worshiped. The people group—what we call "ethnicity"—was another expression of cultic identity, a people's worship of their own particular gods. In a world of so many peoples connected to so many gods, in a world where good government depended on good relations between heaven and earth and where public worship was a sort of civil defense, in a world where local gods presided over specific cities and where disregarding the honor of the gods risked sharp celestial reprisals, a practical religious pluralism had long prevailed. How, then, over the course of four centuries, did one particular god end up the focus of late Roman imperial law and piety?

Answering this question requires identifying some of the defining peculiarities of Jewish religious culture. Jews shared much with their pagan contemporaries. They too, saw their god as in a parental relationship with his people, their "father." They, too, conceived of cult as an ethnic designation, and ethnicity as a cultic designation. They too inherited customs and commitments, both religious and social, which they regarded as "ancestral traditions"—or, as Paul says, "the traditions of my fathers" (Galatians 1.14). And they, too, like their scriptures, acknowledged the existence, and thus the reality, of non-Jewish gods. They considered these other gods lesser or lower than Israel's god ("All the gods bow down to him," sang the Psalmist in Psalm 97.7). But in a world where any god was more powerful than any human, these other superhuman forces had to be treated with a certain caution. In the Greek translation of Exodus, Moses himself advised as much: "Do not revile the gods" (Exodus 22.28). Commenting on this passage, the Jewish philosopher Philo of Alexandria, a contemporary of Paul's, endorsed it, observing matter-of-factly that "reviling each other's gods always leads to war" (*Questions in Exodus* 2.5).

But the Jewish god was also different from other gods in some respects. In a culture where gods were often worshiped before their cult images—frequently depicted as idealized, out-sized, beautiful humans—the Jewish god had insisted on imageless worship. Neither his temple in Jerusalem nor the many Jewish assemblies ("synagogues") outside of the homeland held his divine image, a fact that pagan observers remarked on. And in a culture where the city's well-being depended on displays of respect and loyalty to local presiding deities, the Jewish god demanded that he be the sole recipient of his people's worship.

God's insistence on exclusive worship thus could cause complications for those Jews—the vast majority—who lived outside the land of Israel, and who had to deal with the gods of their cities of residence. Their general avoidance of civic cult occasioned some arch comment from pagan observers: both the Jews and their god, pagan critics complained, were antisocial. Indeed, said some, Jews were guilty of "atheism," that is, of not showing respect to the gods of the majority. One Alexandrian pagan, Apion, annoyed by Jewish residents pushing to be recognized as full citizens of that city, asked, "Why, if they are citizens, do they not worship the same gods as the Alexandrians?" (Josephus, *Against Apion* 2.65). If we remember the way that heaven and earth lined up over the ancient city, and the way that civic cult was a part of civil defense, we can see the reasonableness of Apion's question.

Some streams of prophecy, however, took this idea of exclusive Jewish worship even further. They universalized it. Texts that ultimately became part of the Jewish canon (like Isaiah, or Micah, or Zechariah) and those that did not (like Tobit, or 1 Enoch, or the Sibylline Oracles) looked forward to the day when normal time would end, when the gentile nations would destroy their cult images, disavow their own gods, and turn, too, to worship Israel's god alone. In the two centuries to either side of Jesus's and Paul's lifetime, we see an intensification of this type of prophecy about the coming of God's kingdom. Its scope enlarged. Its time frame shifted from "someday in the future" to "soon" to "*now*."

"Apocalypse" is the Greek word for "revelation." An "eschaton" is a final thing. *Apocalyptic eschatology* is the term that scholars use to describe this particular genre of end-time sensibility. Such prophecies expressed a baggy bundle of expectations, hopes, predictions, visions. They suggested ways to discern the signs of the times. Celestial and terrestrial anomalies—earthquake, eclipses, darkness at noon—might herald the approach of the End. The End might be preceded by a final battle between the forces of good and evil. Sometimes the apocalyptic battle is fought by legions of angels, sometimes led by a messiah, sometimes by an archangel, sometimes by God himself. Some traditions speak of an ingathering of the tribes of Israel, of the rebuilding or aggrandizement of Jerusalem's temple, of the resurrection of the dead and a final judgement of all humanity. Others speak of the transposition of the redeemed into the starry firmament. And these prophecies conclude with the conviction that the whole world—human and superhuman—will acknowledge the sovereignty of Israel's god. Jewish apocalyptic eschatology, in other words, broke antiquity's normal and normative bond between peoples and pantheons, between ethnicity and (what we call) "religion."

It is from this seedbed of Jewish apocalyptic expectation in the first century that the movement around Jesus of Nazareth bloomed and spread. Early in its formative period, Greek became its primary linguistic medium, the ancient city its social matrix. It is from these apocalyptic traditions that Paul and other apostles constructed their "good news," *evangelion* in Greek, which they brought to Jews—and, surprisingly, to non-Jews as well. Within four centuries of constant adjustment, reinterpretation, and change, this message would eventually reconfigure traditional relations between government and religion, between peoples and their gods, between heaven and earth.

When and how do these movements that formed around the memory and message of Jesus grow into something that is recognizably *not*

Judaism—indeed, that is occasionally even virulently opposed to Judaism? Where and why does such individuation begin? How does a message centered on the impending end-time redemption of Israel become a message centered on the idea of a stable, uniform, universal Roman church?

We begin with late Second Temple Judaism, the world of both Jesus and Paul. Chapter 1, "The Idea of Israel," tracks the ways that the gospel message developed and altered once the movement(s) spread out from Jerusalem into the wider Greco-Roman world. Some Jews were Christ followers, and some gentile Christ followers assumed Jewish practices; but the future lay with those gentile communities that disengaged, in various ways, from their Jewish heritage. And as different gentile communities evolved different theologies, so too did different social relations evolve between Christians and Jews. Ultimately, the church sponsored by Constantine would claim the title "Israel" for itself.

Chapter 2, "The Dilemmas of Diversity," explores these different theologies. Already audibly in the late first century, increasingly loudly in the second, diversity was repudiated, difference condemned as "heresy." Contesting communities each developed their own definitions of true Christianity. What began as intracommunal invective became, with Constantine, an indictment with real social consequences. Christian diversity, in the course of the fourth century, would be criminalized, actively suppressed by the Christian Roman state.

Empire could prosper, ancient people were convinced, only if heaven were happy. Proper religion went far toward maintaining good relations between heaven and earth. Chapter 3, "Martyrdom and Persecution," investigates the ways that this conviction led to Roman anti-Christian actions, both before Constantine and (perhaps surprisingly) even after. The memory of these actions, preserved and cultivated in the stories of the martyrs, came to serve as powerful vehicles for communicating idealizations of Christian identity.

Veneration of martyrs led to the development of the cult of the saints: joyous, even raucous celebrations around the tombs of the martyred dead in anticipation of life in the Kingdom of God. Chapter 4, "The Future of the End," surveys these millenarian enthusiasms, and the ways that bishops eventually channeled them. Ultimately, the Christian message of salvation, and proclamations about an end-time resurrection of the body, were broadcast through stories about heaven and hell.

What does it mean, for a god to have a "son"? And why would a theological question become, ultimately, a concern of the state? Chapter 5, "Christ and Empire," untangles the political, social, and intellectual complexities that led to controversies over the nature of Christ, and thus of God. The interventions of imperial government, far from settling these issues, only compounded them.

Chapter 6, "The Redemption of the Flesh," explores the ways that convictions about the end of time, and the experience of its delay, combined with ideas about the soul's relation to the body to produce not only novel Christian teachings—about sexuality, about asceticism, and about voluntary poverty—but also novel Christian behaviors. Men and women experimented with different kinds of spiritual achievement: lifetime virginity; celibate marriages; individual and communal forms of radical asceticism. The evidence of sermons and the canons of church councils, meanwhile, affords glimpses of the conduct of "the silent majority."

When and why is the word and the concept "pagan" invented? When is ritual expertise a sacrament; when is it "magic"? What makes an amulet un-Christian, a saint's relic Christian? Why does the notional heart of the empire, the city of Rome, become the premier Christian capital of the West? What beliefs and behaviors, in short, give the measure of "Christianization"? Chapter 7, "Pagan and Christian," considers all these questions. In the end, Christianity offered not an alternative to traditional Mediterranean Roman culture but, finally, an expression of it.

Each chapter treats the evidence originating in the first century as inflections of late Second Temple Judaism. What we think of as "Christianity" began to emerge, in different ways and in different places, only in the late first and early second centuries, as the ethnicity of the movements' members began to shift from predominantly Jewish to predominantly gentile.

To trace these developments, we begin where Jesus and Paul began: with the idea of Israel.

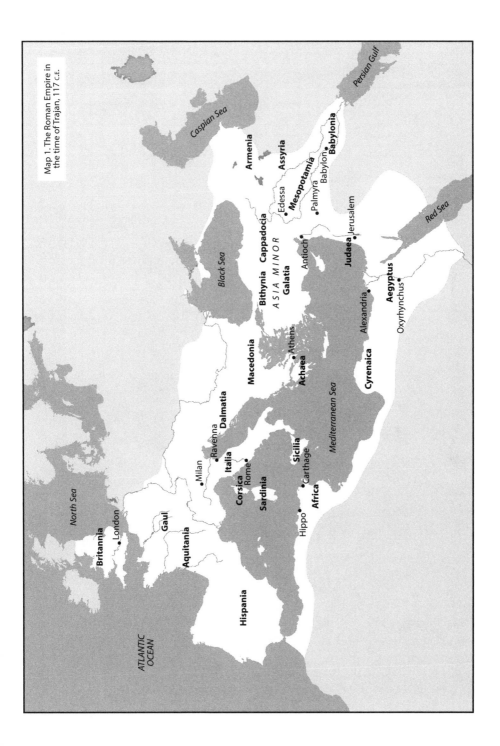

Map 1. The Roman Empire in the time of Trajan, 117 C.E.

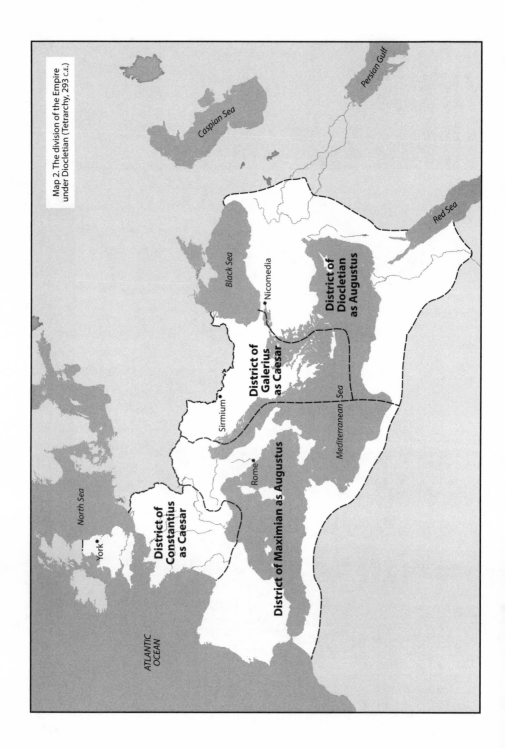

Map 2. The division of the Empire under Diocletian (Tetrarchy, 293 C.E.)

Persian Gulf

Caspian Sea

Red Sea

Black Sea

Nicomedia

District of Diocletian as Augustus

District of Galerius as Caesar

Sirmium

Mediterranean Sea

North Sea

York

District of Constantius as Caesar

Rome

District of Maximian as Augustus

ATLANTIC OCEAN

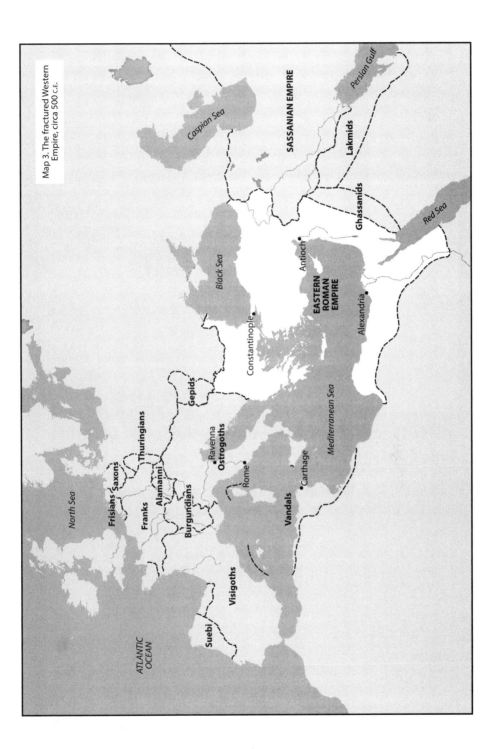

Map 3. The fractured Western Empire, circa 500 C.E.

SASSANIAN EMPIRE

Persian Gulf

Lakmids

Caspian Sea

Ghassanids

Red Sea

Black Sea

Antioch

EASTERN ROMAN EMPIRE

Alexandria

Constantinople

Mediterranean Sea

Gepids

Ravenna
Ostrogoths

Rome

Carthage

Vandals

Thuringians

Saxons
Frisians

Alamanni

Franks

Burgundians

North Sea

Visigoths

Suebi

ATLANTIC OCEAN

ANCIENT CHRISTIANITIES

1

THE IDEA OF ISRAEL

My brothers, my kinsmen by flesh—they are Israelites.

PAUL, ROMANS 9.3–4

Israel is a race of souls, and Jerusalem is a city in Heaven.

ORIGEN, ON FIRST PRINCIPLES 4.3.8

How did a Jewish message of a Jewishly conceived end of time—a coming messiah, the resurrection of the dead, the defeat of pagan gods, the ingathering of Israel, the turning of the nations to Israel's god—spill over to pagan auditors? How, after the apostolic generation, did this message shift, grow, and change into what would eventually become gentile Christianities? And how did such a Jewish message finally transmute into anti-Jewish theologies? To answer these questions, we first need to orient ourselves within two worlds: that of the Roman Mediterranean, and that of the Jews who lived within it. Late Second Temple Judaism was the seedbed from which all later Christianities sprang.

+ + +

The Second Temple Matrix

"The times are fulfilled, and the Kingdom of God is at hand. Repent, and trust the good news!" Thus the message of Jesus of Nazareth, according to the late first-century Gospel of Mark (1.15). So too, according to Matthew, the proclamation of Jesus's predecessor, John the Baptizer (Matthew 3.2). So, too, in the mid-first century, Paul's message to an assembly in Rome: "Salvation is nearer to us than when we first believed. The night is far gone; the day is at hand" (Romans 13.12).

What did their auditors need to do to prepare for this end-time event? All three men called for repentance. But they issued this call to different audiences. John and Jesus proclaimed their message to fellow Jews in Judea and the Galilee; Paul, to non-Jews, in the cities of the eastern Mediterranean. Preparing for the Kingdom—and coming judgement—entailed repentance. John's and Jesus's hearers had to repent of Jewish sins. Paul's hearers had to repent of pagan sins.

"Repentance," accordingly, in light of these different audiences, was also configured differently. John and Jesus, in the late 20s and early 30s of the first century, seem to have called fellow Jews to rededicate themselves to their interpretation of the Ten Commandments—thus, to Jewish ancestral custom. In Mark 10.18–19, for example, Jesus recites these commandments; in Mark 12.28–31, he synopsizes them. The Ten Commandments stood at the core of the Sinai covenant (Exodus 20.2–17; cf. Deuteronomy 5.6–21). In biblical narrative, they were directed to Israel.

But Paul saw himself as preeminently a messenger to non-Jews—*ta ethnē*, as he calls them. This Greek word, which translates the Hebrew *goyim*, can come into English in several different ways. One way is as "nations," which number can include Israel. (Humanity after the flood was divided into seventy different goyim/*ethnē*, Genesis 10.) More commonly in Jewish literature, however, the word refers to non-Jewish nations—the vast majority of humankind—as distinguished from Israel. Here English has two translation choices: "gentile," and "pagan."

"Gentile" is a religion-neutral term, simply indicating non-Jewish ethnicity. But in the first century there was no such thing as a religion-neutral ethnicity: people groups were defined in part by the gods they worshiped. By definition, a non-Jew worshiped non-Jewish gods.

For this reason, "pagan" might serve as the preferred translation for *ethnē*. The term "pagan" itself is a fourth-century Christian term of derogation, meant to distinguish Christian gentiles from non-Christian ones. But Paul's non-Jewish contemporaries were not religiously neutral: they worshiped their own gods, often through cult to their images. "You turned to God from idols," Paul reminds his assembly in Thessalonica (1 Thessalonians 1.9). "You were led astray to dumb idols," he reminds the Corinthians (1 Corinthians 12.2). "Formerly, when you did not know God," he reminds Galatian assemblies, "you were enslaved to beings that are not by nature gods" (Galatians 4.8). Paul's auditors, in brief, were "pagans."

Paul was able to reach pagans because Jews were so well integrated into Greco-Roman culture.

Israel among the Nations

In early Roman antiquity, it seems, Jews were everywhere. Josephus, a Jewish historian who lived one generation after Paul, reports that the geographer Strabo claimed: "This people has made its way into every city, and it is not easy to find any place in the habitable world that has not received [them]" (*Antiquities* 14.115). Josephus's near contemporary, the author of the New Testament's Acts of the Apostles, filled in some detail. Among the Jews gathered in Jerusalem for the next pilgrimage holiday, Shavuot (Greek "Pentecost"), Luke says, were those hailing from Parthia, Persia, Mesopotamia, Cappadocia, Pontus and Asia and Phrygia and Pamphylia and Egypt, Libya, Rome, Crete, and Arabia (Acts 2.9–11)—which is to say, from present-day Turkey, the area around the Black Sea, Babylonia and western Persia, and the eastern rim of the Mediterranean. This population also settled as well in the Mediterranean islands, the western areas of North Africa, the Iberian and Italian Peninsulas, and in what would one day be France.

We habitually use the word "Diaspora" to identify this population; but for the Mediterranean regions, the term is somewhat misleading. It draws on the idea of involuntary exile: in the Bible, this concept comes especially coupled with the consequences of the Babylonian conquest of Jerusalem in 586 BCE, and the destruction of the first temple, built by Solomon. "Diaspora" is the Greek word for "dispersion," that is, to be scattered, forced to leave the land of Israel, to settle "by the waters of Babylon." "Diaspora" is melancholy displacement.

A different experience, however, stood behind the bulk of this western Jewish population. For the most part, centuries before the Roman destruction of Jerusalem and of its temple in 70 CE, these Jews had resettled voluntarily. They were pulled by the wider world created by Alexander the Great (d. 323 BCE) and, later, by Rome. War builds empires, but peace sustains them. The empires of Alexander and especially of Rome established a new stability, one that enabled and even sponsored the internal migrations of populations. As other peoples relocated, so too did Jews.

Like other peoples conquered by Alexander, Jews adopted Greek as their vernacular. They settled into their new cities and their new culture. Inscriptions bespeak the presence of Jews in pagan educational institutions such as the *gymnasium*, dedicated to the gods Heracles (brawn) and Hermes (brain). Jews showed up in pagan civic structures like theaters (whose performances were dedicated to the gods and given on pagan festal days), and in civic organizations (like city councils, convened by invoking city gods). Jews served in foreign armies. They competed in athletic games (also—like the Olympics—dedicated to non-Jewish gods). They performed as mimes and as actors in the theater. They took Greek names.

Literary evidence reveals the ease with which Jewish elites found their way into the pagan gymnasium, where they learned control of the classical curriculum. Educated Hellenistic Jews literally wrote themselves into pagan culture. One text, *Aristeas*, portrayed a Ptolemaic king so eager for Jewish wisdom that he commissioned the translation of Jewish scriptures into Greek. Another Hellenistic Jewish author attributed the source of the alphabet to Moses; another claimed that Moses taught music to Orpheus. Josephus relates a story of Alexander the Great's coming to Jerusalem, worshiping in the temple, and inviting

Jerusalemite Jews to enlist in his army (*Antiquities* 11.329–39). The point to note is the degree to which Greek-speaking Jews made Greek culture and, for intellectual elites, especially Greek philosophical culture, their own. One pagan philosopher, Numenius, finally famously asked, "What is Plato but Moses speaking Greek?"

Most momentously, beginning sometime in the third century BCE in Alexandria, God himself began to "speak" Greek. The Greek translation of Jewish scriptures, often referred to collectively as the "Septuagint" (LXX), did more than introduce new terms and concepts into the Jews' ancestral writings. Crucially for the development of later Christianity, the Bible in Greek made Jewish traditions available to an ethnically broader audience.

How did Jewish traditions in Greek reach non-Jewish auditors? Jewish immigrant groups abroad organized themselves into assemblies (called "prayer houses" or "colleges" or "synagogues"). These assemblies or associations had many functions: discerning the Jewish calendar; collecting monies to be sent back to the temple in Jerusalem; preserving local records. Jews might gather in community one day out of every seven to hear ancestral traditions read or recited aloud and discussed in Greek. And—crucially, for the later Christian movements—interested pagans might also be among those listening.

Jewish communities welcomed the interest of sympathetic outsiders. Sources both literary and epigraphic (that is, from inscriptions) occasionally refer to such people as "God-fearers." These non-Jews were not "converts." Rather, they were pagans, actively engaged with their own gods, who evinced interest in—and showed respect to—the god of Israel as well. Philo, an elder contemporary of Jesus and of Paul, mentions an annual meal in Alexandria celebrating the translation of Jewish texts into Greek, attended by both Jews and pagans (*Life of Moses* 2.41). One generation later, Josephus speaks of pagan votives and of pagan pilgrimage to Jerusalem's temple, where non-Jews could be received in the largest courtyard of Herod's magnificent building (*Jewish War* 5.190–94; *Antiquities* 15.417; *Against Apion* 2.103). Josephus also comments that the observance of (some) Jewish practices ("Judaizing") had spread among pagan populations, especially women (*War* 2.561; *Against Apion* 2.282).

Complaints about pagan Judaizing—of pagans acting like Jews—stand in pagan sources as well: Epictetus, Juvenal, and Tacitus all comment sourly on the phenomenon. Some outsiders adopted the one-day-out-of-seven weekend. Others avoided eating pork.

Inscriptions from Asia Minor (modern Turkey) and elsewhere note pagan patronage of various Jewish structures and communities. One first-century aristocratic Roman lady, Julia Severa, who was a priestess in the imperial cult, built a place of assembly for Acmonia's Jews. Two centuries later, Capitolina, another pagan lady, refurbished a synagogue interior: her donor inscription identifies her as a "God-fearer"—again, a pagan who took an active interest in things Jewish. (Capitolina's husband was a senator and a priest of Zeus.) A Jewish inscription from Aphrodisias from the fourth or fifth century indexes donors by affiliation: born Jews, voluntary Jews (converts, *proselytoi*), and "God-fearers" (non-Jewish sympathizers, still pagan), nine of whom were members of the town council.

Added to this we have the literary evidence of both pagan and, eventually, Christian writers who complain about other gentiles (both pagan and Christian) who maintained an interest in things Jewish: celebrating Jewish holidays, taking vows in synagogues, observing Easter according to the Jewish calendar for Passover. In other words, if we find Jews in pagan places doing pagan things—and we do—we also find pagans (and, later, gentile Christians) in Jewish places doing Jewish things. Community boundaries were porous. Just as the larger Greco-Roman city was a site of broad pagan-Jewish interaction, so too was the urban Jewish assembly, the "synagogue." The extraordinarily wide spread of established Jewish communities outside of the homeland ensured an equally wide spread of outsider audiences, throughout the Mediterranean, for Jewish traditions. These would provide the seedbed for later Christian movements.

The Spread of the Gospel

What is the Kingdom of God? It was an idea that represented a collocation of hopes and expectations that arose out of Jewish prophecy. Its core message was redemption. The Kingdom would bring the culmination of history, a time when God would wipe away every tear. According to some traditions, the forces of good—sometimes led by battling angels; sometimes led by a messiah—would overcome the forces of evil. Those Israelites who had been swallowed up by centuries of conquest would be reassembled, so that Israel would again have all its tribes. The dead would be raised. All would be judged; the wicked punished, the good vindicated. And the gentile nations would cease worshipping their own gods and be gathered along with Israel to worship Israel's god.

Judea in the late Second Temple period, Josephus tells us, saw many popular movements formed around charismatic leaders who were predicting God's coming Kingdom. Many of these leaders—Theudas; the "Egyptian"; a Samaritan prophet; the "signs prophets"—together with their followers, were cut down by Rome. Jesus, who was himself hailed as messiah, met a similar fate in Jerusalem. But uniquely among these popular movements, Jesus's followers were convinced that Jesus had been raised from the dead. This conviction served to confirm his message of the coming Kingdom. The resurrection of the dead was a signature miracle expected at the end-time, one that Jesus had emphasized in his own teaching. If Jesus had been raised, then the Kingdom, his followers reasoned, truly must be at hand.

Their experience of Jesus raised explains two other odd facts about the original community. The first is that Jesus's followers did not hesitate to settle in Jerusalem, despite his recent execution there, despite Pilate's regular reappearances there (he was governor until the year 36), and despite the constant presence of the priests (named in the Gospels as Pilate's collaborators). This community's commitment to the city indirectly indicates their apocalyptic convictions: in Jewish end-time traditions, Jerusalem stood as the terrestrial epicenter of the Kingdom.

Their experience of Jesus's resurrection, for this community, tipped time into a new phase. They lived in a spiritually radioactive zone between the risen Christ's private revelation to a few insiders—some five hundred people, says Paul (1 Corinthians 15.3)—and his imminent, public, cosmic Second Coming. The returning Christ would then confront and defeat pagan gods, redeem both the living and the dead, and establish God's kingdom (e.g., Philippians 2.10–11; 1 Corinthians 15.20–58; Romans 1.4). According to the New Testament's Acts of the Apostles, this community continued to proclaim Jesus's message of the impending Kingdom from the very courts of the temple itself.

Within a few years of their consolidation in Jerusalem, however, some members of this community took their message out on the road. Leaving behind their old territorial ambit in Judea and the Galilee, they struck out for the great coastal cities, Joppa and Caesarea; thence, further abroad, to Damascus and to Antioch. There, traveling through the network of diaspora synagogue communities webbing the eastern Mediterranean, they encountered a social reality that their earlier work in the villages of rural Galilee and Judea had not prepared them for: they met pagan God-fearers who were involved in the life of the synagogue. And these pagans, too, responded positively to the gospel message. This explains the second odd fact about this movement: soon after Jesus's death, his message of the coming Kingdom reached pagans as well.

Acts, an early second-century text, narrates a dramatic story about this moment. It stars the God-fearer Cornelius "who feared God with all his household, gave alms liberally, and prayed constantly" (Acts 10.2). As a Roman officer, Cornelius (fictive or not) would also have been a pagan. Peter hesitates to deal with him, and it takes a lot of visions and angelic prompting to move the story along. Luke's apostle also says that it is "unlawful for a Jew to associate with or to visit anyone of another nation" (Acts 10.28). This is nonsense, as we have just seen: Jews routinely associated with pagans—unclothed in the baths, in athletic competitions, in the gymnasium; clothed, in professional associations, in town councils, in the temple courtyard, and not least, in Jewish diaspora assemblies. And Acts elsewhere presents (pagan) God-fearers as a regular part of diaspora synagogue populations. Luke presumably gave Peter this line in Acts 10 for dramatic effect. We should not confuse it with historical description.

It was in the Diaspora, most likely in Damascus, that members of this movement first encountered Paul the Pharisee. Paul is the individual who, in his lifetime and certainly thereafter, would do more than any other figure to promote the spread of the gospel to non-Jewish listeners. Initially resisting this movement and trying to halt it, Paul abruptly changed from adversary to apostle when he, too, had a vision of the risen Christ. His experience proved to be a hinge of history. From that moment on, Paul was himself a committed champion of the gospel mes-sage. But he deliberately broadened his audience. Paul proclaimed the coming Kingdom to non-Jews.

Paul's letters, written mid-first century, implicitly confirm what early second-century Acts repeatedly portrays: the already Judaized pagans of the diaspora synagogue provided the most likely non-Jewish population that would respond to the gospel message—or even understand it. "Messiah," "David," "Abraham," "the Law," "the writings," "the prophets," "resurrection," "Kingdom"—and for that matter, God the Father, the god of Israel—Paul fires off these terms in his epistles. They are invoked with the presumption of understanding and presuppose a fair degree of "biblical literacy," that is, at least aural familiarity, with these elements of Jewish tradition.

The Jewish scriptures in Greek, through the social matrix of the di-aspora synagogue, thus enabled the spread of the gospel to the ethnē. And Paul taught to these already Judaized pagans a yet more radically Judaizing message: these God-fearers would have to abandon their do-mestic and civic deities, he urged, if they would be adopted, via Christ, into the family of Abraham, thus becoming heirs together with Jews to God's promises of redemption. In order to be received into the approach-ing Kingdom, insisted Paul, these non-Jews had to make an exclusive commitment to the Jewish god. These pagans listened.

What accounts for the appeal of the gospel? What persuaded listen-ers, whether Jews or gentiles, to trust in the good news of the coming Kingdom? Its message of eternal life, released from sin, certainly played a role. And in the meanwhile, members of the movement, according to Paul, received divine spirit, empowering them to prophesy, to work miracles and cures, to speak in the language of angels and also to inter-pret it, and to discern between good spirits and bad. The later Gospels, written at least a generation or two after Paul's lifetime, also depict Jesus as prophesizing, controlling demons and "unclean spirits," curing the ill, raising the dead, and interpreting scripture, abilities that Jesus confers on his traveling apostles. The spirit empowered both this movement's spokesmen and its hearers—another sign that redemption approached. "And it shall be in the last days," proclaimed the prophet Joel, quoted in

Acts, "that I will pour out my spirit upon all flesh, and your sons and your daughters shall prophesy" (Joel 2.28; Acts 2.17).

But this active pagan (or ex-pagan) interest in the gospel message created an internal problem for this new Jewish movement. On the evidence, Jesus had left no instructions for such an eventuality. The audiences for his teaching, according to the gospel accounts, were overwhelmingly Jewish. Arguments about *whether* to circumcise, which roil some of Paul's letters, could be relevant only to non-Jews. The fact that the question stirred controversy strongly implies that no "gentile policy" had ever been originally in place. The inclusive prophetic paradigm of Jewish scriptures, however, of Isaiah in particular, had proclaimed that, at the end of days, the pagan nations would renounce their idols and worship God alone. *Two* ethnic populations were thus anticipated in the Kingdom: not only Israel, restored to the Davidic plenum of twelve tribes, but also the nations, who according to these prophecies will have renounced their native worship for exclusive allegiance to Israel's god.

Christ-following non-Jews, on the evidence of Paul's letters, evidently committed to this allegiance. Their new behavior in turn validated this first-century movement's message: if pagans abandoned their own gods, then surely the Kingdom was dawning. These people were still *not* Jews—no circumcision for male ex-pagans. But they were no longer, in our terms, "pagans" either. They were not religiously neutral: their new allegiance was quite specifically to Israel's god through his messiah. Who or what were they then? They were *eschatological* gentiles, end-time others: non-Jews who had renounced their gods for Israel's god in anticipation of the coming Kingdom.

As such, these eschatological gentiles represented a social anomaly. They were turning their backs to gods that were theirs by birth. Their nonparticipation in civic cult and culture thus occasioned pushback from pagan neighbors, worried that the gods, alienated by this lack of respect, would strike back in anger at the city. Diaspora synagogues, too, were occasionally less than welcoming: alienating the pagan majority in their cities of residence put synagogue communities at risk. Angry pagan mobs, anxious synagogue authorities, Roman magistrates working to keep the peace: Paul complains about his interactions with all these people (2 Corinthians 11.24–27). And he also complains about active resistance on the part of pagan gods (2 Corinthians 4.4). But he—as his apostolic competitors—pressed on, convinced of history's impending happy resolution.

At a crescendo in his final letter, Romans, Paul invokes the full scope of this final redemption. Attempting to explain why, midcentury, the demography of the movement seemed weighted toward gentiles, he ventured an elaborate reinterpretation of apocalyptic prophecy. The gospel had indeed first come to Jews, he said. Then it had gone to gentiles. Then God had deliberately rendered much of Israel insensible to the message, so that Paul and other Jews like him would have more time to reach more gentiles. Only after the "fullness of the nations" was attained would God unblock Israel's ears. "Behold, I tell you a mystery," Paul concludes. Israel's partial insensibility was only a temporary measure. Ultimately "all Israel will be secured" (NRSV "saved"; Romans 11.25–26).

The "fullness of the nations" in Jewish tradition refers to the plenum of seventy nations descended from Noah, as described in Genesis 10. "All Israel" means the Davidic kingdom, the twelve tribes—which is appropriate, since Jesus himself, claims Paul, is the Davidic messiah (Romans 1.3; 15.12). Ultimately the "fullness" of Israel, he asserts, will receive the gospel as well (11.12). The current "remnant, chosen as a gift" (11.5) are those "Israelites," "God's people," with whom Paul agrees, and who agree with Paul—the same group that he elsewhere calls "the Israel of God" (Galatians 6.16). This current remnant is the down payment on the redemption of the whole: God does not break his promises (Romans 11.29; 15.8). The mystery of redemption concealed in prophetic writings has "now" been revealed, Paul proclaims, mid-first century. The final events, he insisted, will take place "soon" (13.11; 16.26, 20).

Jews and Jesus

In the mid-first century, Paul and his colleagues, propelled by their apocalyptic convictions, taught a radical form of Judaizing to ethnic others, a kind of Judaism for gentiles. Despite the social difficulties that their message occasioned, they pressed on, convinced by their very success among (ex) pagans that the Kingdom was indeed at hand. And they argued loudly with each other about the correct interpretation of Jesus's message—arguments that shape both Paul's letters and the later Gospels.

By the early second century, however, gentile forms of Christianity begin to dominate our sources. How this transition occurred is still a mystery. From the first, Jewish generation of the movement we have no word other than Paul's few midcentury letters. We have no writings from the original Aramaic-speaking base; no record, preserved in the New Testament canon, of what ultimately became of Christ's original Jewish followers in Jerusalem. Presumably the Roman destruction of the city in 70 CE swept away the founding community there, whether through death, through captivity, or through forced migration. The fourth-century bishop and historian Eusebius relates that it fled to Edessa in Syria before the destruction, and eventually returned to Jerusalem. His story seems to be motivated, however, by his desire to construct an unbroken line of episcopal succession from the apostles to his own day (*Church History* 3.5.3; 4.5.2). In fact, we do not know the fate of this original group.

What of Jewish Christ followers in the Galilee? Again, we have no original writings from them. If they were living as Jews among Jews—why would they not?—they would be virtually invisible in our evidence, such as it is. Archaeological data are reticent: a room dedicated to special use might suggest the presence of Jewish Christ followers in Capernaum, perhaps as early as the late first century. And such Christ followers might very well have continued to frequent regular synagogues—again, why would they not? Jesus himself had done so. The invisibility of Christ-following Jews in our Galilean evidence is perhaps what we should expect.

What about outsider reports on such people? Non-Christian literary sources from this region, in Hebrew, are relatively late. The earliest, the Mishnah, a body of rabbinic traditions, was not edited until circa 200. It might provide us with glimpses of contemporary Christ-following Galilean Jews.

At issue is the interpretation of the rabbinic terms *min/minim/minut*. Often translated as "heretic/heretics/heresy," the word means "type" or "sort." A rabbinic text redacted (probably) in the mid-third century mentions a *birkat ha-minim*, a "benediction against Those Other Jews." Within a liturgical sequence to be said in daily prayer, this text pronounces a malediction on Not-us, that is, on "them," the minim. May they be unrooted (that is, by God). Some scholars—triangulating between the late first-century Gospel of John, which speaks of Jewish Christ followers being put out of the synagogue (John 9.22; 12.42; 16.2); Justin Martyr's *Dialogue with Trypho* (a mid-second-century gentile Christian text), which claims that "you Jews" curse "us" (gentile Christians) in the synagogue; and the mid-third-century Galilean birkat ha-minim—conclude that John and Justin attest to earlier social fact. The rabbinic minim, in this interpretation, were Christian Jews.

One problem with this conjecture, however, besides the vagueness of the Hebrew term *minim* itself, is the mechanism of the malediction, which would rely on *self*-exclusion. The Jewish Christ-following male would have to recite the prayer in the synagogue, discern that it referred to himself and to his group, and then presumably walk away. Self-exclusion is not being "cast out." And we cannot say with any confidence that Christ-following Jews were the intended objects of this malediction: the profile of the minim is very hard to make out. All we can say with assurance is that the rabbis were drawing distinctions between their type(s) of Jewishness and the type of some other group(s).

This was scarcely unusual. Intra-Jewish argument about the right way to be Jewish is a standard feature of Jewish texts, one rooted in the biblical story itself. From Exodus to Deuteronomy, Moses complains about and corrects his people. The prophets exhort, scold, and warn; Ezra and Nehemiah enact sweeping reforms. Much later, in the period of the Maccabees (160s BCE), Jewish diversity of practice in Judea eventuated as much in civil war between Jews over acceptable ways to be Jewish as in revolt against pagan Syrian Greeks. In Jesus's period, Philo of Alexandria criticized other Alexandrian Jews whose interpretation of the commandments to observe circumcision, Sabbath, and festivals differed from his own (*Migration of Abraham* 89–93). Spiritual understanding, said these people, was sufficient to fulfill the commandment. Philo heatedly disagreed. The Dead Sea Scrolls famously reviled unaffiliated Jewish outsiders, and particularly the Jerusalem priesthood. "There was in Judaism a factor which caused sects to begin," commented a later Christian teacher, Origen, "which was the variety of the interpretations of the writings of Moses and the sayings of the prophets" (*Against Celsus* 3.12).

Mid-first century, Paul railed against his circumcising competitors within the movement, though he acknowledges that they, too, are also, like him, Hebrews, Israelites, and descendants of Abraham (2 Corinthians 11.22). A generation or two later, the Gospels present Jesus as arguing with all comers—scribes, Pharisees, Sadducees, priests. John's Jesus reviles other Jews throughout that gospel ("You are of your father, the devil," John 8.44). John of Patmos—writing, perhaps, in the period of the first Jewish revolt (66–73 CE)—condemns those who "say they are Jews and are not." These false Jews, he says, belong to "the synagogue of Satan" (Revelation 2.9). All these intra-Jewish texts would have a long afterlife in the echo chambers of later gentile Christianities.

Perhaps the most consequential instance of intra-Jewish argument presented by the Gospels occurs in the Passion narratives, which date to the period after the Roman destruction of Jerusalem in 70 CE. These stories shift the responsibility for Jesus's death from Pilate—the only authority, historically, who could have ordered a crucifixion—to the chief priest, Caiaphas, to the priestly council, and eventually to the population of Jerusalem as a whole. In the "seen-together" or synoptic tradition (Mark, Matthew, and Luke), antagonism between Jesus and the priests develops once Jesus is in Jerusalem and causes a scene in the outermost court of the temple precincts, overturning the tables of the money changers. But the same tradition also reports that Jesus was so popular with Jerusalem's Passover crowds that the priests had to arrange his arrest by night, in order to avoid tumult (Mark 14.1–2). The gospels nowhere resolve this paradoxical presentation. In John's gospel, the priests' motivation is practical and political: they want to avoid confrontation with Rome. The reason they fear such, however, is unlikely: they worry that Jesus's abilities to perform "signs" (like raising Lazarus from the dead) would trigger Rome's negative attentions (John 11.47–48).

However we parse these post-70 traditions, they do seem to attest to three historically plausible events: Jesus's popularity, Pilate's intervention, and priestly cooperation with Pilate. Had Jesus *not* been popular with the restive holiday crowd, Pilate would have had no reason to move against him: Jesus could have been safely ignored. And given the priests' familiarity with Jerusalem, they could very well have cooperated with Pilate, to head off further Roman reprisals against those gathered in the city for Passover. Paul's puzzling statement in 1 Thessalonians 2.15 condemning those Jews "who killed both the lord Jesus and the prophets," may support this conjecture.

As these Passion traditions grow and develop, however, priestly agency becomes ever more pronounced as Rome's diminishes. Pilate as a narrative character waxes increasingly sympathetic—washing his hands of Jesus's blood in Matthew's gospel (Matthew 27.24), protesting that Jesus is innocent of any crime in John's (John 18.38). Matthew's Jesus indeed accuses Jews of murdering the historical prophets (Matthew 23.30–36), a bloody behavior that will crest, in Matthew's story, with Jesus himself. Luke's Pilate forthrightly declares Jesus's innocence three times (Luke 23.4, 14, 22: at issue is a false charge of sedition). John's Jesus, speaking with Pilate, is even more forthright: "He who delivered me to you"—that is, Jerusalem's chief priest—"has the greater sin" (John 19.11). In John's Passion narrative, the Jews seem to do the crucifying themselves (19.16, though in 19.23, the soldiers reappear).

Matthew's chilling malediction, "His blood be upon us and upon our children!" (Matthew 27.25), is backlit by the fires of Jerusalem in 70. Jesus's contemporaries and their children had constituted the two generations present in Jerusalem during Rome's destruction of the temple and the city. The city's fall, in Matthew's view, had been their punishment. This passage in his gospel, written well after the city's downfall, was essentially a prophecy about the past.

Acts extends responsibility for Jesus's death to include Jews who were not present in Jerusalem at Passover: Luke's Peter, speaking to a crowd of pilgrims gathered for the next major holiday, Shavuot ("Pentecost" in Greek, observed fifty days after Passover), accuses them too of crucifying Jesus (Acts 2.22–23, 36). Again, these stories relate *intra*-Jewish arguments, not *anti*-Jewish ones. Matthew's own community seems to be both Jewish and Law observant. Acts presents a Law-observant Paul who worships in the temple (Acts 23.26) and depicts an apostolic council that requires ex-pagan affiliates to keep some version of kosher food laws (Acts 15.20). These authors, writing in Greek, could very well represent communities of Jewish Christ followers.

Later gentile Christian interpretations, however, will turn Jewish involvement in Jesus's death into a standing intergenerational indictment. Not only are all subsequent Jewish generations punished for Jesus's death, say these later traditions: they are actually personally guilty. Not only are Jews guilty of Jesus's death "in the background," as the Gospels depict: in later traditions—the *Gospel of Peter*; Melito of Sardis's sermon *On Passover*; in book three of Irenaeus's *Against Heresies*—the Jews are presented as themselves the agents of Jesus's crucifixion, displacing the Romans as Jesus's executioners. Noncanonical texts—*The Ascension of Isaiah*, *The Apocalypse of Peter*, *The Testament of Levi*, the Christian recensions of the *Sibylline Oracles*—all inculpate Jews. A fourth-century priest in Antioch, John Chrysostom, frustrated that members of his congregation continued to celebrate Jewish fasts and feasts, to frequent synagogue assemblies, and to avail themselves of Jewish healers, will heatedly exclaim, "Is it not folly for those who worship the Crucified to celebrate festivals with those who crucified him?" (*Against the Judaizers* 1.5). This toxic charge of universal transgenerational guilt for the death of Christ continued to mark Christian theology through the midtwentieth century. It was renounced by the Catholic Church only in 1965, with *Nostra Aetate*.

Who Is Israel?

In the second and third centuries, gentile Christians will look to Judea's catastrophic revolts against Rome—in 66–73 CE and again, under Bar Kokhba, in 132–35—and see the punishing hand of God. Bereft of their temple, driven from their land, said these authors, Jews were in a perpetual second exile because of their role in Jesus's death. A cascade of later Christian theologians repeats this idea. "These things have happened to you in fairness and justice," Justin explains to his Jewish interlocutor Trypho, "for you have slain the Just One, and his prophets before him" (*Trypho* 16, ca. 150). "Rome would never have dominated Judea," Tertullian asserts, in a writing ostensibly addressed to Roman magistrates, "if she had not transgressed in the utmost against Christ" (*Apology* 26.3, ca. 200). The Jews' greatest sin of all time, comments Origen a generation later, was their killing of Jesus. After that, God abandoned them entirely (*Against Celsus* 4.32, ca. 240). Meanwhile, Pilate continued his development as an appealing figure. "In his secret heart already a Christian," Tertullian writes, Pilate reported the whole story about Christ to another sympathetic Roman, the emperor Tiberius (*Apology* 21.24). Eventually, Pilate would become a saint in the Ethiopic Church.

Accusations of Jerusalemite agency behind the crucifixion had served the evangelists as a way to explain and to justify why God had permitted his temple to be destroyed: those representatives of the temple, Jerusalem's priests, had rightly been judged. Later Christian writers regarded the Roman destruction of Jerusalem in 70 CE through the lens of the Babylonian conquest in 586 BCE, when the first temple had been destroyed and Judaeans indeed forced into exile. The memory of that catastrophe was hardwired in Jewish scriptures, especially in the writings of the prophets.

As with Babylon, said these later Christians, so too, again, with Rome: destruction meant displacement. Second-century Christianity, in other words, invented the idea of a punitive Jewish "second exile." In reality, however, the claims of later church fathers notwithstanding, the Roman destruction of the city had occasioned no "second exile." Jewish communities outside of the land of Israel had flourished for centuries prior to this period, and would continue to do so for centuries afterward. Jewish communities in the Galilee (thus, not "in exile") would thrive well into the post-Constantinian period.

The writings of the church fathers—"patristic" writings, from the Latin *patres*, "fathers"—went on to broaden the evangelists' indictment. The themes of God's punishment for the priests' and the people's failure to accept Jesus as the messiah, proclaimed in the Gospels, later swelled into lurid repudiations of Jewish tradition itself. Paul's angry insistence that gentile Christ followers should not start circumcising, in this new context, transmuted into arguments that all Jews, themselves, should stop. The core texts eventually collected in the New Testament thus shifted from being instances of *intra*-Jewish arguments to statements of principled *anti*-Jewish arguments. Writing in Paul's name, the author of Ephesians (late first century? early second?) will state bluntly that Christ abolished "the law of commandments and ordinances," thereby making a new universal humanity—one that had no place for Jewish ancestral traditions (Ephesians 2.4).

Sometime in the second century, keyed off of Paul's writings, letters ascribed to Ignatius of Antioch give further evidence of this polarization. "If we continue to live in accordance with *Ioudaïsmos*," Ignatius warned the Magnesians, "we admit that we have not received grace. . . . For *Christianismos* did not trust in Ioudaïsmos, but Ioudaïsmos in Christianismos" (*Magnesians* 8.1; 10.3). The two groups are conceived as mutually exclusive abstractions. Less abstract—indeed, perhaps giving us a glimpse of Ignatius's social world—is his advice to the Philadelphians. "If anyone expounds Ioudaïsmos to you, do not listen to him. For it is better to hear about Christianismos from a man who is circumcised than about Ioudaïsmos from one who is not" (*Philadelphians* 6.1). Would the "circumcised man" speaking about Christianismos be a Jewish Christ believer? Would the "uncircumcised man" speaking about Ioudaïsmos be a pagan God-fearer? Perhaps. The very fluidity of his situation may explain the harsh clarity of Ignatius's ideological position: he insists that a person cannot be both Jewishly observant and Christian. Other Christians clearly thought otherwise.

Justin Martyr's mid-second-century *Dialogue with Trypho the Jew* is a foundational text for subsequent patristic traditions *adversus Iudaeos*, "against the Jews." God, Justin said there, had never wanted blood sacrifices. He had only legislated detailed sacrificial ritual in order to distract Jews from their perennial attraction to idolatry. Sacrifice in itself, he insisted, was a practice characteristic of idol worship (*Trypho* 32). Further, Jews had never understood that the active deity depicted in their scriptures—"rather, not yours, but ours" (29)—was actually the eternal Christ, before his incarnation (e.g., 56; 59; 126). God the Father had never interacted directly with Israel, Justin insisted. It had always and

only been the pre-incarnate Christ, "the other god" (56), who had spoken to scriptural heroes and prophets—Moses, David, Isaiah.

What seemed to be biblical prescriptions for behavior, Justin insisted,
were actually allegories, coded stories about Christ, as was evident to
those (like Justin) who read these texts with "spiritual" understanding.
But Jews, ever obdurate and carnal, Justin complained, understood their
scriptures in a "fleshly" way: for that reason, Moses had also given them
laws (the ones, that is, that could not be read as prefigurements of
Christ) as punishment for their stubbornness (11–14; 18; 21–22; 27, and
frequently). Failing to understand the "old law," Jews now failed to see
that Christ has given a "new law" (11–12). "What then?" asks Trypho.
"Are you Israel?" At some length, Justin answers, "Yes" (*Trypho* 123; 135).

This mode of "thinking with Jews" as the defining Christian "other"
while claiming the positive prerogatives of "Israel" for the church became
a drive wheel of patristic theology. Traditions *contra Iudaeos* or adversus
Iudaeos went on to serve multiple purposes. By identifying Jewish interpretations and Jewish enactments of Jewish scriptures with (inferior)
"flesh" and Christian understandings with (superior) "spirit," theologians
pried these prestigious ancient writings loose from their communities of
origin, eventually by the fourth century turning them into the "Old Testament" of the church. These interpretations validated Christian allegori-
cal readings of Jewish scriptures as codes for Christ. They gave Jesus a
huge biblical backstory, one extending back to creation itself. They explained why and how Christians could value Jewish texts while enacting
so few of the ("fleshly") practices that they promulgated.

Anti-Jewish rhetoric could also serve in gentile intra-Christian fights,
to articulate constructs of Christian "orthodoxy" against "heresy." Indeed, patristic writings against Jews and against heretics form a double
helix of invective, the arguments against the one fortifying those against
the other. And finally, by so effacing the Jewish context and content of
core New Testament texts, by transmuting intra-Jewish arguments into
anti-Jewish arguments, these later theologians understood Jesus and
Paul as themselves teaching against Judaism. These two figures thus became, in second-century retrospect, the founders of the gentile
church—in Justin's view, of Justin's church.

But there never was a single "gentile" church. Some gentile communities continued to observe aspects of Jewish tradition, to adapt and to adopt them. Still others actively—and variously—insisted on difference. Valentinus of Alexandria (fl. 130) who, like Justin, relocated to Rome, established another approach to Jewish scriptures, seeing in them highly symbolic codes for a mystical cosmogony and a spiritual redemption. Marcion (fl. 140), who also relocated for a while to Rome, urged that Jewish scriptures be left to the Jews, and that Christian revelation be sought specifically in the letters of Paul (including some of the current New Testament's deutero-Paulines) and in one of the gospels (a version of Luke's). Both theologians contended that the god revealed in Jewish writings was not the father of Christ. The biblical god was a different and a lower deity, they said, one who in fact represented Jesus's cosmic opposition.

A thick cloud of antiheretical rhetoric shrouds these latter Christian figures, making them harder to see. We do know, from the arguments of their Christian opponents, that they buttressed their insistence that the god depicted in Jewish scriptures was a lower god, not the divine father of Christ, by appeal to empirical fact: the Roman destruction of Jerusalem.

The Jews' defeat by Rome's armies in 70—augmented some sixty years later by the defeat under Bar Kokhba—strengthened these "heretical" gentile Christians' case that Jerusalem's temple had nothing to do with the highest god. Had the temple really been allied to the highest god, they reasoned, it never would have or could have been destroyed. These political and military events suggested that the Jews worshiped a god other than the highest god, the one who was the father of Christ. And their theologies, standing at some remove from Jewish scriptures (which in their view did not reveal the highest god), seem less directly engaged with Jews themselves.

Justin and Tertullian, by contrast, in claiming Jewish scriptures for their respective churches, had to work harder to account for Jerusalem's destruction in a way that did not demean or diminish Jerusalem's god. Their answer was that God himself had worked through Rome to end the temple cult: God had never wanted blood sacrifices anyway. In destroying the Jews' temple, they explained, God had in effect repudiated the Jews.

But this argument was itself susceptible to empirical disconfirmation. It was all but upended in 361–63 CE, when, after some fifty years of patronage for one sect of Christianity, Constantine's nephew Julian assumed the purple. Raised Christian, Julian once he became emperor advocated a return to traditional pagan cult and culture. Besides ending the most favored status of orthodox bishops, he conceived a more serious threat: Julian determined to rebuild the temple in Jerusalem.

His motivation was less pro-Jewish than it was anti-Christian. Orthodox tradition—with which Julian was intimately familiar—had emphasized the theological importance of the temple's destruction, interpreting the Gospels' predictions of its downfall ("there will not be one stone upon another that will not be thrown down," Mark 13.2) to mean its permanent demise. By rebuilding the temple, Julian would undermine the authority of that prophecy and embarrass the church. (We can only speculate what Jews might have thought of the pagan emperor's sponsorship.) In the event, his plan came to naught. Julian died on the battlefield against the Persians; the rebuilding effort was stymied and, with his death, abandoned. But his efforts only made subsequent patristic insistence on the significance and the permanence of the temple's destruction—and of the Jews' "exile"—that much louder.

Still, such theologies adversus Iudaeos do not tell the whole story. Other Christ-following communities were more positively engaged with Jewish sensibilities. We catch glimpses of these in now-marginalized texts: the pseudo-Clementine *Homilies* and *Recognitions*; the *Didascalia Apostolorum*; the *Epistle of Peter to James*. These fourth-century writings perhaps rest on earlier second- or third-century foundations. Some remain in their Greek original, some in Syriac translation; one, the *Recognitions*, exists in full in an early fifth-century Latin rendition. Their emphases are interestingly different from what we encounter in "proto-orthodox" Greek and Latin fathers. "Clement," for example, the protagonist of *Recognitions* and *Homilies*, is presented as a student of the apostle Peter. Paul is nowhere mentioned, but perhaps referred to obliquely as Peter's "enemy" (*Epistle of Peter to James* 2.2). And indeed, this literature seems free of Paul's contentious comparison of "law" to "gospel."

This Clementine literature foregrounds Jesus as "the prophet," one whose transgenerational activity stretches from Moses to himself—though Jesus, as messiah, is also superior to Moses (e.g., *Homilies* 3.20). Salvation is preached by Moses to Jews, by Jesus to gentiles (*Recognitions* 4.5): each pathway is legitimate and efficacious for each people group. (Intriguingly, the word "Christian" nowhere appears with reference to Christ-following gentiles, who are identified rather with the repurposed term, "God-fearers.") Indeed, "Jesus is concealed from the Hebrews who have taken Moses as their teacher. . . . Moses is hidden from those who have trusted in Jesus" (*Homilies* 8.6; cf. *Recognitions* 4.5). Peter and James are the central apostolic characters (with a strong cameo appearance by Barnabas). And proper practice—concerning purity, marriage, food, community discipline—is emphasized, perhaps paralleling the same concerns that appear in contemporary rabbinic literature. The *Didascalia Apostolorum* even criticizes other Christians who evidently observed Jewish food laws and traditions concerning menstrual purity. Clearly for some communities, then, keeping "the law" was a vital part of Christian praxis.

Who were these people? Are they ethnic Jews who also revere Jesus? Are they Judaizing gentile Christians? The ambiguities of our evidence collapse the question. Despite the clarity with which Law-observant "Jewish-Christian" groups are denounced as heretics by Constantinian and post-Constantinian authors like Eusebius, Epiphanius, and Jerome, they are evidently alive and well, evincing alternative voices in the contest over definitions of right teaching (orthodoxy).

Contestations over the identity of "Israel" long continued. Passages in the Old Testament and, in the New, Paul's insistence on the redemption of all Israel and the permanence of God's gifts and promises to Israel continued to trouble thoughtful churchmen. In the early decades of the fifth century, Paulinus, bishop of Nola in Italy, wrote of his puzzlement to his North African colleague and correspondent Augustine, bishop of Hippo.

Addressing Augustine as "blessed teacher of Israel," Paulinus cited several problematic passages in scripture. "Slay them not, lest they forget your law," sang the Psalmist. "Scatter them with your might" (Psalm 59.12). Why, asked Paulinus, did Psalms speak of scattering "them"—meaning "the Jews"—"*lest* they forget your law"? If God had repudiated the Jews, "what good does it do them not to forget the Law," since salvation is acquired "solely by faith?" (*Letter* 121.1, 7). Further, Paulinus asked, how can Paul state that Jews are "beloved of God because of the forefathers" (Romans 11.28)? If they are damned for being enemies of Christ, how can they be "beloved"? "If the Jews are beloved of God, how will they perish? And if they do not believe in Christ, how will they not perish?" (*Letter* 121.2, 11).

Augustine himself had long wrestled with these passages, and with the deeper question of the theological status of the Jews vis-à-vis Christian revelation. In *Letter* 149, he summed up his conclusions for Paulinus. The Jews indeed, he says, had been "scattered" with the temple's destruction in 70. But this scattering had been to the benefit of the church. Jews providentially continued not to "forget the law" because their attachment to their ancient books meant that, as they wandered, they spread the Bible everywhere they went. Jews thus served as witness to the church, since (in Augustine's view) the law itself had predicted that the Jews would not receive the gospel. The prestigious antiquity of their books, their continuing attachment to them, their wide dissemination of them thanks to their eternal exile: all served to convince skeptical pagans of the gospel's truth—*that* was the utility of the Jews' "not forgetting" their law.

As to Paul's statement on the redemption of "all Israel," Augustine explains, that cannot refer to Israel *secundum carnem*, fleshly Israel, but only to Israel *secundum spiritum*, spiritual Israel, the church (*Letter* 149.2, 19). And God's "call," further, is irrevocable only with respect to those whom he *both* called *and* "chose" (nodding to Matthew 22.14: many are called, but few are chosen; *Letter* 149.2, 21). Redeemed Israel, "spiritual" Israel, are those few from within the church who are so predestined. According to Augustine, not even all within the current church were redeemed, only those whom God had "foreknown."

Rhetorical "Jews" and Historical Jews

The patristic image of Jews is most often a still life sketched from biblical sources. It does not represent a social portrait of Jewish contemporaries, but a scripturally generated depiction that could be deployed for various ends.

The Christian critique of Jewish blood sacrifices provides a premier example of this rhetorical technique, whereby gentile writers used Jewish scriptures to criticize and to repudiate (a defunct) Jewish practice. The *Epistle of Barnabas*, a pseudonymous second-century sermon, inveighed heatedly against blood offerings. According to the author, Israel had never received the true covenant at all: Moses in his fury at Israel's idolatrous adoration of the Golden Calf had shattered it (*Barnabas* 4). Christ is the true, the uniquely effective blood offering (*Barnabas* 5). Food laws are not about food, but expressions of ethical allegories. "Do not eat swine" censors wallowing in luxury; "do not eat hare" warns against sexual profligacy; "do not eat hyena" condemns adultery (*Barnabas* 10). Circumcision is about the heart, not about body parts (*Barnabas* 9). The temple's destruction proved what is evident from a right reading of scripture: God had never wanted blood sacrifices anyway, as is obvious to anyone with spiritual understanding (*Barnabas* 16). The true temple is the community of (right) believers (*Barnabas* 16).

Belabored though Barnabas is, it displays a good training in Hellenistic rhetorical technique, using parts of a text to undermine a different reading of that same text. And, like Justin's *Trypho*, its antisacrificial arguments undercut a Marcionite perspective. Marcion, another second-century gentile Christian, had argued that the highest god, the father of Christ, had never wanted sacrifice: only lower gods, *daimones*, sought them out. Therefore, Marcion concluded, the highest god could not be the deity described in Jewish scriptures, who did go on at length about what offerings he required. The Jews' god was a lower god. That god clearly could not be the father of Christ.

Against Marcion, appropriating Jewish scriptures positively for their churches, allegorizing Christians like Justin and Tertullian infused them with new meaning while repudiating sacrifice as well. The Jews' god, they insisted, *was* the father of Christ, but he had never *really* wanted sacrifices, either. Then why all the detail about sacrifice in these texts? Tertullian, around the year 200, agreed with much of Marcion's position. He, too, held that Paul himself had repudiated Judaism, and that blood sacrifice was intrinsically bad worship, linked invariably to the worship of idols and demons. But, Tertullian explained, a bad god had not given bad laws in a bad book (the interpretation that he attributes to Marcion). Rather, the good god had given bad laws to a bad people, to distract them from their ever-active proclivity (as proved by the episode of the Golden Calf) to worship idols.

Tertullian's rhetoric against sacrifices obscures three points. First, Jews in the Diaspora—those Jews who were immediately proximate to these Christian writers—had not been sacrificing to begin with. Offerings being in principle restricted to Jerusalem, Jewish sacrifice abroad did not exist. And after 70, even in Jerusalem, sacrifices had ceased: the temple was no more. That Jews were constitutively obsessed with blood sacrifices was an image generated by hostile readings of ancient Jewish biblical texts. It was primarily useful as a polemical trope, to lambast putative Jewish literal-mindedness as incipient idolatry—and to accuse Christian competitors of the same.

Second, surrounding contemporary cultures in the second and third centuries *did* actively sacrifice: offerings were made before the images of gods. This social context underscored gentile Christian accusations that Jews were themselves inclined to the premier pagan sin, that is, idol worship. Only pagan gods were receiving such cult. No wonder God had allowed the destruction of Jerusalem's temple: he had wanted such sacrifices to cease. To this argument, patristic authors appended another. If Jewish sacrifices were ended, then by definition the practice of all the rest of Jewish law should end as well. This ancillary argument was aimed not only at Jews, but also against those other gentile Christians who, like their pagan contemporaries, continued to frequent Jewish communities and to adopt some Jewish practices.

Third and, in some ways, most interestingly, the scriptural generation of arguments against sacrifices masks one foundational source for this rhetoric: *pagan* arguments against animal sacrifice. Centuries before this period, Platonic philosophers had critiqued the anthropomorphic deities, their cults, and their defenders, the Stoics. The highest god, they insisted, had no use for such worship: he (or it) should be approached not through cult but through mind alone. Only lower gods, said these philosophers, were attracted to blood sacrifices. (Porphyry, a third-century pagan critic of Christianity, had himself repeated this ancient argument contra animal offerings.) In short, tried-and-true verbal ammunition on the general topic against sacrificing lay ready to hand. Educated Christian authors easily repurposed it for use against their scripturally sketched representations of Jews—as indeed Hellenistic Jews, also well educated in the pagan curriculum (the only one there was) had earlier repurposed this same pagan argument against pagan sacrifices.

Eventually, "rhetorical Jews" will wander into all forms of Christian literary production. They will be conjured in martyr stories, there teamed up (no matter how improbably) with pagan mobs howling for the death of the martyr (*The Martyrdom of Polycarp*). They will be presented as obsessed with blood sacrifices (thus Justin). They will be described as infested with demons (so John Chrysostom). They will serve as a constant counteridentity in Christian sermons, invoked in constructions of Christian identity—especially in arguments with and against other gentile Christians who, as "heretics," will be denounced as "just like the Jews," "worse than the Jews," or indeed, most directly, as "Jews."

Yet for all this, there was a type of *pro Iudaeos* stream within imperial ecclesiastical rhetoric as well. Judaism and knowledge of things Jewish were sometimes conjured as validation in intra-Christian contestations. In popular stories about the recovery of relics in the Holy Land, a "Jew" would often appear as the guide to the holy object: he served as a narrative device, testifying to the relic's genuineness. Jerome in Bethlehem, translating parts of the Old Testament not from the traditional Greek text but from Hebrew, appealed to the *veritas Hebraica* in support of his controversial effort. And he authorized his endeavor by publicizing how he had learned the language from local Jewish instructors. Augustine, against the Manichees, repeated the older polemic equation of "Jews" with "flesh"—and then stood that polemic on its head, arguing that the fundamental message of (true) Christianity focused precisely on the flesh: its creation by God, its assumption by Christ, and its redemption in the Resurrection. The Jews, he argued, had therefore been correct to interpret the law secundum carnem, not allegorically but "literally." Only the Jews' fleshly circumcision, urged Augustine, could have adequately foretold the mystery of fleshly resurrection. Only actual blood sacrifice adequately foretold the crucifixion of the incarnate Christ.

More radically, Augustine insisted that Jesus, all his disciples, and even the apostle Paul for this reason had continued to live traditionally Jewish lives and to observe Jewish law. This was a matter of pastoral principle, he said, precisely to serve as a lesson for gentile Christians. The source of their former religion, he explained, had been demons, but the source of Jewish law was the true God. (Jerome, convinced that Jesus and Paul had renounced Jewish law, pushed back against this reading. Augustine stood his ground.)

In denying the title "Israel" to Jews, the fourth-century imperial church appropriated the idea of Israel as a "chosen people" for itself. This enabled the church to coherently reread the (now) Old Testament, referring positive statements about Israel to (orthodox) Christians, and negative statements to "the Jews." And by seeing Christ as encrypted in Old Testament figures, expressions, and events, theologians could draw on an interpretive pattern of prophecy and fulfillment, putting these notionally contrasting, notionally bounded communities in a developmental relationship to each other, with the new, "Christianity," superseding "Judaism," the old.

The Jews themselves, and the idea of Israel, however, could never be left alone. The originary Jewishness of the imperial church's double canon—the Old Testament, and much of the New—meant that Christians were constantly dealing with representations of Jews and of Judaism whenever they turned to their own sacred texts. In the canonical gospels, read regularly in community service, Jesus of Nazareth appeared as an observant Jew, frequenting synagogues; keeping the great Jewish pilgrimage festivals; reciting Judaism's central prayer, the Shema; wearing the Jewish prayer fringe on his garment; giving instruction on fasting and prayer, on offerings at the temple, on the appropriate dimensions of Jewish ritual objects. The supersessionist rhetoric of the contra Iudaeos traditions notwithstanding, many gentile Christians evidently saw Jewish practice as continuous from the Old Testament through the New Testament to their contemporary Jewish neighbors—or so Christian sermons complain. Indeed, some Judaizing Christians justified their voluntary observance of some Jewish law by pointing precisely to the example of Christ, whose practice they wanted to imitate.

The continuing existence of flourishing Roman-period Jewish communities attracted both clergy and laypeople, even after Constantine. We hear the reproaches to these behaviors in sermons as well as in the canons of church councils and in the provisions of imperial legislation, all of which attempt to regulate and to minimize such "interfaith" socializing. These prohibitions reveal the situation on the ground. Some Christians kept the Jewish Sabbath as their day of rest and worked on Sundays. They received festal gifts from Jews, accepting matzah and participating in Jewish "impieties." They shared in Jewish fasts and feasts, tended lamps in synagogues on feast days, joined with Jews in prayer, and gave their children to Jews in marriage. And the lunar Jewish calendar—especially the date of Passover—long continued to influence Christian communal celebrations of Easter.

In Sardis, a huge synagogue, capable of holding upward of a thousand people, was integrated into the town's central gymnasium complex. Non-Jewish God-fearers contributed to its upkeep. It flourished until flattened by an earthquake in the seventh century. In Aphrodisias, in the fourth or fifth century, a monumental inscription proclaimed the active membership of converts and of non-Jewish God-fearers in the Jewish community. In the Galilee, large and well-furbished synagogue buildings continued to be erected well into the post-Constantinian period.

In Roman Palestine, pre-Constantine, the mysterious institution of the Jewish patriarchate emerged, headed by sages who claimed Davidic lineage. Acknowledged by Rome, the patriarch collected taxes, ruled on community issues, and (according to Origen) even exercised judgment in capital cases: "The power wielded" by the patriarch, wrote Origen in 240, was so great "that he differs in no way from a king of a nation" (*Letter to Africanus* 14). The position only ceased—for reasons obscure—in the early decades of the fifth century. In the broader social sphere, the continuing presence of Jewish town councilors and magistrates, of Jewish civic patrons, and of sought-after Jewish exorcists, ritual experts and healers, all problematized the insistent patristic pronouncements of Jewish decrepitude. Perhaps, indeed, because of this very gap between negative theological depiction and positive social interaction, the rhetoric of separation and supersession boomed so loudly in the literature of the church.

Fourth- and fifth-century Roman imperial legislation was itself marked by the ecclesiastical rhetoric of contra Iudaeos tropes. Laws characterized Judaism as a "feral" and "nefarious sect" and as a "polluting contagion." Jews were increasingly barred from positions in the military, in law, and in imperial service. But the harsh rhetoric to one side, these laws also protected Jewish religious assembly and forbade the appropriation or destruction of synagogues. "The sect of the Jews," ruled Theodosius I, "is prohibited by no law" (*Theodosian Code* 16.8.9).

Relations between Jews and (various sorts of) Christians were not always sunny. As the empire ages in the course of the fourth and fifth centuries, as bishops become increasingly empowered, as their urban base becomes increasingly radicalized and codes and councils strain to regulate acceptable Roman *religio*, Jews will be increasingly lumped together with pagans and heretics, two other groups that demarcated the limits of religious respectability. Christian Roman law will demote Jewish ancestral tradition to a *superstitio*, and to a "perversity . . . alien to the Roman Empire" (*Theodosian Code* 16.8.19). Orthodoxy meant not only the right way of being Christian. It increasingly came to mean the right way of being Roman. Depending on the temperament of the local bishop, Jewish communities and property—like that of heretics and of pagans—could become the targets of opportunistic coercion: the seizure of synagogue buildings, the intimidation of populations, the choice between forced baptism or exile.

Yet there was a difference. In the rhetoric of Roman law, heretics were denounced as "insane" false Christians, pagans as clear outsiders. The legal rhetoric itself sought to establish clear and stable boundaries between groups. But unlike paganism and heresy, and despite certain legal disabilities, Judaism itself was never forbidden. Legally, socially, religiously, Jews within a now-Christian society retained an ambiguous status and experienced an unstable and inconstant tolerance, one that would follow them into the Middle Ages and beyond.

2

THE DILEMMAS OF
DIVERSITY

When you come together in assembly,
I hear that there are divisions among you.

PAUL, 1 CORINTHIANS 11.18

Heresy shall be considered a public crime, since whatever is
committed against divine religion redounds to the detriment of all.

THEODOSIAN CODE 16.5.39

*From the earliest sources we have, Paul's letters and the later Gospels, the
message of salvation in Christ was clearly interpreted in a variety of ways.
This very variety became a source of bitter internal arguments. Later gentile
Christianities also produced many different interpretations of the Christian
message; its spokesmen condemned diversity as deviance, "heresy." Once imperial politics, with Constantine, came into play, charges of heresy had serious social consequences. Heretics were considered a danger not only to the
church, but also to the state.*

+ + +

The War of Words

"Not everyone who says to me 'Lord, Lord,'" warns Matthew's Jesus, "will enter the Kingdom of Heaven." He continues: "On that day"—the day of judgment—"many will say to me, 'Lord, Lord, did we not prophesy in your name? And cast out demons in your name? And do many deeds of power in your name?'" Not good enough. "Then I will declare to them, 'I never knew you. Go away from me, you evildoers'" (Matthew 7.21–23).

This passage provides an interesting glimpse at a formative moment in the gospel traditions. Already by the time of Matthew's writing— circa 85?—the movement in Jesus's name was clearly developing in various directions. Matthew does not celebrate this diversity. These other Christ followers might acknowledge Jesus ("Lord, Lord"). They might even work miracles in his name. But such confessional loyalty and charismatic power endowed no legitimation. To be counted among the redeemed, the Christ follower presumably had to adhere to Matthew's view of things, which his Jesus describes as doing "the will of my father in heaven" (Matthew 7.21).

Some three decades earlier, mid-first century, Paul had already voiced similar sentiments against other members of the movement—also Christ-following apostles, like himself, who were going to gentiles; also Jews like himself. ("Are they Hebrews? So am I! Are they Israelites? So am I! Are they descendants of Abraham? So am I! Are they servants of Christ? . . . I am a better one!"; 2 Corinthians 11.22–23.) In his view, these "super-apostles" (said with heavy sarcasm) were teaching a different message from his own. He too threatens them with a bad result: "Their end will match their deeds"—their deeds, evidently, being to speak the message about Christ in any way different from Paul's.

What precisely these super-apostles taught in Corinth is now impossible to say. We are in a better position to assess the situation when Paul loses his temper with his gentile assemblies in Galatia. Opening his letter with a rousing anathema against any gospel different from his own (Galatians 1.6–9), Paul only eventually names the problem with his Galatian competitors: they are urging proselyte circumcision on Paul's ex-pagan communities (Galatians 5.2; circumcision would presumably not be an issue for adult Jewish males). Paul is having none of it. His letter contains his most strident and polarizing rhetoric. The law, flesh, slavery, and circumcision fall to one side; faith, spirit, and freedom, to the other. Through Christ's spirit, he says, these non-Jews have (already) been adopted into the lineage of Abraham, and thus can be heirs, along with Israel, to God's promise to Abraham (4.4–7). Flesh—the site of circumcision—cannot effect this eschatological adoption and cannot effect these gentiles' being made righteous: only spirit, Paul insists, can do that. Through Christ's spirit—and through spirit alone—are gentiles rendered a "new creation" (6.15).

When we reflect on how few Christ followers of any sort there must have been in the mid- to late first century, this level of heated hostility—Paul's, Matthew's—might seem astonishing. But condemnation of difference characterized the intersectarian infighting that marked much of late Second Temple Judaism. The Dead Sea Scrolls, in this respect, provide a useful comparison. They too condemned other Jews of different persuasions; they too focused on internal community discipline. Unanimity bolstered claims to revelation. Divergence, in this view, was damnable and dangerous. We see similar responses to such splintering in other texts that were eventually collected in the New Testament. The letters of John, for example, condemn those who go "out from" John's group. Says this writer, such people are no less than antichrists (1 John 2.18–19).

Eventually some second-century gentile Christian authors will provide internal diversity with a name and a pedigree. Adapting the Greek word *hairesis*, which had originally meant "school of thought," these writers will lambast Christian difference as a late deviation from "orthodoxy" ("right teaching") into "heresy." The true church is the (only) one founded by Christ. "Other" churches, in this rhetoric, deviating from the original apostolic orthodoxy, were founded by errant individuals and sustained by their wayward followers. They were "heretics."

This emphasis on unanimity, *homonoia* (concord), and *homodoxia* (same opinion), replicated concerns current in second-century pagan philosophical circles, known as the Second Sophistic. Pagan thinkers were no less focused on keeping "pure" those traditions conceived as stemming from Pythagoras or from Plato. Diversity implied error. Truth is one. One claimed unanimity for one's own side, while asserting that diversity and mutual contradiction characterized another side.

"Heresy" preserves the language and the outlook of history's winners, those second- and third-century writers whose usefulness for the fourth-century imperial church ensured their texts' later survival. These earlier authors—Justin, Clement of Alexandria, Irenaeus, Hippolytus, Tertullian, and, with a difference, Origen—we designate as "proto-orthodox." That in itself is an anachronistic label, since their "orthodoxy" was a status conferred on them by fourth-century thinkers who chose to place them retrospectively within the intellectual lineage that they were constructing for themselves. (Some of the teachings of these proto-orthodox thinkers will, in the fourth-century context, be quietly ignored as not quite orthodox; and Origen himself will not weather the changed historical context. His works will be condemned.)

In their own day, however, as this heated rhetoric attests, there was no one single authoritative interpretation, only vigorous variety. The churches condemned we know by the names of their teachers: followers of Valentinus are called "Valentinians"; of Marcion, "Marcionites"; of Montanus, "Montanists," and so on. Their "proto-orthodox" critics, by contrast, are called, simply, "Christians." The implication is that these other teachers—goaded by pride, said their critics; or by demons; or by too much philosophy; or by Jews; or by philosophy misunderstood; or by unseemly and destabilizing curiosity—deviated from a stable and defined original doctrine laid down by Christ, guaranteed by apostolic succession, and preserved once for all in the writings of the "proto-orthodox" author himself.

Many of these other groups have been characterized by historians as "Gnostics," "knowers." But that label was itself contested in antiquity: proto-orthodox writers sometimes claimed it for themselves, too, while imputing false knowledge to their competitors. Valentinus and others like him (or those lumped together with him) clearly thought of themselves simply as followers of Christ—not as "Gnostics" and not, for that matter, as "Valentinians." And all these intellectuals characterized their respective interpretations of Christ traditions as imparting knowledge of salvation.

Further, despite the notion of "apostolic tradition," all forms of second-century Christianity had to differ from any form of the original Christ movements of the mid-first century, the generation of the apostles, not least because of the simple passage of time. The due date of apocalyptic prophecy was necessarily readjusted and postponed, its message of redemption rethought. Different ways of thinking philosophically produced different theologies. And as these movements spread, they were inflected locally: different places had different cultures, and their own vernaculars (Coptic in Egypt; Syriac in eastern Syria). The individual temperament and training of their spokesmen mattered: different thinkers voiced different commitments and convictions. A unified translocal church, in short, was a notion created not by social reality but by the demands of rhetoric—my side, since true, is uniform; yours, false, must therefore be pluriform. And, by the fourth century, this idea of translocal uniformity was also demanded (if never achieved) by imperial politics, which sought to support a unified empire.

One thing that all these second-century intellectual contestants had in common was a high level of pagan rhetorical education. That curriculum, surprisingly stable across centuries, had spread in the Hellenistic period after the conquests of Alexander the Great (d. 323 BCE). It had continued, augmented by Latin texts and grammars, in the Roman schools. The learned and the literate were trained in the art of oral argumentation. They practiced presenting a persuasive case for or against a given proposition by orally rehearsing traditional arguments and their coordinating traditional counterarguments. Arguments particularly about the meaning of a text—a law, a treaty, a will, a passage of poetry, a valued philosophical writing—were imagined, practiced, and performed as an *agōn*, a trial or contest. (The word originally derived from athletic competitions.) The goal of oral exercise was not to present a fair picture of an opposing view, but to make one's own view as persuasively as possible. Indeed, the construction of a view *as if* it were opposing—the proverbial straw man—was itself a stratagem of agonistic rhetoric, the better to present clearly one's own position.

This fact explains both the contentious tenor of so much early Christian literature, and the reason why we cannot take its presentation of alternative Christian views at face value, as a fair description of those views. The goal of an agōn was to win, to persuade the listener that one's own interpretation was the only correct interpretation. The more incoherent or offensive one could make one's opponent look, the stronger one's own position appeared. Indeed, we might consider ancient agonistic rhetoric as the art of skillful misrepresentation. Since we rarely have the documents of those "heretical" others who lost the fourth-century power sweepstakes, we are left with the second-, third-, and fourth-century characterizations by their ideological opponents. These must be taken with more than a grain of salt. Agonistic rhetoric offers caricature, not description.

One last caveat. Since we deal with rhetorical texts when we deal with heresiological writings, we ipso facto deal with the views of a literate upper crust. Literate elites in antiquity wrote mainly to and for and against each other. Christian communities, especially in the second century, were porous, unbounded, without strong institutional structures. This very porousness accounts for the loudness of the learned invective: these writers were insisting on (indeed, in a certain sense, "performing") principled, clear difference in a period when ideas and ideologies were under construction.

In the second century, for example, Christian "institutions" were often, at higher social registers, more like literary salons. Texts were read within the social networks of the author. Many different teachers floated between these salons. The goal of the heresiologist—the Christian rhetorician, if you will, a "specialist" of heresies—was to cement allegiance to his point of view. Accusations of intellectual incoherence and of moral profligacy, of a lack of unanimity and discipline, of female dominance in leadership roles (a gendered code for confusion and disorder): all were tropes of derogation aimed variously at pagan, Jewish, and especially Christian contemporaries. Intra-Christian diversity, if we consider how heresiology bulks in Christian literature, was perceived as the gravest threat of all.

We have little access to the thoughts of the un- or undereducated illiterate members of any Christian group. The ideological clarity and stylized belligerence of learned heresy hunters do not translate into broad social fact. As we will see when we look to other bodies of evidence—later sermons and church councils complaining about and interdicting actual social behaviors; magical papyri, invoking a dizzying array of divine forces; amulets, protecting the wearer from demons and, thus, disease; descriptions of singing and dancing around martyrs' tombs—most people's heads were positioned well below the intellectuals' line of fire. Despite the ideology of unity, diversity—even within the notionally same community—always prevailed, no less after Constantine (his best efforts notwithstanding) than before.

The rhetorically charged works of the heresiologists, nonetheless, cast a long shadow over modern attempts to write a history of the growth and development of Christianities. It is their works that are canonized as "orthodox," and, thus, it is their works that have remained. It is their conceptualization of a unitary "Christianity" that has been normalized. It is their texts that are readily available online in English translation. It is their view that dominates reconstructions. The works of those Christians they characterized as "heretics" have largely been lost.

The Knowledge of God

A recent book on second-century Christianities names twenty-six different teachers who were denounced by their patristic contemporaries, the "church fathers." Some of them are known only through piecing together the hostile reports of their repudiators. Like their more familiar counterparts, these other Christians too drew on various Jewish writings in Greek both ancient (especially Genesis) and more recent (such as assorted gospels, revelations, and Pauline letters). And again like their more familiar counterparts, these Christians also built their worldview with ideas current in philosophy and, thus, in science. We might look at all this intellectual production as Christian versions of *paideia*, Greco-Roman higher learning.

Elite Christian ways of reflecting on the nature of the physical universe well illustrate this point. For ancient thinkers, the order of the cosmos bespoke metaphysical truths. Astronomically and geologically, their map of reality brought together what we consider the separate domains of "religion" and "science." With earth at its center and the sphere of the fixed stars at its outermost edge, the ancient cosmos reflected both value and order. The higher up one passed from earth, the more stable, luminous, and beautiful, the *better* both morally and metaphysically, the heavenly spheres became.

The moon demarcated a cosmic zone between the confused and chaotic conditions on earth (where the heaviest matter had sunk) and the increasing perfections of the sun and five known planets (made of better matter, beautiful and eternal). Beyond the spheres of the moving planets, the fixed stars—luminous, immortal, and (a mark of their superiority) unmoving—described the edge of visible cosmos. All these celestial bodies were regarded as divine intelligences. Philo of Alexandria, the first-century Jewish philosopher, had referred to these stars and planets, quite simply, as "manifest and visible gods" (*On Creation* 7.27)—created by Philo's god, the god of Israel, thus subordinate to him; but "gods" themselves, nevertheless.

"Manifest and visible," however, implied "lower and lesser." For those thinkers (like Philo) of Platonic bent, these visible celestial bodies depended for their existence on an invisible god, a god beyond space, time, and matter. Solitary; transcendent; unique; immaterial; unembodied; self-generated; radically changeless and, therefore, perfect; visible to the mind alone: this deity was the "unborn," the "highest god." Philo identified this deity with the god of Israel. Some later gentile Christian thinkers were not so sure.

How was one to obtain knowledge, *gnōsis*, of this highest god, the "One"? Such was the goal of theology, a specialized subfield of philosophy—thus, the concern of an educated elite. Pagan thinkers turned to their treasured texts, especially to Plato's story of creation, the *Timaeus*, to work out the relation of divinity (*theos*) to the organized material universe (*cosmos*). Jewish thinkers such as Philo, esteeming Jewish writings as their revelatory texts, read Genesis through a Platonic lens.

According to Christian theologians, knowledge of God was particularly revealed through Christ. How that revelation had occurred, and what the content was of the knowledge so conveyed, were (inevitably) matters of dispute. The importance of cosmogony, however, of "universe making," was not. This issue drove them to consider and to reconsider the text of Genesis. How did this Jewish text relate to Christian revelation? But the driving question for all these intellectuals was the problem bequeathed by Platonism itself: If the highest god was perfect, immutable, and immaterial, how and why had material cosmos come to be at all? What is the relation of the One (that is, the highest god) to the many (that is, to everything else)? And why, if the world was the creation of an all good and all powerful deity, were things as bad as they were?

Pagan philosophers, free of the narratives of Genesis, had provided answers to these questions. Matter, they said, was the substratum of visible cosmos. Matter too was coeternal with theos, "God," though it had been originally unformed and utterly without aspect. As such, unformed matter, called *hylē*, was virtually the opposite of theos. This eternal formless matter logically protected the highest god from any imputation of change: in the time before time, theos and hylē had always coexisted. But then, how had hylē become organized as cosmos? That was a work tasked to a lower deity, a *demiurge* or (as in Philo's thought) God's *Logos*, a sort of contractor god and principle of divine, organizing rationality. (*Logos* can be translated as "word," as "speech," or as "reason.") The demiurge or logos in the time before time had brought the impress of divine form to hylē, thus transforming shapeless matter into order (cosmos).

In pagan and Jewish systems, this contractor god was the lieutenant of the highest god. In Christian systems, however, the question of the relation between the highest god and the lower deity became more complicated. Clearly—so philosophy—the god of Genesis could not be the highest god: his very activity told against that identification. (Philo had avoided this conclusion by positing God's Logos as his creative surrogate.) The Jewish deity, said these Christian thinkers, clearly functioned as a demiurge, the lower god who ordered cosmos. ("In the beginning, God created the heavens and the earth," Genesis 1.1.) How then could this scriptural god's activity cohere with the characteristics of highest divine being? What, indeed, was the identity of this demiurgical deity? Was he working in concert with the highest god? Or was he in some sense merely a dim subordinate, or a defective craftsman, perhaps even an opponent of the highest god? Further: did the defects of this demiurge account for evil—thus, for the situation from which Christ was to redeem the believer?

Three highly educated theologians struggled with this cluster of questions: Valentinus (fl. 130), Marcion (fl. 140), and Justin Martyr (fl. 150). Their influence lingered long after their lifetimes. Valentinus hailed from the philosophical powerhouse of Alexandria in Egypt; Marcion, from Pontus on the Black Sea; Justin, from Neapolis in Roman Palestine. Their places of origin attest to the wide spread of gentile Christianities already in the second century. For a time, all three men lived in Rome. All three grappled with the identity of the god depicted in Genesis, and with the relation of that god to their respective versions of Christianity. Thus, all three dealt with the fundamental problem of cosmogony, "world making," and of the ways that knowledge of God brought through Christ corresponded to concepts of cosmos.

Valentinus

Valentinian Christianity was at once more elaborate and more poetic than other, more familiar forms of Christian tradition. Some of the texts of Valentinus's "school," long lost, have been recovered in the fourth-century Nag Hammadi library, translated from their original Greek into Egyptian vernacular, Coptic. With these retrieved texts, and with cautious use of the characterizations of their heresiological opponents, we can reconstruct Valentinian cosmology and, thus, theology.

Valentinus stretched out the cosmos considerably by positing a whole new order of nonmaterial being, a spiritual world above and preceding the material one. He called this upper world the Pleroma, the "Fullness" or the "All." At the apex of this immaterial universe was the ineffable god, the Father. He was the ultimate source of all else. Out of him, in gendered pairs, spilled personified aspects of his divinity: Depth (a masculine noun in Greek) and Silence (a feminine noun), from which emanated Mind (masculine) and Truth (feminine); thence Logos (masculine) and Life (feminine), and so on. According to the *Gospel of Truth* (associated controversially with Valentinus), these entities—"aeons," meaning "ages" or "eternities"—emanated effortlessly from the ultimate divine

One; according to Nag Hammadi's *Tripartite Tractate*, they were generated by the highest god's self-contemplation.

In a daring revisioning of the template of Middle Platonism, Valentinian Christians asserted that matter was *not* coexistent with the
Father. It was, rather, the result of a mistake, an error committed by
one of the personified divine attributes, erring Wisdom (Sophia). Sophia had quit her place in the Pleroma, the upper heavens, in her desire to know the Father. The fog of error and anxiety; the unnerving
ignorance of the Father; the passion that characterizes the longing for
knowledge of God: all these personified emotional states filled Valentinian cosmogonies, characterizing Sophia's quest for the highest
god. Matter, in this view, had a beginning: it was the cast-off consequence of Ignorance. The immaterial upper world, the Pleroma, was
the really real. The lower, material realm was a distorted shadow cast
by the upper world. Indeed, it was something to be escaped altogether
by the knowing believer. In his or her postmortem state, the saved
Christian would slip beyond matter's grasp and ascend to the spiritual
world above.

Knowledge—gnōsis—separated the saved from the doomed. And this
knowledge was brought to the lower, material world by Christ. But how?
Reading Genesis as an allegory of redemption, the *Gospel of Truth* reversed the meanings of the story. Only a lower god would prevent humans
from eating of the tree of the knowledge of good and evil: a good god
would want humans to have such knowledge. Accordingly, said this gospel, Jesus was the fruit of Eden's tree of knowledge, "the fruit of the knowledge of the Father" (*Gospel of Truth* 18.20). The fruit/Jesus "did not cause
ruin because it was eaten." Rather, to eat of the fruit of this tree was to gain
saving knowledge of God, available only through Christ.

What then is the relation of God the Father, and thus of Christ, to
the god of Jewish tradition? Thanks to the report of a fourth-century
heresy hunter, Epiphanius, we have preserved a second-century Valentinian text, the letter of Ptolemy to his Christian "sister," Flora. Ptolemy's
reading of Jewish scriptures structures his catechetical lesson. The Ten
Commandments, he explained, nodding to the Gospel of Matthew, was
"pure legislation unmixed with evil . . . which the Savior came not to

destroy but to fulfill." This law was ordained by the Jewish god, a god of justice, whom Ptolemy identifies as this world's demiurge and maker. This god was thus distinct both from the Father (the unmoving god above this god) and from Christ (the Father's divine Son). But he was also distinct from another divine force, "the adversary, the devil."

Note: Ptolemy is no "dualist," positing two separate and equal spheres of divine being. One highest god presided over the whole. Like his pagan, Jewish, and other Christian contemporaries, Ptolemy was a monotheist, though an ancient monotheist. Ancient "monotheism" spoke to the hierarchical structure of heaven, not to its absolute population. As long as a single highest god reigned on top, many other subordinate divine forces could range beneath. Ptolemy names three other chief divine powers below the Father: first, Christ; then, the demiurgical god associated with the god of the Jews; and last, the devil. Basilides, another Christian thinker, posited 365 lower divine forces. The ancient cosmos was a crowded place. Hierarchy, however, preserved divine unity: the highest god was One.

Ptolemy assures Flora that more "apostolic tradition" will be forthcoming, "which we have also received by succession, because we can prove all our statements from the teaching of the Savior" (Epiphanius, *Medicine Chest* 33.7, 9). To appeal to apostolic succession was to assert authority, invoked here by Ptolemy as it will be invoked against him by heresiological opponents like Irenaeus. We see here, also, how Jewish scriptures (in Greek) are held as mediating knowledge of Christ if they are read "correctly"—that is, in light of the gospel (itself variously interpreted). And we also see how the main narrative character of Jewish scriptures, the god of Israel, is not, in Valentinian teaching, the father of Christ. Israel's god has been demoted to the status of the lower, contractor god of Middle Platonism.

Marcion

Marcion's theology was both like and unlike that of Valentinus. Like Valentinus, Marcion distinguished God the father of Christ from the god of Israel, whom he—again, like Valentinus—identified as the lower world maker and world ruler. But Marcion conceived a sharp moral distinction between these two gods. In his lost writing the *Antitheses*, Marcion contrasted passages in Jewish writings to those now deemed Christian: a version of Luke's gospel, and a collection of letters by Paul and by later authors who wrote in Paul's name. Marcion posited a purely benign, all good, unchanging god, the father of Christ, and another, lower god who was unrelievedly "just." That lower god was invested in blood sacrifices and in sexual procreation ("Be fruitful and multiply"): he was the god of the Jews. Part of Christ's mission had been to unveil this lower god, to annul his laws, and to reveal the prior, unknown god, highest and best, the epitome of moral and metaphysical excellence (so characterized by Tertullian, *Against Marcion* 1.6, 1).

One of our earliest sources of information about Marcion is the five long books of his bitter opponent, Tertullian of Carthage (fl. 200). Tertullian accused Marcion of "mutilating" Christian writings by excising offending "Jewish" passages from them. This was a good rhetorical accusation: if an opponent could not make sense of a text as it stood, claimed his opponent, he would cheat by changing it. Justin had resorted to a similar complaint against "the Jews" who, he claimed, had deliberately excised Christian passages from Jewish scriptures (*Trypho* 71.1; 73.1–6; the verse in question seems to have been a Christian interpolation). In fact, Marcion's gospel, which lacked a birth narrative, might attest to the textual fluidity of these second-century written evangelical traditions. On this reconstruction, Marcion did not cut up Luke's text. Rather, he used the text as he knew it.

Marcion particularly emphasized the letters of Paul, *the* apostle. His other lost work, the *Apostolikon*, collected a grouping of ten Pauline letters. Seven of these represent letters genuinely dictated by Paul: in (probable) chronological order, these are 1 Thessalonians, Galatians, 1 Corinthians, 2 Corinthians, Philippians, Philemon, and Romans. Three others—Colossians, "Laodiceans" (a version of Ephesians), and 2 Thessalonians—were written in Paul's name by later followers. This last letter, intriguingly, itself contains a warning against pseudonymous letters circulating under the apostle's authorship, urging its recipients "not to be quickly shaken in mind or alarmed, either by spirit or by word or by letter, *as though from us*" (2 Thessalonians 2.2)—further attestation to the known fluidity of texts in a manuscript culture.

It is difficult to overstate the importance of Marcion's thinking for later Christian theologies. Marcion's creation of a delimited gathering of specifically Christian texts—gospel plus letters—had a long future as later communities, even those opposed to him, took up the idea itself. Opposing churches would have their own collections of Christian authoritative writings. Indeed, modern New Testaments, though larger than Marcion's, duplicate his basic structure of gospel plus letters. Marcion in this sense can be credited with composing and conceiving of the Christian canon, a first New Testament. Before him, scriptural authority resided in Greek Jewish scriptures. Even after him, Justin Martyr still referred to apostolic writings as "memoires" (*Dialogue with Trypho* 29.2). Only once the idea of a "New Testament" took hold could Jewish writings in Greek become the Christian "Old Testament."

Marcion's emphasis on Paul's letters, with their polemical contrasting binaries of law and gospel, flesh and spirit, works and grace, supported his theological polarization of the higher (good) god and lower (just) one. His renowned championing of celibacy—a pagan philosophical ideal as well as a Pauline one (1 Corinthians 7)—certainly pitted Marcionite ethics against those of the creator god, the god of Genesis, who had enjoined people to "be fruitful and multiply." Was Marcion introducing a new teaching, deliberately distancing Christianness from Jewish traditions and practices? Or was this the form of Christianity familiar to him from his native Pontus, which he sought to protect, preserve, and promulgate by constructing a delimited, specifically Christian canon? It is hard to say.

Later opponents held that Marcion was forced out of Rome, frustrated by having been denied the position of "bishop." In his own day, however, mid-second century, there was no central authority in Rome or anywhere else. Networks of household assemblies—whether overlapping or competing—comprised various members with various interpretations of the Christian message and various forms of organization. Stable institutional infrastructure built around ordained church offices would be a while in coming. Marcion did eventually quit Rome, founding

many of his own assemblies (like "wasps build nests" complained Tertullian, *Against Marcion* 4.5, 3). Later church fathers attest to the Marcionite presence throughout the Roman Mediterranean: in Rome, Italy,
North Africa, Egypt, Asia Minor, Roman Palestine, and Syria; on
through the Mesopotamian region touching Persia. Despite the best
efforts of his opponents, and the stringencies of his teachings on Christian celibacy, Marcion's communities continued to thrive. Through the
missions of a third-century Christian teacher, Mani, many of Marcion's
theological principles would go on to affect no less a figure than
Augustine.

Justin Martyr

Justin fumes that Marcion's people are called "Christian." He complains
similarly about Valentinians, Basilidians, "and others by other names"
(*Trypho* 35.6). Such "so-called Christians" are "really godless and impi-
ous heretics" who "teach blasphemy, godlessness and stupidity in all
respects." Justin goes on to impugn their ethics, to question their intel-
ligence, and to deride their impiety for teaching about a god above God.
"Do not consider them Christians" (*Trypho* 80.3–4).

   To Celsus, a thoughtful late second-century pagan critic, all these
querulous sects certainly looked Christian, while their mutual recrimi-
nations attested to the movement's intrinsic lack of coherence and unity.
Christianity thus compared poorly, he said, with the concord that characterized philosophy, the "true Logos," the title of Celsus's work. "These
[Christians] slander one another with dreadful and unspeakable words
of abuse," Celsus notes. "And they would not make the slightest concession to reach agreement, for they utterly detest each other" (*Against
Celsus* 5.63). Of course, Christian writers mobilized this same rhetoric
against pagan philosophers, whom they accused of a similar lack of unanimity: they "express opinions that contradict each other . . . for each
one hates the other," says Justin's student Tatian (himself later accused
of heresy; *Oration to the Greeks* 3). The force of this argument—that
factionalism undermined truth claims—in turn accounts for the heresiologists' assertion that "heretics" were, ipso facto, *not* Christians. To

concede the name would have been to concede the pagan critics' point: that Christianity was itself multivocal, thus in an essential way untrue.

For all his insistence on difference, however, Justin as Christian philosopher—a persona that he indeed claimed for himself—thought with the same Middle Platonic template as had Valentinus and Marcion. The highest god, he said, "abides eternally in the heavens, invisible, holding personal intercourse with none . . . the Father of All" (*Trypho* 56.1). Unbegotten and without passion, this god was also without form, unchanging, unnamed (1 *Apology* 9.1; 10.1; 13.4; 25.2). Then who was the busy god so active in Genesis? It was "another god," Justin said, in this way agreeing with his two competitors. Another god was by definition a lower god. But this second god, Justin explained, was in fact God's Logos, Christ, before his incarnation. Justin's divine Christ, in other words, assumed the role of cosmic demiurge. It was he who had spoken with Moses; it was he who had given the Law (1 *Apology* 63.1). That the Jews did not read the texts this way did not trouble Justin's position: the prophets, as Justin read them, had foretold that their people would not understand.

With this argument, Justin killed the proverbial two birds—Christian rivals (to him, "heretics") and Jews—with one rhetorical stone. To those arguments made by his competitors that the Jews' fate at the hands of Rome proved that Jews worshiped a lesser god, Justin could respond: No. The Jews were punished by the highest god through the agency of his son, whom they killed—for which sin they were now in "exile," proving Justin's multiple points.

Like his Christian competitors, Justin too could deplore blood sacrifices, and fault the Jews for having performed them. But Jewish blood sacrifices, he insisted, did not prove his rivals' point, that the god worshiped in Jerusalem was a lesser god. It simply proved that the Jews did not recognize an allegory when they saw one: such sacrifices as were detailed in scripture were actually prophetic models or "types" pointing ahead to the sacrifice of Christ. It was the Jews' (mis)understandings of their own texts, rather than the texts themselves, that were "lower," "fleshly" rather than "spiritual." Of course, argued Justin, God had never wanted blood sacrifices to begin with. Had Jews been less inclined to

idol worship, they would not have needed so much distracting legislation seemingly about sacrifices. That Jews disagreed with Justin's reading, insisted Justin, merely proved Justin's case—which he made as
much against Valentinus and Marcion as he did against "the Jews."

Strategies of Control

Philosophy, cosmology, traditions of biblical interpretation, constructions of canon: all were configured coherently but differently by different Christian intellectuals. In the arguments of the heresy hunters, these
other theologies represented madness and sickness, lowly misreadings
of scripture, demonic inspiration, pride muddled with excessive philosophy, merely knowledge falsely so called.

In order to sharpen their own views, these heresiologists also sometimes invented teachings that they then attributed to theological rivals.
Heretics, they claimed, preached a "docetic" Christ, one who only appeared to have flesh but actually had not. (*Dokeo* is the Greek verb for
"appear.") Both Valentinus and Marcion were pilloried for holding such
a teaching. Valentinus however had in fact taught that Christ had a body,
though it was of a special sort. Jesus, he maintained, "ate and drank in a
special way, without evacuating food. So great was the power of continence
that food was not corrupted within him" (*Miscellanies* 3.7). So similarly
Marcion. His version of Luke lacked a nativity, and his vision of the
resurrected body (whether that of Jesus or of the believer) was spiritual,
not fleshly, in keeping with Paul's statement in 1 Corinthians 15.50: "flesh
and blood cannot inherit the Kingdom." Opponents accordingly accused Marcion of claiming that Christ did not have a fleshly body and
that he did not truly die. Both theologians had emphasized Christ's role
in revealing the knowledge of salvation. Their opponents' accusations of
Docetism served by way of contrast to emphasize Christ's fleshly incarnation, the better to foreground his death as a blood sacrifice and his
resurrection as a physical, embodied event—as indeed, they insisted, the
believer's would also be.

Heretics emphasized gnōsis, "knowledge," complained the heresy-
hunting Irenaeus toward the end of the second century. The true Chris-

tian, he insisted, emphasized obedience to the rule of faith: universal apostolic teaching, the assertion of the identity of God the Father with "the creator" (though creation was worked through Christ); belief in Christ's Second Coming, in the bodily resurrection of the dead, and in the eternal punishment of the damned (*Against Heresies* 1.10). Against both the Valentinians (who wrote many revelatory texts, and who especially favored the Gospel of John) and Marcion (who championed a single gospel, a version of Luke), Irenaeus invoked the fourfold gospel. "Four," after all, corresponded to the number of zones of the world, to the four principal winds, and to the number of faces borne by the cherubim (11.8). A generation earlier, Tatian had asserted the authority of these four evangelists in a different way. He rewrote them, combining them into a single continuous narrative, the *Diatessaron*. This harmony remained the standard form of the gospel in Syria until the fifth century.

False Christians, conceded Irenaeus, might indeed work miracles, but such powers only proved that they consorted with spirits and demons. False Christians, like "true" Christians, might advocate celibacy, but this only masked their secret decadence. The authority of apostolic tradition, he insisted, was the only safeguard against the deceits of false teachers and pseudoprophets. But as we have seen, other teachers also invoked apostolic tradition. The Valentinian Ptolemy, instructing Flora, had appealed to exactly the same rhetoric of authentication.

Another weapon against diversity—though contributory to it—was pseudepigraphy, writing in the name of a past authoritative figure. Within this tradition, the figure of Paul holds pride of place. The second epistle of "Peter"—itself a late first- or early second-century Greek pseudograph—attests to the apostle's literary afterlives. Warning against end-of-the-world enthusiasms and their opposite, disconfirming despair ("Where is the promise of his [second] coming?," referring to Jesus), "Peter" cautions that Paul's letters contain "some things hard to understand, which the ignorant and unstable twist to their own destruction, as they do the other writings" (2 Peter 3.16). "Peter," similarly to but differently from 2 Thessalonians, attests both to Paul's posthumous authority and to the plasticity—and reinterpretability—of his written legacy.

Other authors controlled Paul's message in new and changing con-
texts by continuing to write in Paul's name. Almost half of the fourth
century's New Testament Pauline canon—2 Thessalonians; Ephesians
and Colossians; and 1 and 2 Timothy and Titus, the so-called pastoral
Epistles—preserves these writings. Hebrews was anonymous, but early
on, Pauline authorship was assigned to it, too. Second Thessalonians
reconfigured apocalyptic eschatology, introducing a cycle of trouble
around a dark figure, the "man of lawlessness," who will "proclaim himself to be god." The author reassures his listeners that Christ will ultimately prevail over this end-time villain. By introducing another whole
cycle of final events, this author—while warning against pseudonymous
letters himself!—stretched out Paul's own apocalyptic scenario to accommodate the continuing delay of the End.

Ephesians, echoing Pauline vocabulary, picked up the themes of cosmic conflict and of ethnic difference, which, for this author, resolved in
ethnic erasure, the annulment of Jewish law. Colossians trumpeted the
already accomplished heavenly triumph of the Christ assembly, while
directing stable household relations on earth ("Wives, be subject to
your husbands; . . . children, obey your parents; . . . slaves, obey your
earthly masters."). "I, Paul, write this greeting in my own hand," claims
the otherwise anonymous writer. The Pastorals—perhaps written in
response to Marcion—emphasize hierarchical community structures
and the importance of male leaders who were married. (Marcion's
group—as, indeed, many groups—championed celibacy as a preferred
lifestyle.) Another writing that domesticated Paul for later heresiological tradition is 3 Corinthians. Its "Paul," too, positions himself clearly
against those other forms of Christianity that placed less emphasis on
incarnation, and which held that creation was the work not of God but
of subordinate powers, "angels."

If writing in Paul's name was one way to control how Paul was interpreted, writing about Paul provided another means. Canonical Acts, composed probably in the early second century (when it was *not* "canonical"!)
had carefully coordinated Paul's message with the directives of the Jerusalem community: no fissures in the foundation of the movement,
whose apocalyptic eschatology the author also tamped down. Still later

writings, like the *Acts of Paul and Thecla*, present Paul as the perfect celibate, a miracle worker, and a master missionary. A fourth-century Latin correspondence has Paul trading learned compliments with the Stoic philosopher Seneca. Direct attack and disavowal; pseudepigraphy; insistence on a closed body of authoritative texts; credal interpretive positions; creative narrative compositions: in all these ways, the contested figure of the apostle could be pulled into line with later constructions of Christian "orthodoxy."

Neither Male nor Female

At the end of his letter to Rome, Paul had sent greetings to acquaintances who were currently in the capital city. Among them he named Phoebe, a "sister" (meaning a follower of Paul's message), a "helper" in one of Paul's assemblies, and a "patron" of many as well as of Paul himself. He likewise greeted Prisca and Aquila, a married couple (according to Acts) and Paul's "co-workers," evidently people of some means, because they host a Christ assembly in their house. "Mary" was noted as an active member of this group; Junia designated a messenger ("notable among the apostles"); he also greeted Tryphaena and Tryphosa and Persis; and Julia and Olympas (Romans 16.1–16).

This is an intriguing roster of female names. Elsewhere, Paul mentions that Peter and other apostles traveled with their "sister-wives" (1 Corinthians 9.5). Philippians names Euodia and Syntyche among "co-workers" (Philippians 4.2–3). And women in Paul's assemblies in Corinth clearly prophesied and enacted other charismatic deeds along with the men (1 Corinthians 11, 12, and 14). Paul seems ambivalent about this: he says both that women should be quiet in the assembly (1 Corinthians 14.33–35: is this a later interpolation?), and that when they prophesy, they should be veiled (1 Corinthians 11.20: Paul is concerned about the presence of male angels). Clearly, women as well as men were involved with spreading and sustaining this first generation of the evangelion.

Other female figures are named in later first-century gospel traditions: Mary and Martha, Mary the mother of James, Mary Magdalene,

Joannna, Salome. Were these women also itinerant? Or did they stay in situ in villages, hosting the traveling members of Jesus's followers? They clearly went up to Jerusalem as pilgrims (as did Jewish women who were not Jesus followers). Women appear in the crowds that listen to Jesus; they also appear as characters in parables. Women as well as men, it would seem, are depicted as participating in the earliest Jesus movements, both in the homeland and in the Diaspora.

Did this participation distinguish the Christ movements from the broader culture, whether Jewish or pagan? Modern scholarship has often painted a dark picture of ancient patriarchy, both pagan and especially Jewish, the better to highlight a supposed gender egalitarianism in what would become Christianity. Research into women's lives in Roman antiquity more broadly has laid such caricatures to rest. As always, social class, financial status, education, and legal status (especially whether one was slave or free) had determinative effects on the lives of all women. Elite women served as important benefactors within both pagan and Jewish communities, not just Christian ones. All elite women enjoyed privileges and freedoms, and tolerated constraints, that lower-class women did not. Property law and family law everywhere favored men. Mediterranean gods of all ethnicities seem most concerned with the public behaviors of Mediterranean males, though gods and priests could be male or female, depending on the particularities of a given cult.

The language of value was itself highly gendered. Whether in medicine or in philosophy or in literature, when deploying gendered binaries, "male" was construed positively, "female" negatively. For medical science, the male seed provided the rational and organizing principle of human being, organizing the passive matter of the female. Men and women were constitutively different: men were hot and dry, women cold and wet—also less intellectually endowed, more emotional, less rational, easily duped or led astray, and so on. (Foreign men, ethnic "others," could also be characterized as effeminate. To be feminine was to be lesser.) Virtuous women were praised for transcending their sex, displaying male excellences: indeed, the Latin *virtus* has as its stem the word for male, *vir*. (One fourth-century male Christian writer praised the aristocratic and intellectual Melania the Elder as a "female man of

God.") So many of these stereotypes survive today that they scarcely need review here.

But it is exactly these stereotypes that make difficult our assessment of the historical role of Christian women within Christian communities of all sorts from the second century onward. Heresiological writers frequently claim that women were prominent in "heretical" Christian circles. Irenaeus had named Simon Magus, a character in Acts of the Apostles 8.9–24, as the founding father of Christian heretics; Simon, according to Justin, took as a coworker a former prostitute, Helena. A century later, Origen of Alexandria reports on Simonians who also call themselves Helenians. Another disputed Christian teacher, Carpocrates, was associated with one Marcellina who (so Irenaeus) came to Rome, where she gained a notable following. Harpocratians follow Salome, says Origen; others, Mariamne; others, Martha—names generated from the gospel stories. The Valentinian Ptolemy, as we noted, exhorted Flora to receive apostolic tradition. Another Valentinian, Marcus (supposed founder of the eponymous Marcosians), encouraged women in the Rhône Valley and in Asia Minor to prophesy and have ecstatic experiences (so Irenaeus). The Marcionite Apelles wrote down the prophecies of one Philumena. The spirit gave revelations, in Phrygia, not only to Montanus but also to Priscilla, Maximilla, and, later, to Quintilla. His own Montanist sympathies notwithstanding, Tertullian ridiculed other Christian sects as being dominated—to their detriment—by females. "The women of these heretics, how wanton they are! For they are bold enough to teach, to dispute, to enact exorcisms, to undertake cures, perhaps even to baptize!" (*Prescription against Heretics* 41).

How reliable is heresiological polemic for social description? The accusation that women have leadership roles in "the other" community does not tell us, directly, whether women indeed had leadership roles in that other community. It does tell us that the accuser—Justin, Irenaeus, Tertullian, Origen—is gendering confusion, bad management, intellectual muddiness, and social disorder, imputing those flaws to the rival group that he so describes. The same author can flip these stereotypes, and praise his own form of Christianness for making "even women" self-disciplined and virtuous; this trope especially shapes martyr narratives. Again, the goal of the rhetoric determines how a trope is used. Pagan critics—Celsus in the second century and Porphyry in the third—ridiculed Christianity in general as appealing to slaves, women, and minors: their intention is insult, not description. We do know from a letter of Pliny, the Roman governor of Bithynia in the early second century, that two enslaved women served a local community as "assistants" or "deaconesses." But *which* Christian communion did they serve? And what, within their church, did they do? Nothing that Pliny says about them can help us to identify them further.

The Nag Hammadi codices have yielded many texts that were not received into the fourth-century imperial canon. Some of these, like *The Gospel of Mary*, seem to elevate the status of women. (Jesus gives her special teachings, contested by Peter.) But other writings, like the *Gospel according to the Egyptians*, seem to do the opposite. "I came to destroy the works of the female," Jesus teaches in that gospel, preserved in Clement (*Miscellanies* 3.63). *Gospel of Thomas* 114 presents Jesus as promising to make Mary male so that she can gain the kingdom of heaven. Esteem for female figures in Valentinian myth, like that of Wisdom/Sophia, no more maps onto social terrain than does the medieval veneration of the Virgin Mary. And it is perhaps relevant to this question of actual female agency that the women teachers named by the heresiologists are usually depicted as linked to heretical males: they seem not to be completely independent authorities.

What *was* the status of women within Christianities? The answer we find depends on where we look. We have the names of only a few women teachers, repudiated by heresiologists. We have examples of female Christians who, possessed by a spirit—or by the spirit—were enabled to utter prophecies. Itinerant ascetic charismatics and desert solitaries might be of either sex, and we later hear of mixed groups both wandering and stationary. For heresiologists and, later, bishops, females literally embodied the dangers of unregulated charisma. Roman aristocratic women had a lot of freedom of movement, but this was because of their wealth and their status, not because of their Christianity.

Could women hold church offices? Male prelates dominate our literary sources. Inscriptions, though (and not many), hint in other directions,

where women are designated *presbytera* or *episcopa*. Later church canons will rule that women should not hold ordained office; perhaps this
means that some did. Our slender evidence cautions against generaliza-
tion. And the tendencies of the broader cultural context are clear: Roman
antiquity was not marked by gender egalitarianism in any register,
whether within Christian communities or outside of them.

Mani and Pelagius: The Politics of Orthodoxy

Constantine's conversion in 312 resolved some of the confusions of Christian diversity. Orthodoxy was what the emperor said it was. Charges of
"heresy" became a weapon in the hands of enterprising bishops.

Some heresies were born; others were made. That is, Christianity as
we see it emerging in the second century sponsored many genuinely
different (and competing) visions and versions of the gospel, with all
sides condemning the others. But later Christians who were themselves
originally committed to imperial (i.e., "orthodox") Christianity could be
targeted as deviants as well. Manichaeism exemplifies the first type of
heresy. Donatism and Pelagianism exemplify the second. Interestingly,
Augustine (354–430) figures prominently in the stories of all three.

Manichaeism was a genuinely new form of Christianity, one that
combined elements of Zoroastrianism (an ancient Persian religion that
posited the cosmic opposition of Light and Darkness, Good and Evil)
and of Buddhism with the Christian message. It thus had a genuinely
different metaphysics from that of western Christianities. Light and
Darkness, or Good and Evil, were locked in an ongoing battle. The universe as currently constituted was the result of and witness to this eternal
antagonism: particles of Light had become entrapped in dark matter,
captured in an ancient skirmish between these two kingdoms. Collectively, these particles of captive goodness constituted the divine presence
in the cosmos, the "suffering Jesus" or the "Cross of Light." Through
ascetic discipline and rituals of purification, the believer could liberate
these divine sparks to return to their native sphere.

Mani, a visionary ascetic in Persian Mesopotamia, had received this
revelation sometime in the early decades of the third century. He then

set about organizing and promulgating a new universal form of Christianity, modeling himself on the apostle Paul. Influenced by Marcionite sensibilities, Mani repudiated Jewish scriptures as unsuited for the true Christian; and he also held that Paul's letters and the Gospels had been corrupted by Judaizing interpolators. Against this compromised literary legacy Mani juxtaposed books of his own revelations, establishing a new canon of scriptures. And he took his mission out on the road. Teaching in Persia—where, in 276, he was executed at the behest of Zoroastrian clergy—Mani spread his message far and wide. It eventually spanned from Spain to China.

Mani taught a strict asceticism to a church organized in two tiers: a celibate, vegetarian, mendicant elite, the Elect—both male and female—and a lay group, the Hearers, who supported them. This latter group, bound by less drastic vows, attracted Augustine's loyalty in the early 370s when he was a student in Carthage. He remained with this church for years, converting to imperial Christianity only in 386. It is thanks to his later, informed antagonism that we can reconstruct so much of the western sect's teachings.

Both the pagan emperor Diocletian in the late third century and the Christian emperors Valentinian and Theodosius in the late fourth targeted the Manichees for persecution: their leaders were to be exiled, their books burnt, their property seized, their communities disrupted, their legal rights abridged. In a period marked by wars on Rome's eastern front, both pagans and other Christians reviled Manichaeism as a "Persian" poison. Manichees nonetheless carried on proselytizing, continuing a clandestine existence within the empire. Their answer to the problem of evil—that sin was a force independent of the individual, who was an internalized miniature instance of the cosmic struggle of good against evil—would continue to haunt Augustine's own later theology of original sin.

Manichaeism represented a genuinely new form of Christianity. Pelagianism, by contrast, was largely invented by Augustine. Pelagius himself was a reformer, moving among the same Roman aristocrats as would Jerome. His teachings emphasized the importance of human effort to living a truly Christian life, by which he meant a dedication to asceticism (both moral and, accordingly, financial, meaning a commitment to support of the poor). In bringing the importance of individual effort to the fore of his message, Pelagius likewise foregrounded the importance of the freedom of the will, aided by divine grace. Sin was not a condition, but a choice; otherwise, God would not be just in punishing the sinner. Sin to be justly punishable, in other words, had to be committed freely.

Pelagius and his circle were pushed from Italy into North Africa, refugees from Alaric's siege of Rome in 410. It was there that his way of thinking clashed with traditions of African thought on the nature of sin. Augustine, against Pelagius and his younger spokesperson, Julian of Eclanum, thought in terms of the transmission of sin: human nature, he held, had been compromised after Adam's fall, and the guilt of the original sin had been inherited by each following generation. In consequence, human will as now constituted suffered from diminished capacity: it could choose *only* to sin unless grace intervened. Sin in this sense was not a choice, but a condition. And because all humanity had been contained "in" Adam, God was just in punishing all later generations for Adam's sin.

Augustine's political context explains the success of his anti-Pelagian actions. North Africa, where he was bishop, by this point had long been mired in a local ecclesiastical civil war. The orthodox church had split over issues of community discipline in the wake of the last great pagan persecution under Diocletian, between 303 and 306. Some prelates had complied with the government's demand to turn over the scriptures; others had refused. Once the persecution was over, the question lingered: which clergy was valid? Constantine, entering this controversy shortly after his victory in 312, had ultimately decided in favor of those who had handed over the scriptures: theirs was the side that was "universal," *catholica*. His decision only hardened the will of the opposition, now called the "Donatists" after one of their bishops, Donatus. They proclaimed their community the only true church. But the Donatists were actually and only dissident catholics: both sides were doctrinally all but identical. A century on, in 405, this polarized situation was brought under the control of the catholics who, after heavy lobbying of the emperor, had their schismatic opponents legally declared heretics by imperial decree.

Augustine was primed, in other words, to use the same techniques of censure against Pelagius as he had used against the Donatists. He accused Pelagius and his followers of heresy. Julian of Eclanum responded that Augustine was the heretic; indeed, that he was still a Manichee. The North African bishops then attempted to interfere in the decisions of two councils called in the East to determine Pelagius's status, where he was adjudged to be orthodox. Importuning the bishop of Rome (who initially sympathized with Pelagius), again heavily lobbying the imperial capital, Ravenna, Augustine finally triumphed: in 418, Pelagius was banished from Rome by the emperor's decree. The pope was constrained to oblige. He excommunicated the losing side. The question of Pelagius's "orthodoxy" had been settled by imperial fiat.

Etiologies of Error

Orthodoxy's true enemy is time. What is right belief in one period becomes wrong belief in a later one. For Justin as for Irenaeus, right thinking encompassed a vivid commitment to millenarianism, the belief in a final thousand-year reign of the saints in an earthly Jerusalem (*Trypho* 80–81; *Against Heresies* 5.25–36). To Origen, a scant century later, such thinking was too fleshly, too "Jewish" (*On First Principles* 2.11.2). A champion of Christian sexual self-discipline, Tatian will eventually be condemned as an extremist "Encratite" and posthumously excised from the "orthodox" fold. The ecstatic, apocalyptic prophecies of the Montanists, too, will be edged out of acceptability by later imperial communion. And the name and work of the great Origen himself, a prodigious champion of the "true" church, will be devoured in the fourth century by controversies that he could not have imagined in the third. Despite its rhetoric of radical stability, "*the* faith" is itself a labile concept. "Orthodoxy" has a shelf life.

Before Constantine's unanticipated decision to align himself with the Christian god in 312 (to be explored in chapter 5), accusations of deviance from "true" Christianity were hostile exchanges between contestants, be they Irenaeus or the (Valentinian?) author of the (no less heatedly heresiological) *Testimony of Truth*. With Constantine, things change.

What was once a species of internal name-calling now had serious social consequences. Championing one Christian denomination—and trying mightily to weld it into the unity that it so insistently claimed for itself—Constantine turned on those other Christian communities condemned by his church. He ordered their assemblies outlawed, their leaders exiled, their buildings confiscated, their books impounded. Eusebius of Caesarea, the emperor's biographer and historian, reports with satisfaction that, subsequently, "the parts of the common body were united together and joined in a single harmony, and alone the catholic [that is, "universal"] church of God shone forth gathered into itself, with no heretical or schismatic group left anywhere in the world" (*Life of Constantine* 3.66.3).

This rhetoric of unity and victory did not correspond to the reality of diversity, as Eusebius himself full well knew. Constantine's chosen church was fractured by dissention and would indeed be ripped apart by disagreements over the theological status of Christ, the so-called Arian controversy (discussed in chapter 5). Disenfranchised communities long continued, and new forms of Christianity like Manichaeism evolved, joining the ranks of the repudiated. The rhetorical bark of imperial legislation, then, seems not to have corresponded closely to social bite. Yet such laws could be mobilized by motivated bishops. In the late fourth century, Priscillian, the bishop of Ávila in Spain and a charismatic ascetic, was denounced to the secular authorities by episcopal rivals. They accused him of Manichaeism and witchcraft. Despite protests from other bishops, the charge of ritual malfeasance, "magic," stuck. In 385, Priscillian the Christian bishop was executed by the Christian state.

It is in this period after Constantine, when constructions of community were wed to appeals to state power, that heresiological writings reach their apex. Eusebius catalogues "false Christians" in his *Church History*, tracing a genealogy of error from Simon Magus (Acts 8.9–24) while listing as well those works to be accepted as "sacred," distinguishing them from the books of the heretics. Later, and exhaustively, Epiphanius in his *Medicine Chest against Heresies* will identify (and in some cases, generate) no fewer than eighty categories of religious error, twenty pre-Christian and sixty post. Demons and overdependence on philosophy were called to account. Augustine, in his late work *On Heresies*, will catalogue eighty-eight religiously deviant groups, spanning in time from the ancient biblical past up to his own day.

Unless we imagine Christians committing these categories to memory and peering at other Christians like birdwatchers keying out birds, the practical import of these heresy catalogues seems largely elite and internal. That is, these writers construct "wrong" Christianities as a way to articulate, by means of contrast, the principles of their own "right" revelation. The focus on heresy only intensified with the empowerment of imperial patronage. Nondoctrinal distinctions between theologians and communities, under the glare of hostile scrutiny, will be magnified to the point that schisms—divisions within a single church—will come to be regarded as "heresies" as well. In the wake of anti-Christian persecutions, several communities advocated a higher bar for readmission of the lapsed: the Novatianists after Decius mid-third century, the Melitians and Donatists after Diocletian in the early fourth. These schismatic groups, too, will eventually be pressured as "heretics" to join the "universal" church. Such reclassification had real benefits: rival churches could be stripped of their assets.

Imperially sponsored creeds, generated by imperially sponsored councils, ultimately set the limits of Christian theological diversity. In principle the product of consensus, creeds functioned to signal episcopal allegiance to the emperor's will. After Constantine, whether by withholding of financial benefits or by applications of force, concord could be coerced—though often only with mixed results.

Eventually, heresy in the late imperial period will become a legal category, with defined disabilities, part of the taxonomy of religious deviance detailed in book 16 of the fifth-century compendium of Roman law, the *Theodosian Code*. "The insanity of the heretics must be restrained" declared the code: assemblies outlawed, property confiscated, careers in imperial service forbidden, inheritances annulled (16.5.65).

Yet, while the code's conceptualization of religious deviance is specifically Christian, the motivation for articulating these laws seems entirely and typically Roman. Rome from before the days of empire had always been fastidious about right *religio*: the best way to secure well-being on earth was to ensure that no impiety alienated heaven. This was why, since the days of Augustus, the emperor was also the *pontifex maximus*, "greatest priest," charged with overseeing right religio in Rome. After 312, the denomination of heaven may have shifted, but this practical concern to promote religio and to suppress dangerous superstitio remained paramount. Good relations with heaven were the key to security and well-being—*salus*—on earth. Religious uniformity, now specifically Christian, and a specific kind of Christian, had with Constantine become a concern of the state.

3

PERSECUTION AND MARTYRDOM

Giving themselves over to the grace of Christ, they despised
the tortures of this world, purchasing for themselves in the space
of one hour the life eternal.

MARTYRDOM OF POLYCARP 2.3

All Africa is filled with holy bodies.

AUGUSTINE, LETTER 78.3

Wherever there is part of a saint's body, there, too, his power emerges.

PAULINUS OF NOLA, CARMINA 27.445

*Ancient people did not distinguish between religion and politics. The two
spheres overlapped intimately, since the well-being of cities and of the empire,
themselves religious institutions, was thought to rely on good relations between heaven and earth. Good relations meant proper observance of pious
rituals. By opting out of traditional Mediterranean observances, by insisting
on worshiping only one god and no others, gentile Christians sometimes drew
down on themselves the negative attention of their pagan neighbors, of
Roman magistrates, and eventually of Roman emperors. Some were persecuted to the point of death. The memory of these persecutions was greatly*

*magnified in the period after Constantine, when the ideology of martyrdom
became an essential component of Christian identity.*

+ + +

Celestial Diplomacy

How do humans maintain good relations between heaven and earth?
And what is at stake in their relationship?

Proper attention to revealed protocols for showing affection, loyalty,
and respect to deity is the answer to the first question. *Sōtēria* (Greek) and
salus (Latin)—"well-being"—is the answer to the second: true for cult in
the city of Rome itself; true for traditional Mediterranean cults in general;
true for Judaism in all its many modalities; true ultimately for imperial
forms of Christianity as well. At the level of statecraft, relations between
empire and gods were configured as a pact or an entente: the *pax deorum*,
"peace of the gods" or, post-Constantine, the *pax dei*, "peace of God."
Ritual etiquette articulated the rules of divine/human reciprocity. Humans
solicited divine benefactions through cult; gods, engaged through cult,
responded (one hoped, positively). Showing honor to heaven in societally
sanctioned ways was of concern "not only to religion," Cicero observed,
"but also to the well-being of the state" (*On the Laws* 1.2.30).

But such rituals do not exhaust the category "religion" in antiquity,
relations between heaven and earth. What moderns think of as "religion"
ancient people considered an ethnic inheritance, "ancestral custom."
Gods came bundled together with other indexes of one's ethnicity: homeland, language, kinship, cult. It was for this reason that peoples were
born into their relationship with their people's gods.

Numberless ethnic groups constituted ancient empire. Empire accordingly accommodated a numberless population of gods, worshiped
according to the various inherited traditions—similar, but different—of
different ethnic groups. The antiquity of custom conferred respectability. Rome did not "tolerate" religious diversity: religious diversity was a
simple fact, and a consequence of empire. For the most part, a practical
religious pluralism prevailed. In a world of so many people groups and

so many gods, matters could scarcely have been otherwise. "Different nations have different customs and laws," observed the late second-century Christian writer Athenagoras. "And no one is hindered by law or fear of punishment from following his ancestral practices, however ridiculous these may be" (*Legatio* 1).

Rome was nonetheless famously fastidious about cultic activities within the city itself. In the second century BCE, the senate banned nocturnal celebrations of the Greek god Dionysus (Latin: "Bacchus"): they were foreign, thus "un-Roman." Accusations of criminality and debauchery no doubt also informed the senate's decision to restrict the cult. But such accusations were a standing aspect of Roman xenophobia: the problem with any foreign superstitio was that it was foreign. Isis's fortunes fluctuated as did Rome's political relations with Egypt. And foreigners of all sorts were the objects of classical ethnic stereotyping. Metaphors of disease and contagion; accusations of sexual profligacy, incest, cannibalism, and ritual murder; imputations of "unnatural," antisocial, or uncivilized behaviors—all these tropes could be mobilized to describe the cult and culture of the ethnic "other."

Yet foreign cults were also deliberately established. Roman armies performed the ritual of *evocatio* when pressing assault on a hostile city, "calling forth" the city's presiding deity to the Roman side with the promise of worship back in the capital. The Syrian Cybele, "mother of the gods," was brought to Rome when an oracle had revealed that such a measure would ensure victory over Carthage. Magistrates consulted the books of the Sibylline, visions attributed to an ancient seeress through whom Greek divinities once spoke. And new deities arrived also through the unofficial channels, with waves of immigrants. That was more than some patriotic Romans could bear. "The Syrian Orontes," grumbled Juvenal, "has long overflowed into the Tiber" (*Satires* 3.58).

The ancient city—like the ancient empire—was a religious institution. Governance was itself a religious activity. Urban elites, charged with leadership, functioned as priests; and the emperor himself, charged with responsibility for overseeing proper Roman cult, was the pontifex maximus, the empire's "greatest priest." Public safety, indeed, public order, depended on heaven's goodwill. When things in the sublunar realm went wrong, responsible government sought for the root reason in heaven. Human well-being—of the household, the city, or the empire—depended on placating the gods. For this reason, ritual protocols were a first resort both to discern the causes of divine alienation and to restore harmonious relations between heaven and earth. But better not to be in that situation to begin with. Public piety went far toward ensuring the common good.

Pre-Christian "Christian" Persecutions

How, in a culture characterized by a general and pragmatic religious pluralism, did Christians become the object of pagan coercive force? Why and when were Christians persecuted? To answer these questions, we have to look back to the "pre-Christian" phase of these initiatives, to the letters of Paul.

Paul describes himself as having "persecuted" the Christ assemblies, by which he must mean the Jewish members thereof. (As an agent of his own Jewish community, he would have had no authority over non-Jews.) Unfortunately, he nowhere reveals what he means by this term.

The Acts of the Apostles, in the early second century, filled in this lacuna: it located Paul in Jerusalem, consenting to the death of Stephen. Stephen, like Jesus, is the victim of priestly enmity; Stephen, unlike Jesus, is killed by mob violence. The Paul of Acts, consenting to Stephen's death, maltreats Jerusalem Christ followers and drags them into prison (Acts 8.3). Later, he solicits the high priest to deputize him to bind Christ-following Jews in Damascus for punishment back in Jerusalem. It is while on the road to Damascus, according to Luke, that Paul receives his summons from the risen Christ.

Acts takes novelistic liberties. First, as a matter of historical fact, Jerusalem's high priest at no point had any authority over diaspora Jews. Second, Acts depicts Paul in Jerusalem as "still breathing threats and murder against the disciples of the Lord": this fanaticism dramatizes his impending change of heart. But Paul in his own letter presents himself as already in Damascus when he "persecutes" the assembly, and he is already in Damascus when he receives his call (Galatians 1.13–17). Finally, Paul nowhere mentions imprisoning anyone, much less murdering them. What then does he mean by "persecute"? Perhaps the same thing that he complains about receiving: disciplinary lashing by synagogue authorities, up to the permitted maximum of thirty-nine blows (2 Corinthians 11.24).

But in this same passage in his letter to Corinth, Paul names more than synagogue authorities as the agents of his woes. Roman magistrates beset Paul with juridical punishments. ("Three times I have been beaten with rods.") Paul has been stoned (pagan mob violence?), shipwrecked, adrift at sea, in constant danger "from robbers, from my own people, from pagans" as well as from other members of the Christ movement with whom he disagrees. ("False brothers," he calls them.) He encountered superhuman resistance as well. High winds and rough water are the domain of lower gods, about whom Paul complained elsewhere—for example, at 2 Corinthians 4.4, where he protests the interference of "the god of this age."

It is this last group of ancient social actors—pagan deities—that explains the behavior of all the others. As a messenger for an apocalyptic, messianic movement, Paul demanded that gentile Christ followers cease showing respect to their native gods and worship the Jewish god alone. No other gods, and no offerings before cult images. But disrupting relations between gods and their humans in this way meant disrupting ancient relations between heaven and earth as well. Such behavior, in the view of the majority, risked divine wrath. It insulted and alienated both the gods and the gods' peoples: hence Paul's being stoned, as well as being in a generalized condition of "danger."

But why would diaspora synagogue communities also object to Paul's message? After all, they had long accommodated the interest and enjoyed the support of pagan sympathizers. The synagogue had never demanded sympathetic pagans to abandon their own gods: they were simply encouraged, as God-fearers, to show respect to the Jewish god as well. This capacious arrangement actually stabilized the synagogue community's position within its larger pagan environment.

Paul's demand destabilized it. The sole worship of the Jewish god was a social marker of ancient Jewishness, one that pagan culture was prepared to honor. The synagogue would invariably be associated with such a message's spreading to pagans. If alienating the gods put the city at risk, then alienating the urban majority would put the synagogue at risk. Small wonder the diaspora Jewish communities sought to distance themselves from this disruptive message—indeed, this may well have been Paul's own motive for "persecuting" the Jewish members of the Christ assembly back in Damascus, before his experience of Christ turned him from adversary to advocate. And as his own complaints attest, he drew the negative attention of everyone: Jews, Roman magistrates, pagans, other Christ followers, and also pagan gods.

The relatively tranquil existence of the Christ community in Jerusalem indirectly makes the same point. From within weeks of their leader's crucifixion until, forty years later, the destruction of the city by Rome's troops, the members of the original community experienced no harassment from pagan authorities. Why not? Because Jerusalem was overwhelmingly Jewish. No problem with pagans becoming ex-pagans ever arose. No one in Jerusalem feared the angry intervention of a pagan god: its own god enjoyed liturgical monopoly and supreme local authority. In the Diaspora, of course, things were otherwise.

Paul and his cohort of Jewish apostles, at work in the Diaspora, would thus have encountered resistance from all quarters, human and superhuman. Paul considered such resistance "persecution." That resistance stemmed not from these apostles' own refusal to worship the gods—in light of the known antiquity of their ancestral traditions, Jews had long been excused—but from their efforts to turn non-Jews away from their native pantheons.

In Paul's generation, mid-first century, Christ following had been a form of Judaism for gentiles. Its demand that the god of Israel be the sole recipient of worship was born of its apocalyptic convictions. It looked to the imminent return of Christ, who would defeat or subjugate the lower pagan gods and errant forces of the cosmos. First Corinthians 15 gives a dynamic picture of Christ's defeat of these divinities; Philippians 2 heralds it. The *longue durée* was not in view. It was only as time continued that negative pagan attention came to focus decisively on gentile Christ followers. By becoming ex-pagans in order to follow Christ, this anomalous gentile population called forth from their cities of residence an anxious and angry response. In the eyes of their neighbors and of the government, they were deviant pagans.

The Matrix of Martyrdom

The traditional story of the rise of Christianity is well known. From its beginnings—seen with the crucifixion of Jesus and Stephen's stoning—Christians were persecuted violently because of their beliefs. Withdrawn from society, avoiding civic celebrations like public shows and gladiatorial combats, keeping to themselves, Christians in this telling met in secret. When brought before the Roman governor, they stalwartly stood by their commitment to witnessing to "the name." Time and again, they responded to the governor's request to sacrifice by declaring, "I am a Christian." They endured unthinkable torments, whether juridical torture or condemnation to beasts in the arena. At issue was their principled refusal to make offerings to pagan gods and to the genius of the emperor. Leaving a trail of blood through the first three centuries of the empire, untold numbers suffered rather than betray their faith.

Eventually—so this version of Christian origins—the jeering pagan crowds were brought round by admiration for the martyrs' courage and the strength of their convictions. "The blood of the martyrs," as Tertullian proclaimed, "is seed" (*Apology* 50.13). Finally, prompted either in a dream or by a vision before a battle for control of Rome, Constantine himself was suddenly converted to the Way. Anti-Christian persecutions immediately ceased. Pagan cult dissipated. The empire, in the short space of some three hundred years, had converted to the church.

This is the triumphant narrative presented especially by two Constantinian authors, the rhetorician Lactantius and the church historian Eusebius. It has had remarkable staying power, enduring well into the twentieth century, both in Hollywood films and in academic publications. And martyrs, indeed, have occupied a central place in Christian culture, from antiquity's celebrations around martyrs' shrines to devotion to martyrs' relics to pilgrimages to martyrs' memorials to liturgical calendars dominated by the death days of these saints. The memory of the experience of persecution is to this day one of the load-bearing pillars of Christian identity.

This traditional narrative, however, has been complicated by historical research. For one thing, while there is no doubt that some Christians suffered from the hostile attentions of Roman officials—we have pagan as well as Christian statements attesting to this—historians have had trouble reconstructing an actual legal charge. Before Diocletian's early fourth-century initiatives, no specific law banned Christianity. Most religions, indeed, were neither legal nor illegal: they simply *were*, a defining part and parcel of the ethnic packaging of people groups in the ancient empire. How then, did a Christian end up before a magistrate? And why?

According to the Roman historian Tacitus, Christians had served the emperor Nero as convenient scapegoats back in 64 CE, when a devastating fire consumed the city of Rome. Looking back from his vantage in the early second century, Tacitus described how Nero had deflected blame for the blaze from himself to "the Christians," a group that was disliked, he said, for their infamous, abominable, and pernicious superstition. The term "Christian" is itself an early second-century coinage: in Nero's day, no collective noun identified Christ followers as such. (Acts, which does impute the term "Christian" to the first generation, is itself an early second-century text.)

Popular dislike of Christians is mentioned also by Tacitus's younger contemporary Suetonius, who describes them as a class of men given to a new and malicious superstition. Nero, he says, subjected Christians to physical torments. Both historians echo the language of another contemporary, Pliny the Younger, governor of Bithynia in this same period. Writing to the emperor Trajan about a trial of Christians, Pliny likewise characterized the movement as a *superstitio* both extravagant and depraved.

In later Christian tradition, Nero will loom large as the pagan persecutor par excellence, first and worst, killing Christians just because they were Christians. Eventually, he will be blamed for the deaths of Peter and of Paul. But while a generalized dislike may explain why Nero could with impunity target some Christ followers for responsibility for the fire, it does not make his action an anti-Christian persecution as such. His victims were prosecuted as arsonists, not as "Christians." They were punished not for being Christians, but for lighting fires. In other words, though some Christians may have been caught up in Nero's face-saving diversionary action, they did not motivate it. Had there been no fire, there would have been no arrests, and thus no "persecution."

When, where, and why, then, does the deliberate persecution, or prosecution, of Christians begin, and for what reasons? As usual, origins are murky. The later writings eventually collected in the New Testament will make frequent allusion to "persecution." The apocalyptic whore of Babylon in the book of Revelation, clearly a figure for Rome, is "drunk with the blood of the saints and the blood of the witnesses of Jesus" (Revelation 17.1–6). But the dating of this text is uncertain, and it is nonspecific about what its community was actually enduring, from whom, and why.

With Pliny's letter to Trajan, composed circa 110 CE, we gain some traction on the issue. Pliny had evidently executed a group of Christians. Someone had brought an accusation of their being Christians to the governor: at issue seems to have been their imputed "secret crimes" (*Letter* 10.96, 2). Pliny had asked them to recant no fewer than three times. When they refused, Pliny sent the ones who held Roman citizenship off to Rome, while dispatching the others, punishing them for their "obstinacy." They had defied his authority by stubbornly refusing to recant.

But now another, larger group was in his court, having been anonymously denounced. Some of these people asserted that they had never been Christians; others, that they had once been Christians, but for some time had ceased being so. They established their disaffection by obeying the governor's orders, offering before the emperor's image and those of the gods, and cursing Christ.

In this connection, Pliny adds that these (former) Christians gathered together to eat, but had ceased meeting when the governor's order banning political associations was issued. His offhanded remark about Christian group meals—that the food consumed was of "an ordinary and innocent kind"—gives us a glimpse at some of the accusations attached to this new movement. Christians were rumored to eat human flesh. Pliny's examination has established their innocence in this regard. Investigating further, Pliny tortured two enslaved women who, he says, were "deaconesses," some sort of community assistants. (Torture was a legal and a class-specific way of eliciting testimony in Roman courts.) Pliny reports that nothing more than an outlandish superstitio was revealed.

This second group of defendants proved to Pliny's satisfaction that they were Christian no longer. They were released. When Trajan wrote back, he praised Pliny's procedure, observing that the situation allowed for no hard and fast rules. Former Christians were not to be prosecuted. Trajan advised that Christians not be sought out. (Roman law in general was primarily reactive—in this instance, responsive to the anonymous denunciation—not proactive: Christians were not arrested at government initiative.) Anonymous accusations, the emperor concluded, were absolutely inadmissible, "unworthy of our time" (*Letter* 10.97).

According to Christian apologists, Christians were accused of incest, murder, and cannibalism. Some scholars have tried to explain these accusations situationally. Christians called each other "brother" and "sister," and would exchange the "kiss of peace." Eucharistic celebrations, misheard from a middle distance, might imply cannibalism—eating flesh and drinking blood. Imagination embroidered rumor, filling in details: babies sprinkled with flour before being sacrificed for the common meal; dogs tied to lamps that, overturned by a canine lunge, brought the darkness necessary for sexual misconduct.

What we see here, however, is another version of the accusations common to ethnic stereotyping, wherein different groups of foreigners— Egyptians, Jews, Persians, Germans—were similarly characterized. These tropes presented an all-purpose way of saying, "Unlike *us*, *you* are morbidly antisocial and uncivilized. We don't like you." And such detailed accusations occur only in Christian sources. Indeed, Christians also accused each other of such enormities. Justin, disavowing such behaviors for his own group, comments, "whether *they*"—other Christian groups— "do those shameful things . . . we do not know" (1 *Apology* 26.7). Perhaps, then, some of those bringing accusations against one group of Christians were Christians of another stripe.

These lurid rumors of cannibalism and of sexual malfeasance put to rest, what dominates the stories about martyrs is their refusal to make offerings. How these people would have been put in such a situation is unclear. Ancient Rome was not a modern police state: in the normal course of events, no one was monitoring cultic behavior. Nor, until the mid-third century under the emperor Decius, would there be mechanisms in place to do so.

Nor, on the evidence of the martyr stories themselves, was simply being Christian sufficient reason to be arrested. In *The Passion of Perpetua and Felicitas*, other Christians go in and out of the prison in regular contact with the martyrs. If simply being a Christian were actionable, the governor was losing a great opportunity to round up more. In *The Martyrdom of Pionius*, the hero is surrounded by his admiring flock: the same observation obtains. So too with the story of the martyrs of Lyon: the Christian community gathers to watch the events occurring in the arena, evidently to no ill effect. So too when the bishop Cyprian was martyred, surrounded by his very vocally supportive flock: no widespread arrests were made.

Spectacles of Death

The factual improbabilities posed by these narratives hint at how they functioned socially. The term "martyr" means "witness." But to be a martyr, martyrs themselves needed witnesses. The witnesses presented in the story create a bridge to the text's secondary witnesses, the story's later hearers. "Martyrdom" in this view is not an event—the violent death of a Christian—but a form of discourse, a literary genre. These owed much to the depictions of violence against those Jews who resisted forced Hellenization during the Maccabean Revolt of the mid-second century BCE. Second Maccabees 7 presents *in nuce* the stylized descriptions that will shape later Christian martyr acts. (The Maccabean "martyrs" themselves will eventually be appropriated as saints for and by the later church.)

Martyr acts as literature were communal performances of memory. They were read aloud in commemorations of the martyr's death. They did ideological work, both constructing and presenting idealized exempla of Christian identity. Again and again in these stories, the hero insists,

"I am a Christian." Stalwart refusal to offer to the emperor or to the gods or to both seals the hero's fate, which he or she embraces enthusiastically ("Thanks be to God!") and endures with equanimity. Indeed, so much are the martyrs in control of their circumstances and of themselves that they seem not to suffer at all.

What is the relation of these stories to the events that they purportedly describe? How much time stands between the putative event and its narrative retelling? The dating of these stories is uncertain, which makes it difficult to establish a chronology for early anti-Christian initiatives. Compounding this problem, we also have multiple versions of a given story, a datum that testifies to their continuing textual fluidity. Their claims to be eyewitness reports, their self-presentation as trial transcripts, their accounts of the text's lineage of transmission, can all be understood as techniques of legitimation, strategies for establishing and conveying the authority of the martyr text. As such, these writings represent less a report of actual events than narrative teaching devices, articulating a social identity that created a neat and unambiguous distinction between "pagan" and "Christian." They also provided a way to understand current circumstances *as* persecution—and indeed, to understand "persecution" as the quintessential Christian experience, one literally embodied by Jesus, himself seen as dying for Christianity in order to establish his church.

The development of Christian martyrdom as a type of ideology coincided with a phase in Roman public entertainment. Civic holidays—days dedicated to the gods; celebrations of the emperor and his family; displays of munificence by local grandees—were marked with games, races, various competitions, and theatrical performances. These were tremendously popular, enthusiastically attended, and visually memorialized in mosaics decorating private homes. Some of these contests did double duty. Gladiatorial combats and struggles against wild animals not only marked these holidays with violent blood sports. They also provided a public venue for the execution of war captives and condemned criminals. Enthused spectators visually drank in blood. Christians could provide a source of such victims.

Yet so popular were gladiatorial contests that Christians themselves (to draw on Tertullian's fierce complaints) attended them as spectators.

And these entertainments perdured well into the Christian period. Constantine, signing off on the observances of the imperial cult for a small Italian town, approved the number of gladiators to be engaged. (This was after his conversion to Christianity.) In the late fourth century, Chrysostom was still complaining about the Christian presence at spectacles and games. His younger contemporary Augustine, in book 6 of his *Confessions*, described how the arena's violence had seduced the enthused participation of Alypius, a close friend and latterly a fellow bishop. "He found delight in the murderous contest and was drunk with bloodthirsty pleasure" (*Confessions* 6.8,3).

These urban contests provide the narrative setting for martyrdoms. *Ekphrasis*, the rhetorical tool of vivid verbal visualization, accounts both for these stories' intensity and for their appeal. Condemned to death in the arena as part of these civic celebrations, the martyr him- or herself performs as an athlete of Christ, competing for the "crown," besting pagan persecutors, through death emerging victorious. In *The Martyrs of Lyon*, the victims endure all torments and wear down their torturers. Beaten, burned with red-hot bronze plates, stretched and broken, one hero amazes his tormentors by emerging "unbent and straight." In *Perpetua*, the heroine has a vision wherein she herself becomes a man. Stripped and oiled in the arena, she/he begins to wrestle with a "vicious Egyptian." Fists fly. The Egyptian tries to topple Perpetua; "but," she says, "I kept striking him in the face with the heels of my feet." She kicks and pummels him, and then, as she says, "put my two hands together linking the fingers of one hand with those of the other and thus I got ahold of his head. He fell flat on his face, and I stepped on his head" (*Perpetua* 10). The blow-by-blow description of their contest evinces the writer's familiarity with real-life spectacles while conjuring them for the text's audience.

The martyr's story, in short, offered a verbal spectacle to the pious hearer when the *acta* were read in community. This was in part an effort to entice listeners from attending the actual spectacles themselves. Attend they did. Tertullian, in his treatise *On Spectacles*, inveighs against the Christian presence at the games. Such places are the locale of idols, he insists, the haunt of demons. Christians who frequent them risk demonic possession and even ignoble death. Urging that the Christian avoid such amusements, however, Tertullian mentions almost as an afterthought that arenas should be avoided because they served as sites of anti-Christian persecution. This admonition occurs only in chapter 27 of a thirty-chapter harangue.

Tertullian grants that the pleasures of such pastimes are sweet, but their sweetness, he warns, masks their poison. He further complains that some Christians balked at exhortations to abstain from the games: Scripture, they pointed out, nowhere prohibited them. Tertullian counters with the promise of an eschatological spectacle for the pious. "What sight will wake my wonder, my laughter, my joy and exultation," he enthuses, when he will watch magistrates, philosophers, poets, actors, charioteers, athletes, and Jews burn for all eternity. Be patient in foregoing civic spectacles, Tertullian urged. Hell offered to the Christian the promise of a bigger and better spectacle of death (*On Spectacles* 30).

Tertullian's curiously belated mention in *On Spectacles* of Christian suffering in the arena puts the question: how common and widespread were such events? Before 250 CE, actions brought against Christians seem to have been random, sporadic, and local: there were no empire-wide, imperially sponsored persecutions. How particular Christians ended up before the governor we have no idea. Some were denounced as such to local magistrates, who could rule at their own discretion (as Pliny did). Did some Christians do something to put themselves forward, by defacing a divine image? Perhaps. We have Christian criticisms of such volunteerism—and accounts—like the stories of Lucius in Justin's 2 *Apology* 2, and of Agathonikē in *Martyrdom of Carpus, Papylus and Agathonikē*—that admire such behavior. But Christian teachings on martyrdom were themselves variable. Against an enthusiastic embrace of violent death we have sayings in the Gospels that the Christ follower, encountering opposition, should flee to another place (Matthew 10.23). Whoever does not flee, opined Clement of Alexandria, becomes complicit in the sin of his persecutor.

+ + +

But what brought on this anti-Christian opprobrium in the first place? Here we must look to local circumstances: earthquakes, celestial anomalies, outbreaks of disease. All were easily interpreted as signs of divine anger, a breakdown in good relations with the gods. Such events naturally caused alarm and could trigger unrest. If gentile Christians were known not to show respect to the gods, the common understanding was that the gods would of course strike back: the Christians, ergo, were the root reason for the disaster. Origen, commenting on the Gospel of Matthew, remarked that Christians were blamed for famines, pestilence, and earthquakes—on this account "churches have suffered persecutions and have been burnt down" (sec. 39). If the Tiber overflows or the Nile does not, Tertullian complained, if the earth moves or the sky does not, if there is famine or plague, "the cry goes up, 'The Christian to the lion!'" (*Apology* 40.2).

Popular anxiety, in short, fastened on ex-pagan gentile Christ followers not because they were Christians, but because they were, in the view of the majority, deviant pagans, impiously angering the gods, destabilizing the concordant between heaven and earth. Such deviance of course had real consequences. "No rain, because of the Christians!" So Augustine, reporting popular sentiment in the early fifth century (*City of God* 2.3). Unhappy natural events could trigger coercion. Styles of civic spectacle encouraged it.

Yet Christianity—or Christianities—were not underground movements. After the Persians captured the emperor Valerian in 260, his son and heir Gallienus put a stop to Valerian's anti-Christian initiatives. Christians were to be unmolested, he ordered, and their property returned—so there was property, including cemeteries, to be returned (Eusebius, *Church History* 7.13). Christians met in buildings, both purpose-built and remade residences. They had books. An inventory of church goods seized during the last great pagan persecution under Diocletian listed two gold chalices, six silver chalices, six silver urns, lamps in a variety of metals, and various items of clothing for distribution to the poor. Later, Constantine could not have ordered the property of criminalized Christian minorities to be impounded had there not been property to seize. In the early 300s, before the outbreak of the "Great Persecution," a significant Christian public building stood across from the emperor's palace in Nicomedia.

By the late third and early fourth century, in fine, Christianities of all sorts had found their place on the public urban map.

We also find further evidence of social integration well before the accession of Constantine. Already by the mid-third century, some Phrygian Christians appear in inscriptions as members of city councils. They were thus involved to some degree with liturgies for the city's presiding deities. A third-century Christian in Bithynia—Pliny's old province—was his town's magistrate, underwriting the civic games. Another Christian competed in several pagan athletic events and also served as a town councilor. One Abercius, toward the end of the second century, erected a lengthy Christian epitaph. By the early fourth century, Eusebius claimed, some Christians served as governors of provinces; and he reports that the Christian intellectual Julius Africanus, in 222, petitioned the emperor Severus to rebuild a Christian shrine. Africanus also worked as an architect for Severus's library in Rome. His contemporary Origen was summoned for a consultation on divine matters by the imperial regent Julia Mamaea. A church canon from circa 300 describes baptized men who also served as priests in the cult of the (pagan) emperor. Nor did Christians hesitate to appeal to the emperor to settle an internal dispute. In the early 270s the church in Antioch, frozen in stalemate, petitioned the pagan emperor Aurelian: the bishop, Paul of Samosata, had been judged guilty of heresy by three episcopal councils, but he refused to vacate his church. (Aurelian said that the community should follow the ruling of the bishop of Rome. Paul was ousted.) In short, well before Constantine, Christianity itself was not illegal, nor was it "underground."

How many Christians, then, of all denominations, suffered violent death? We have no numbers of any sort—not of the total population of the empire, not of Christians of any and all stripes among the population, not of those who, as Christians, would have been the objects of coercion. Some Christians did heroically stand up for their principles, emboldened, perhaps, by the promise of direct ascent to heaven. But an observation of Origen's in the mid-240s bears repeating. In his work against a pagan critic, Celsus, he observed that "a few, whose number could easily be counted, have died occasionally for the sake of the Christian religion" (*Against Celsus* 3.8).

Turning Points

In the year 212, the emperor Caracalla, in an unprecedented move, extended Roman citizenship—thus, Roman law—to most free inhabitants of the empire. Historians debate Caracalla's motive, but not the effect of his edict. The *Constitutio Antoniana* greatly expanded "Romanness." Free residents of the empire were now citizens of the imperial city, and in that sense involved in new ways with Roman law and, thus, with Roman *religio*. As the emperor phrased it, he was gathering people as Romans to the service of Rome's gods (*Papyrus Ginessis* 40, col. I). Rome was not only the eternal city: it was now the universal one, too.

As the century proceeded, the empire experienced tremendous instability and upheaval. Multiple armies acclaimed their own generals as emperors, a sure recipe for civil war. Within a fifty-year period, some twenty-five emperors came and went. Frontiers crumbled. Plague ravaged the population. Finally in 249 the then-emperor, Decius, sounded Caracalla's idea of Roman universalism in an actively and specifically religious key. He ordered residents of the empire to perform uniform public acts of piety, a *supplicatio* to the gods for the eternity of the empire. Tax forms were adapted to document compliance. Enacting the sacrifice before a witnessing government official, the offeror would receive a *libellus*, a certificate testifying to the fulfillment of his obligation. At issue was not a question of belief, but the performance of cult to the divine.

Christians throughout the empire were affected by this imperial mandate. As a "big government" initiative, it caught more Christians in the finer and broader mesh of its legislative net. The admired ideal of martyrdom notwithstanding, very great numbers of Christians complied and made offerings. "At the first threatening words of the Enemy," complained Cyprian, "an all too large number of the brethren betrayed their faith. They were not felled by the violence of the persecution, but fell of their own free will" (*Concerning the Lapsed* 7). Cyprian implies that these "lapsed" suffered from a failure of nerve.

But these Christians may simply have constructed their own Christianness in such a way that they saw nothing wrong, as Romans, in offering for the well-being of the empire. Those Christians who *did* see a problem could order their slaves to act as their proxies. Others feigned mental incompetence (like David when he pretended to be mad, said Bishop Peter of Alexandria approvingly, *Canonical Epistle*, canon 5). The wealthy simply bribed officials to look the other way. (Peter also approved of this, saying that such Christians served God rather than mammon in so doing, showing their contempt for money, canon 12.) Others exploited a legal loophole, designating pagan relatives as proxies. Still others bribed officials for a libellus. (The more stalwart derogated these people as *libellatici*, "certificate holders.") Some Christians (like Cyprian himself) fled. Others stood their ground and refused. Of this latter group, some were exiled, some imprisoned, others executed.

Again, Decius's intent was not, in a first-order way, to target Christians. His goal was to safeguard the empire. He wanted compliance, not martyrs. As long as the Christian obliged the state, he or she could go on being a Christian. But in the perspective (and rhetoric) of Christian martyrdom, Decius had initiated a persecution. And several years later, in 257–60, a successor emperor, Valerian, took more deliberate aim. He specifically targeted Christian property and leadership and mandated penalties for those of the social elite who would not sacrifice. Sacrifice testified to Roman bona fides.

When shortly thereafter Valerian was captured by Persians on the eastern front, these efforts at religiously inflected homeland security ended. But they left in their wake a crisis of discipline within the churches, precisely because great numbers, even among the clergy, had complied with the government's demands. What to do? What exactly constituted a "lapse"? Who were the lapsed, how were they to be identified, and how could they be reinstated in the community? And what about bishops who had fled, or indeed had sacrificed—could they resume their office? Who was to determine who was in and who was out?

Cyprian, bishop of Carthage, well illustrates the divisive effects that these disciplinary problems could cause. Cyprian himself had fled the city and gone into hiding in 250, directing his church by correspondence and occasionally sending back funds. When he returned, Decius's death having ended his efforts, Cyprian's authority was so compromised by lay *confessores* (Christians who had gone to prison, prepared for death, but who had survived) and by angry presbyters (who had stayed put) that seismic internal power struggles ensued. Confessors issued their own *libelli*, certifying the forgiveness of the sin of lapsing on their own charismatic authority. The presbyters backed them up.

Cyprian responded by insisting on hierarchical party discipline, condemning his critics, corralling other bishops to issue directives, famously arguing that *extra ecclesiam nulla salus*, "outside the church there is no salvation." The church, in his view, was embodied in the office of the bishop. Control was to be asserted through the administration of sacraments. Baptism or consecration given by lapsed prelates, Cyprian insisted, was inadmissible: the fallen could not be receptacles, thus channels, of holy spirit. Recipients of such *sacramenta* would have to be rebaptized, or (if clerics) to be consecrated within proper episcopal channels, declared as such by episcopal councils convened under his authority.

Cyprian's community remained bitterly divided. When the emperor Valerian in 258 offered another opportunity for martyrdom, the bishop had little choice. His congregation clustered around him at his execution, crying out to be martyred with him. (Once again, notably, this public proclamation of Christian allegiance occasioned no official response.) By that point, Carthage had no fewer than three bishops, Rome had two—and those were just the ones self-designated as "orthodox and catholic" (that is, "right-thinking and universal"). Schism perdured: Novatian, in Rome, insisting on taking a hard line against the lapsed, formed another long-lived branch of the church.

But—perhaps surprisingly—other Christians saw no problem with pagan observances. The council of Elvira (ca. 303?) had to mandate penalties for baptized Christian men of means who served as priests in the (still-pagan) imperial cult, making offerings to the emperor and his family and organizing gladiatorial games. Again, these men evidently saw no problem with being baptized Christians and serving in the cult. This ruling of the council evinces both the penetration of Christianity into upper classes (participation in these cults took money) and, for some Christians, the abiding normativity of majority culture.

With the death of Valerian, imperial initiatives against Christians ceased. The new emperor, Gallienus, even ordered that church properties should be restored to the bishops. Churches settled into a long period of growth.

Then abruptly, in the closing decades of the third century, in a situation of grinding military turmoil, the empire was recreated once again. The general Diocletian, seizing control, established an innovative imperial power-sharing arrangement: a college of four rulers (the "Tetrarchy"), two Augusti and two Caesars, would govern the wide territories of Rome. Diocletian's reorganization de facto acknowledged a split in the empire between (Greek) East and (Latin) West. And from this point forward, the city of Rome faded as a truly central node of power: the emperors and their entourages would move between imperial capitals closer to the porous frontiers.

As part of his efforts, Diocletian sponsored a religious revival, since— as usual—the empire's safety depended on correct cult. This meant, in turn, identifying and rooting out what was deviant cult. The first Christian group to fall victim to Diocletian's scruples was the Manichees, the extraordinarily vigorous, culturally eclectic Christian missionary church arising out of Mesopotamia in the mid-third century. Its prophet, Mani, had taught and later been martyred in Persia, but the movement that he had founded went on, endured, and flourished. In the West, by the late 200s, it had already crossed Mesopotamia and Syria into Roman Palestine and Egypt, thence into North Africa, and ultimately into Italy, then Gaul and Spain. In the East, via the Silk Road, it eventually reached China, continuing there until the fourteenth century.

Diocletian saw Manichaean Christianity as a depraved foreign incursion, another Persian threat to the Roman state. In 302, Manichaean rites were classified as *maleficia*, black magic, which was itself already banned. Their books were to be burned, their leaders subjected to capital punishment. Aristocratic Roman communicants would forfeit both property and liberty, and the right to make bequests. The ban was harsh, but its application was haphazard: as late as the 390s in North Africa, Manichaean missionaries were able to move around, to missionize, and to participate in public debates.

Still, Manichaean Christianity constituted a criminal offence against the state. The church historian Eusebius, looking back across several decades, approved of Diocletian's initiative. Mani, he said, "stitched together false and godless doctrines that he had collected from the countless, long-extinct, godless heresies, and infected our empire with the deadly poison that came from the land of the Persians" (*Church History* 7.31). Pagan anti-Christian persecution was fine, according to Eusebius, as long as it was directed against the wrong sort of Christian.

Beginning in 303, however, Diocletian turned his attention to more domestic forms of Christianity. Roman Christians were accused of attracting harmful demons to the cities, causing a pollution that interrupted the efficacy of rites directed toward the gods. Divination had been disrupted, the divine/human communications necessary for good governance compromised. The usual sanctions—confiscation of property, destruction of buildings, exile or imprisonment or execution of leadership, demands for traditional sacrifice—ensued.

The prosecution of Diocletian's program was uneven. Preserved in Christian memory as "the Great Persecution"—probably because it came as such a shock following the decades of peace since the emperor Gallienus in 260—it lasted only a few years in the West, where it was summarily suspended by (the pre-Christian) Constantine in 306. In the East it persisted on and off until 311. But by then, the damage once again had been done. Schism erupted within the churches. The ensuing divisions over issues of community discipline would outlast the western empire itself.

In 305, in an unprecedented move, Diocletian retired from his imperial duties. Power once again seesawed between various military contestants. One of these was Constantine who, acclaimed by his army at York, eventually conquered the western half of the empire by 312. By 324, he had consolidated his hold over the East as well. Like his earlier, now-vanquished colleagues, Constantine too pursued policies defining a universalized Romanitas as right religio, and he condemned as superstitio any deviation from proper cult.

But now the shoe was on the other foot. Constantine championed a new construction of piety. The old gods were demoted to the status of evil demons. The Christian god and his son now defined true deity. They alone, Constantine ruled, were the appropriate recipients of Roman worship.

This shift of religious allegiance, however, did not bring the age of Christian martyrdom to a close. On the contrary, the longest and most effective period of imperial Christian persecution was only beginning, this time enacted by the Christian emperor himself, who strove to suppress "heresies" and to root out schism.

North African Christians were the first to feel this blow. The root reason went back to events under Diocletian in 303 to 305. Under pressure to oblige the government's directives, some bishops had handed over scriptures to imperial troops. Others handed off nonsacred texts, complying through subterfuge. Still others resisted and were imprisoned and even killed. Once the dust had settled, internal controversy emerged around the figure of the new bishop of Carthage, Caecilian. His predecessor had appeared excessively pliable, handing over heretical books, as a feint, for destruction: more stalwart clergy criticized him for his compromise. When he died, his deacon Caecilian was consecrated by a lapsed bishop, himself accused as a *traditor* who had indeed handed over holy books. Other African prelates looked back to Cyprian. How could such a compromised agent be a vessel of holy spirit? How could the consecration by a traditor be valid? How could his baptism be legitimate, effective? Caecilian's opposition accordingly consecrated another man, Majorinus, as bishop. The "orthodox" church in North Africa was once again split.

No sooner had Constantine declared his new allegiance than he was pulled into this controversy. Majorinus's side appealed to the emperor in 313 to settle the dispute. Constantine referred the question to the bishop of Rome, who then convened a council of bishops from Gaul and Italy. These prelates, balking at the North African idea of rebaptism, found in favor of Caecilian. The losing side promptly petitioned Constantine again. Constantine himself convened the next council of bishops in 314: they again found for Caecilian. His opponents then appealed to Constantine a third time. Losing patience, Constantine attempted to settle the issue by force, sending imperial troops to Africa to execute these decisions by confiscating dissent properties for the catholics' church. Realizing eventually that such efforts were counterproductive, he left the two parties to fester.

The Caecilianists enjoyed the recognition of the bishop of Rome. It was they, then, they insisted, who were to be regarded as "orthodox" and "universal" (catholica), the true church. Their opponents, aghast at the victory of the traditor clergy, declared themselves the true church. Theirs was the church of the martyrs, the one who had stood up—and who stood up still—to the power of imperial Rome. Their catholic opponents in turn named this communion after one of its members, Donatus. The dissenters were no longer "Christians." They were "Donatists."

The ideology of martyrdom fueled Donatist identity. Doctrinally identical to the Caecilianists, split on the issue of community discipline and sacramental protocols (Donatists hewed closely to Cyprian's position: those baptized by traditor clergy needed rebaptism), they could see their own experience as continuous with that of the church in its heroic age, which for them had never ended. Both sides of this ecclesiastical civil war met around the same memorials to the martyred saints—though to these sites the Donatists could add a roster of their own. Both followed the same liturgical calendars, though to these Donatists added their own celebrations of specifically Donatist martyrs. Both had dense episcopal hierarchies, indeed evenly matched. One century on, by 411, sprinkled across large cities and small towns, 285 dissident bishops faced off with 268 catholic ones. Both sides controlled basilicas, property, martyria, and loyal followings. Both sides claimed sole legitimacy. But with the catholic embrace of state coercive power in the early fifth century, Donatists would produce more martyrs still.

An activist western emperor, Honorius, primed by heavy lobbying on the part of North Africa's catholic clergy, determined finally to break the deadlock. He issued an Edict of Unity in 405, demanding that the Donatists stand down. Donatist bishops had the options of submission, arrest, or exile. The noncompliant would thenceforth be regarded not as schismatics but as heretics, subject to the same legal disabilities as other heretics, the first targets of Constantine's efforts at consolidation almost a century earlier. This meant that wealthy Donatist laymen could

neither hold public office nor avail themselves of legal protection, including passing on property to designated heirs.

Finally, in 410, the emperor posted another order: "We abolish the
new superstitio, and we command that the regulations in regard to
catholic law be preserved unimpaired and inviolate" (*Theodosian Code*
16.11.3). Armed resistance in the countryside persisted, sometimes transmuting into defiant suicides. The Donatist bishop of Timgad, together
with his whole congregation, threatened to burn their basilica down
around themselves rather than surrender it to agents of the state.

Better a few Donatists burn in their own flames, opined Augustine
of this last incident, than their vast majority perish in the flames of hell.
From this principle of pastoral concern, Augustine developed a theological apology for the use of coercion against other Christians. A martyr was
not a true martyr, he argued, if his cause was spiritually flawed. If endured
in defiance of the catholic church, such suffering was merely prideful and
misguided. Coercive force in itself, he continued, was neither good nor
bad: its motivation determined its morality. Born of love, and of concern
for the well-being of its object, violence was sanctioned by scripture itself.
Look, said Augustine, at Moses's occasional harsh treatment of Israel;
look at God's coercion, on the road to Damascus, of the apostle Paul. Such
coercion, administered lovingly, is actually *disciplina*. To rebuke errant
Christians, if necessary by force, was the sacred duty of the true church.

The Communion of Saints

No one knows how many Christians, of any persuasion, suffered at the
hands of the state, be the state itself pagan or Christian. It is the ideology
of martyrdom, developing across the second and third centuries, flourishing fiercely in the fourth, that emerges most clearly from our unoblig-
ing evidence. Whence its power, and its perduring appeal?

Martyrdom as a literary genre provides one answer. These stories
dramatically conveyed idealized principles of faith. The nonheroic
many—be they the narrative audience within the text or its actual auditors when the text was read—could admire the heroic few, while vividly
visualizing the torments suffered by the saints.

As a discourse of identity, the acts of the martyrs configured adversity as persecution in ways that aligned the trials of their protagonists with the charismatic founding figures of Jesus and of the great protomartyr, Stephen. Even more importantly: unlike his less courageous coreligionists, the martyr after death was thought to ascend immediately to heaven. This conviction had real time consequences. Imprisoned for his witness, the potential martyr enjoyed considerable prestige and charismatic authority in the interim between confinement and death. That prestige and authority continued—to Cyprian's chagrin—even if death did not result. Confessors functioned as living martyrs, outside of, beyond, and occasionally against episcopal control.

Martyr stories anchored hearers meaningfully in a cosmic battle waged against demons. Most ancient people of whatever religious affiliation held that superhuman beings, *daimonia*, were drawn by the rituals of sacrifice. For pagans, these beings could be good or bad; for Christians, all these powers were demonic in a negative sense. They lurked around pagan altars, awaiting their feasts of incense and blood. They rode on sacrificial meats, polluting those who lapsed, possessing them, causing disease and death—indeed, causing the outbursts of persecution to begin with.

In the figure of the martyr, the wavering and the lapsed had a model of correct behavior against the temptations of compliance in the worship of demons, a stalwart stance communicated by hearing the martyr narrative read in community. And, should the listener fail his own test, he knew that he had a champion in the martyr. The saint stood as a patron, a well-placed intercessor with the divine, an active advocate for the defense. The exceptional few, having gone directly to Paradise, could plead on behalf of the nonheroic many.

As a form of entertainment, martyr stories appealed immediately to the taste of ancient audiences for spectacles of violence. "The materially minded look on and think how wretched and unfortunate those martyrs are," Augustine preached, "thrown to wild beasts, beheaded, burned with fire." The spiritual listeners do not "fix their attention on the mangling of bodies" but instead marvel at the completeness of faith: "a splendid spectacle offered to the eyes of the mind!" (*Sermon* 51.2). As the culture of martyrdom developed, so too did lurid descriptions of the torments endured. The victory of Constantine retrospectively magnified the severity of Diocletian's persecution, so that, post-Constantine, the number of martyrs—that is, of martyr stories—greatly increased. During this later period tales of earlier martyrs were redacted and sometimes composed. And as the numbers increased, so did grisly details of pagan torments.

Paradoxically, this valorization of suffering presented protagonists whose piety and will triumphed precisely over suffering. Lecturing their judges, these saints were heard but not hurt. And the stylized dialogue between the martyr and the governor gave scope for communicating dogmatic and ecclesiastical claims regarding the perversity of traditional cult, the abiding dangers of associating with Jews, the false faith of heretics, the authority of the bishop, and the efficacy of Christian salvation, this last seen already in the martyr's charismatic desensitization to pain.

The holy dead began to reshape Christian social life. Eating over a family tomb had a long history in Mediterranean culture. The rise of the cult of the martyrs developed this practice in new ways. On the death day of the saint, communities would gather around the grave, a practice so conspicuous that hostile imperial governments had proactively prohibited Christian meetings in cemeteries. More than within buildings, Christians—a vastly greater number—met in graveyards. It was on such occasions that the acts of the martyr could be read aloud. Animals might be killed and butchered for the feasting that followed. Exorcisms, divinations, and spectacular healings might occur. Eventually, post-Constantine, large basilicas, "cemetery churches," would be built over the graves of the saints.

By the fourth century, the evening vigils preceding these gatherings could become raucous celebrations, marked by dancing and singing as well as eating and drinking, all of which were normal aspects of ancient worship. The amount of food and drink consumed on such occasions offended the high-brow: "carnal gorging," Augustine complained. Yet the feasts continued, shaping a new urban calendar around the saint's day of death.

Eventually, bishops would domesticate the martyrs' wild charisma, enhancing their own prestige by serving as impresarios of these cults. The old pattern of civic elites ritually demonstrating respect to presiding deities for the well-being of the city was repeated, now with bishops in the stead of pagan aristocrats and saints as local heavenly patrons in the place of the old gods—a point not missed by noncatholic Christian critics. "You have changed pagan sacrifices into your love-feasts, their idols into your martyrs, whom you pray to like they pray to idols!" observed Faustus, a Manichaean bishop (*Against Faustus* 20.3). Faustus was both wrong and right. The metaphysics were different—martyrs were elevated humans, not local gods—but the social function of celestial patronage was precisely the same.

Present already in heaven, the special dead also exercised power on earth. Martyria became sites for healings, especially for exorcisms. The ill and the demon possessed flocked to these shrines. In fourth-century Egypt, ambiguous demons also gathered around saints' tombs, enabling divination for the faithful. Again, bishops objected. "They dare to question unclean spirits!" Athanasius fumed, offended by such confusions of charisma (*Festal Letter* 42).

Power concentrated particularly in the body of the martyr, leading not only to celebrations in cemeteries, but also to the physical partitioning of the dead. These body parts, "relics," were the hard currency of Christian piety. They were infused with healing powers and lavished with pious attention. Catholics claimed that the Donatist schism had erupted when Caecilian reprimanded a local *grande dame*, Lucilla, for her public display of piety: she ostentatiously kissed a saint's bone before receiving communion. (The offended Lucilla—so the story— responded by sponsoring Majorinus, a man of her own household, as an alternative bishop.) The truth of the tale matters less than the etiquette of piety that it reveals: physical proximity to sanctity was empowering. In Milan, Bishop Ambrose's surprising discovery of the bodies of two obscure saints galvanized Milan's catholic community, enhancing his prestige and local clout against the resident imperial family.

In 415, in Jerusalem, the presbyter Lucianus miraculously recovered the body of Saint Stephen. The prestige of Jerusalem's bishop soared.

Furtively divided, parts of Stephen's body then journeyed west. On Minorca, in 418, the saint inspired and enabled a local bishop to forcibly convert the island's Jews. Reaching North Africa, Stephen's remains were further parceled out. Wonders occurred even through contact with the dust around his various memorials. Augustine dedicated the last book of his great intellectual masterpiece *The City of God* to recounting the miracles that Stephen's relics worked. Healing in this life anticipated the restoration of the body at the final resurrection.

The body of the ultimate martyr, Christ, could not be brought directly into this divine economy: he had ascended bodily into heaven. Things that he had touched, however, had remained behind, premier objects of adoration. Most spectacular was the discovery of his cross, a wonder attributed to Constantine's mother, Helena, when she toured Jerusalem. Over Christ's recovered tomb rose the magnificent church of the Holy Sepulcher.

Great works of public architecture had long been a traditional feature of the imperial repertoire of power, one that Constantine himself had readily embraced. Christian construction projects bloomed around biblical sites, especially those named in the Gospels, which had been sanctified through their contact with Jesus. Pilgrims—the foot soldiers of the Christianization of Roman Palestine—appeared in increasing numbers. Socially and architecturally, the old Jewish homeland was transformed into the new Christian Holy Land, itself become a kind of relic: a nexus, like the saint's body, for contact between heaven and earth.

Rhetoric of Martyrdom

The rhetoric of martyrdom proved impressively elastic. In the fourth century, when theological controversies racked the imperially sponsored church and emperors attempted to enforce doctrinal unity, exiled bishops presented themselves as the new "martyrs," suffering for their witness to the true faith (that is, to the particular doctrinal position that they espoused). Opposing Christian rulers were extravagantly vilified as "persecutors" on the order of Nero and of Decius. Champions of the council of Nicaea (325) against "Arian" opponents, and later defenders of the council of Chalcedon (451) against imperial efforts at building consensus, were quick to label the experience of opposition as "persecution." By claiming to be martyrs, they seized the rhetorical and ideological high ground.

The Donatists, objects of the successful Caecilianist manipulation of imperial coercive force, took their situation as evidence that theirs was the right position: the true church was the persecuted church, the true Christians those who suffered rather than compromise their faith. Later, with the Vandal invasion of North Africa, the tables were turned on their catholic opponents: the newcomers were "Arian" Christians, representing the threat of establishing another local rival church. The Vandals mobilized earlier Roman legislation originally drawn up against the Donatists to now undermine catholic dominance and to appropriate catholic properties. The catholics duly framed their new circumstances as "persecution," their own side as the church of martyrs. *Christianus sum*—"I am a Christian"—the signature statement of witness in the earlier martyr narratives, was reappropriated by the catholics against the Vandals (who were themselves, of course, Christian).

The language and the ideology of martyrdom could also shape less dramatic situations, such as that of personal illness. Inveighing against his flock's dependence on amulets, Augustine presented illness as an opportunity for martyrdom. By declining to resort to such a practice (the efficacy of which Augustine does not question), the ill person becomes a martyr on his sickbed (*Sermon* 18.7–8 Dolbeau). For the true Christian, Augustine urges, death would be preferable to resorting to such aids. Even Christian amulets should be avoided: physical death is to be preferred to "dying forever," since recourse to such practices, Augustine insisted, was tantamount to a denial of the faith.

Internal doctrinal disputes, political setbacks, even individual illness: all could be framed with the rhetoric of martyrdom. In this way, what might seem a personal difficulty could be perceived as a part of a larger struggle, as the positive pole in an unambiguous confrontation between good (the side of the "persecuted") and evil (the side of rival authorities, including that of extra-ecclesiastical ritual experts and healers). Current problems thus took on a religious dimension of tremendous theological resonance, enabling and expressing an identification with the martyred saint and with the figure of Christ himself. And martyr narratives, proliferating especially in the period after Constantine, also served as a way for the church now favored by the emperor, indeed now empowered by the emperor and identified with the empire, to construct continuity between its current position of dominance and its idealizations of its own heroic past.

4

THE FUTURE OF THE END

The revelation of Jesus Christ, which God gave him to show to his
servants what must soon take place . . . for the time is near.

REVELATION 1.1–3

Behold, from Adam all the years have passed, and behold, the
6,000 years are completed, . . . and now comes the day of judgment!

AUGUSTINE (QUOTING SOME EXCITED CHRISTIANS),
SERMON 113, 8

*When would the Kingdom of God arrive? Where would it arrive? What
happens to the dead before it comes, and after? And what sort of bodies
would its residents have? Controversy swirled about these questions, from
the time of Paul in the first century to the time of Augustine in the early
fifth. And different answers abounded. For some, persecution signaled the
approach of the End; for others, calculating the age of the world gave the answer. Ideas about eschatology (knowledge of final things) also supported
speculations about the final fates of individual believers. The proclamation
of God's kingdom led to elaborate constructions of Christian ideas about
heaven and hell.*

+ + +

The Second Coming

Followers of Jesus in his own generation—like Jesus himself and, before him, like John the Baptizer—had expected the Kingdom of God to arrive in their own lifetimes. From what we can see in our earliest documentation, this belief was tied to the idea of the impending resurrection of the dead. It was this conviction that prepared Jesus's own earliest followers for their experience of his individual resurrection. That event vindicated and validated his prophecy: "The Kingdom of God is at hand!" (Mark 1.15).

Jesus's resurrection, for this original community, was thus the first robin of the eschatological spring. Surely the Kingdom was now at hand; surely the general resurrection of the dead would soon occur. But now Christ himself would have to return to complete his mission: the earliest movement grew within what it saw as a temporal gap between Jesus's first coming, which ended on the cross, and his second manifestation, in power.

Paul echoes this conviction in his earliest letter, 1 Thessalonians, written almost twenty years after Jesus's death. The community there had apparently become unnerved that some of its members had died before Christ's anticipated return. Paul confidently asserted that things were still on track. "The Lord will appear with the cry of command," he reassured his Thessalonian hearers. "The dead in Christ will rise first; then *we who are alive, who are left,* will be caught up together with them in the clouds" (1 Thessalonians 4.16–17). Elsewhere, he taught his assembly at Corinth, "the form of this world is passing away" (1 Corinthians 7.31). The ends of the ages, he affirms, have fallen "upon us" (2 Corinthians 10.11). Christ's Second Coming, or Parousia ("appearance"), urged Paul, would occur within the lifetime of his hearers.

Implied in this message was an uncoordinated cascade of events prophesied in older Jewish writings. The restoration of all Israel; the turning of the nations to Israel's god; the final judgment; the rebuilding or glorification of Jerusalem or of its temple; the establishment of universal peace: these end-time events figured variously in different Jewish apocalypses. As Jewish prophetic traditions developed, details diverged.

According to the Temple Scroll from the Dead Sea, the final battle would be heralded by two messiahs, one priestly (descended from Moses's brother the first high priest, Aaron) and one royal (descended from David the warrior king). According to 2 Baruch, a first-century Jewish apocalypse, the Kingdom would be established on earth, which would then enjoy superabundance: each vine would have a thousand branches, and each branch one thousand clusters, and each cluster a thousand grapes. A version of this saying will later be attributed by the early Christian figure Papias, via Irenaeus, to Jesus himself (*Against Heresies* 5.33, 4).

Paul associated the arrival of God's kingdom with the return of Jesus as, specifically, the Davidic messiah—that is, as an eschatological warrior. Only after the final battle would the dead be raised. But whom does Paul's returning Christ defeat? In his first letter to Corinth, chapter 15, Paul had specified Christ's apocalyptic opponents: every "ruler" and every "authority" and every "power." What sounds like vague generalities actually refers to cosmic powers, those divine energy shells ringing antiquity's geocentric universe: stars, planets, daimonia, "godlings." Philo of Alexandria had designated the celestial bodies as "gods." For him, their presence was benign. For Paul, they were hostile—the pagan gods who were by nature not-gods, he says, those beings, the elements of the universe, that had previously enslaved his gentiles to their worship. They would submit to Christ at his glorious return.

In Philippians 2, Paul had predicted the defeated acquiescence of these powers: knees "above the earth and upon the earth and below the earth" would bend to the victorious Christ (Philippians 2.10). In the (brief) interregnum between Christ's resurrection and his triumphant return, Paul taught, believers were sustained by having Christ's "spirit" or "holy spirit" within them. That spirit was already moving them toward their final transformation, when both the quick and the dead would rise to the upper air (1 Thessalonians 4.17), thence into the heavens (Philippians 3.20), in bodies made not of dross matter but of material spirit (1 Corinthians 15.44).

This bodily transformation—presumably like the one that Jesus himself, in Paul's view, had undergone—would mark the believer's redemption. But unlike many Jewish eschatological prophets, Paul did not speak of a kingdom on earth. "Flesh and blood cannot inherit the Kingdom of God," Paul explained to the Corinthians, "nor can the perishable put on the imperishable" (1 Corinthians 15.50). Paul's vision of redemption was bodily, but not fleshly. For him, the Kingdom would be celestial, not terrestrial. The believer would ascend to the heavens in a *sōma pneumatikon*, a body made of spirit, above the sublunar realm. There, finally realizing God's ancient promise to Abraham, the redeemed would be like the stars (Genesis 15.5).

Later gospel writers saw things differently. Both Luke and John insisted on the fleshly physicality of the risen Christ. In Luke, Christ eats some fish to persuade the terrified apostles that he is not a ghost; in John, doubting Thomas famously fingers his scars. As the Kingdom lingered, other prophesied events filled in the widening gap between Jesus's first and second comings. First, said the synoptic gospel writers, the temple had to be destroyed; there would be wars and rumors of wars and false messiahs and persecutions and darkness at noon ("predicted" in Mark 13, composed sometime after the temple's destruction in 70, and repeated by Matthew and Luke). The Pauline author of Second Thessalonians, counseling patience in the wait for "the day of the Lord," introduced another intervening apocalyptic episode. A "man of lawlessness" must first appear, said "Paul," exalting himself and taking a seat in the temple. Currently restrained, this evil actor—associated with Nero as Antichrist in later Christian traditions—though abetted by Satan, would be slain by the returning Christ. And Christ's kingdom would come on earth.

Surely the most elaborate apocalyptic scenario involving Jesus appears in the book of Revelation, which now closes the New Testament canon. Its period of composition is debated, but it seems to have been written before the turn of the first century, perhaps during the time of the Judaean rebellion against Rome between 67 and 73 CE. (This dating would explain why the community felt persecuted by Rome.) Revelation represents a pastiche of older Jewish prophecies recombined around the figure of the apocalyptic Christ. An angel reveals to John a message that came heavily encoded in symbols, numbers, and alarming visions. The slain Jesus appears, promising those killed for their witness to him that they will soon be avenged once their full number is attained.

Quakes rack the earth, stars fall, the sun blackens, the moon becomes like blood. The martyred dead cry out for vindication and vengeance. 144,000 Israelites (male virgins all) are sealed from harm by angels; numberless others from all the nations, robed in white and "washed in the blood of the Lamb"—that is, of the slain Christ—worship before the throne of God. Mystical numbers structure the story: for five months, plagues ravage humanity. The nations trample the holy city for forty-two months. They gaze on the dead for three and a half days. Terrible reptiles and beasts prey on the saints, while the great whore of Babylon, drunk on their blood, commits fornication with the kingdoms of the earth.

But finally, dramatically, Babylon is no more. An angel binds Satan as the martyrs awake at a first resurrection to reign with Christ for a thousand years. Fire from heaven consumes the evil Gog and Magog. All the dead are then judged at a second resurrection. A new heaven and a new earth appear with the descent of the heavenly Jerusalem. Death is no more. Spread this prophecy, John's angel urges, "for the time is near. Behold, I am coming soon" (Revelation 22.20).

Yet time stretched on. When, then, was "soon"? How could one know? One way was to study the prophets' and the evangelists' catalogues of catastrophes—persecutions, plagues, earthquakes, celestial and social turmoil—and their allusions to kings, armies, and empires, and match these to the times. Particularly in periods of persecution, such interpretations, promising the vindication of the righteous, could be powerfully persuasive. The link between such suffering and impending redemption came directly from older Jewish traditions originating in the period of the Maccabean Revolt, namely the book of Daniel and 2 Maccabees. These texts, originating in another period of persecution, influenced the evangelists' apocalypses. Their prophetic potency was continually stimulated by events. During the reign of the emperor Severus (193–211), reports Eusebius, a Christian calculation based on numbers derived from Daniel predicted the imminent arrival of Antichrist, "so mightily did the agitation of persecution, then prevailing, shake the minds of many" (*Church History* 6.7).

Private revelations could also trigger apocalyptic hopes. Hippolytus of Rome, in his commentary on Daniel, warned against such responses.

He related two cautionary tales. In Syria, a bishop convinced his flock that Christ was awaiting them in the desert. Quitting their homes, wandering in the mountains to meet the Savior, the community was almost cut down as bandits. In Pontus, prompted by visions, another bishop taught that the final judgment was imminent. His people deserted their farms and awaited the End, which failed to arrive. Poverty and near starvation ensued (*Commentary on Daniel* 4.18–19).

Prophesies of the impending arrival of the Kingdom, spurred by persecution, could take on a pointedly political cast. John's apocalyptic Babylon, seated on seven hills, is clearly Rome. Writing against other Christians who imagined final redemption differently, Irenaeus read the prophesy of the book of Daniel together with Revelation and saw in the apocalyptic creatures the current ruling imperial power. The name of John's apocalyptic beast, encoded in the numbers 666, Irenaeus said, is "LATINUS" (*Against Heresies* 5.30, 3). Victorinus of Pettau, circa 300, awaited "the ruin of Babylon, that is, of the city of Rome" (*On the Apocalypse of John* 8.2). Persecution, to these authors, indicated the approach of the End, when Christ would return to complete his messianic mission, a big part of which would be to avenge his martyred saints.

Taming the Apocalypse

"Where is the promise of his coming?" asked some weary Christians early in the second century. "Ever since the fathers fell asleep, all things have continued as they were from the beginning of creation." The author of this pseudonymous New Testament epistle, "Peter," consoled and exhorted his auditors by recalling a line from Psalms: "With the Lord, one day is as a thousand years, and a thousand years as one day" (2 Peter 3.4 and 8; Psalm 90.4). The Kingdom was not late. God's timekeeping was simply different.

Some Christians later combined this verse from Psalms together with the idea of the first week of creation as presented in Genesis 1, and with the thousand-year reign of the saints promised in Revelation 20, to produce a new way to know what time it was on God's clock. They thus framed a key eschatological concept: the cosmic week, or the seven ages of the world.

As God had created the world in six days, and rested on the seventh, and as a day for him is as a thousand years, so too would the world exist for six ages, each lasting a thousand years. Then at the end of the sixth age, six thousand years since creation, Christ would return to inaugurate the millennial Sabbath rest of his saints. For another thousand years, in a restored Jerusalem, the saints would reign with Christ. To know the time of the End, then, one had only to calculate the age of the world. (No one in this period was dating *anno domini*: that convention was still centuries off.) To know the date of Christ's promised return, one had simply to discern when the year 6000 would fall.

This "scientific" calculation of the millennial week ran counter to the situational stimulation of apocalyptic hopes. These could be triggered by personal prophetic revelations: that was how the "New Prophecy" of Montanism had bloomed in mid-second-century Phrygia, foretelling the approach of the imminent End. Celestial anomalies, too, might presage the coming Kingdom. In the early third century, Tertullian, writing against Marcion, had spoken of the "heavenly Jerusalem" hovering in the Judean sky for forty days: it pointed ahead to the thousand-year reign of the saints, he said, when God would bring the heavenly city to earth. In 351, over Jerusalem, a luminous cross appeared in the sky. According to Jerusalem's then-bishop, Cyril, both pagans and, more especially, Jews were thereby prompted to convert: these events, coupled with the appearance of the celestial cross, were the sign of the coming Son of Man. The eschatological countdown had begun.

Still later, in 418, having forced Minorca's Jews to be baptized, Bishop Severus framed this event, too, as an eschatological sign of the approaching end: "Perhaps that time predicted by the Apostle has indeed now come, when the fullness of the gentiles will have come in and all Israel will be saved" (*Letter of Severus* 31.1). In the same year, Bishop Hesychius of Salona, spurred by a recent solar eclipse that had coincided with a great drought and an earthquake, wrote to Augustine asking whether the End might be at hand. Hesychius also based his hopes on a fundamentally optimistic reading of recent history. Since Rome had become Christian, he argued, most of the signs predicting Christ's

Parousia had been accomplished, and the gospel had been preached throughout the whole world (*Letter* 198.6).

Chronological calculations gained some control over such enthusiasms. Against agitations occasioned by circumstance—persecution, or natural phenomena whether on earth or in heaven, or social occurrences like mass conversions—these calculations had a calming effect. If the year 6000 were still some centuries off over the historical horizon line, current circumstances could not be interpreted as signaling the imminent end of the age.

Christian dating systems proliferated, drawing on the numbers and symbols available both in prophetic texts and in ones that could be read through that lens. One such system, advanced in the early third century by Hippolytus, identified the year 5500 since creation as the time of Christ's first advent. "From the birth of Christ one must count another five hundred years" (*Commentary on Daniel* 4.23–24). The year 6000 was thus pushed off to the equivalent date of 500 CE, a safe several centuries away. But such calculations were themselves fated to age. The date was affirmed by Constantine's apologist Lactantius in the early fourth century: "the entire time left seems no greater than two hundred years," he proclaimed in his *Divine Institutes* (7.25). The due date crept ever closer. In 397 CE, the bishop Hilarianus reiterated that the year 6000 was a scant hundred years off. The millennium loomed.

What would it be like, this earthly reign of the saints? Some Christians believed "after the resurrection that there will be engagements to marry and the procreation of children, for they"—that is, those Christians, complained Origen, who thought in these ways—"picture themselves in an earthly Jerusalem to be rebuilt with precious stones" (*On First Principles* 2.11, 2–3). Contra Origen, drawing again on Jewish prophetic texts and Christianized "pagan" prophecies like the Sibylline Oracles, Lactantius celebrated precisely this terrestrial future, looking forward to the millennial procreation of an infinite multitude of saints, to mountains oozing honey, to wine flowing down in streams, and to rivers running with milk. And contra Lactantius, Augustine especially lamented the material feasting and drinking that the faithful believed would mark life after the first resurrection, during the thousand-year Kingdom. The Kingdom, he insisted, was a nonterrestrial heaven.

Augustine's protests against this vision of future feasting had a precise immediate focus: current celebrations of the martyred dead. Some of these customs were simply carried over from long-traditional Mediterranean observances for family members, who gathered around the tomb of their deceased to partake of a meal. But the celebrations over the special Christian dead took on a life of their own. Dining tables were erected over sacred tombs; eventually, church buildings surrounded these. Singing, dancing, eating, and above all drinking, especially during the vigil the night before the saint's festal day, were all part of enthusiastic expressions of fervent piety. Such Christians, Augustine acerbically commented, "worship tombs and drink with utmost self-indulgence over the dead and set food before them. In so doing, they bury themselves at such graves, and then attribute their gluttony and drunkenness to religion" (*On the Morals of the Manichees* 1.34). These behaviors, he complained, presented ready examples of unseemly carnal-mindedness to watching (and scornful) heretics.

But these festivities also made a theological point: they articulated expectations about what life would be like after the first resurrection. The faithful were enacting the joys of the Kingdom over the physical presence of the martyred saint. Augustine disapproved. Such worshipers anticipated that the raised would "spend their rest in the most unrestrained material feasts," he thundered in the *City of God*, "in which there will be so much to eat and drink that those supplies will break the bounds not only of moderation, but also of credibility" (20.7).

It was just embarrassing, Augustine urged. Manichaean critics especially noted the "paganism" and unelevated quality of the saints' cults. But Augustine also taught that this enacted millenarianism was also theologically wrong. When he worked to transform traditional observances, to turn these "carnal" banquets into a day of preaching and orderly congregational prayer, more than a question of Christian deportment was at stake. The bishop sought to impose a vision of the eschatological reign of the saints, as previewed in these celebrations around their *memoriae*, that was fundamentally different—in his own terms, "spiritual."

Other Christian thinkers had tackled the problem of fleshly constructions of redemption in other ways. Both Valentinus and Marcion (if we can trust Justin's reports about them) had taken Paul at his word: flesh and blood could not inherit the Kingdom. They therefore anticipated redemption as the ascent of the individual soul beyond the cosmic realm (Justin, *Dialogue with Trypho* 80; Tertullian, wielding the text of Revelation 20 like a cudgel, had pummeled Marcion for this view). The sublunar realm was to them beyond salvation. Repudiating the idea of a fleshly resurrection and a kingdom of God on earth, some Christians also appealed to allegory. Such allegorists, complained Tertullian in his work on resurrection, understood death in a spiritual sense: not as the separation of body from soul, but as ignorance of God, "by reason of which man is dead to God, and no less buried in error than he would be in the grave." When, then, and what, according to these allegorizing Christians, is the resurrection? Said Tertullian disapprovingly, when they "are with the Lord, once they have put him on in baptism" (*On Resurrection* 19).

Origen, despite his repudiation of Valentinus and of Marcion, was in fundamental agreement with such allegorizing understandings. The wine that the saints will drink in the Kingdom, he explained (taking a position that Tertullian would heatedly deny) is the wine of divine wisdom. The bread is the bread of life: these nourish the soul and enlighten the mind of the spiritual body. Those Christians who think otherwise, he sighed, whether from poverty of intellect or from lack of education, have an extremely low and mean idea of the resurrection of the body. But the resurrected body, he insisted, must be spiritual, as Paul in 1 Corinthians 15 had taught. These less intellectual Christians reject the labor of hard thinking "and seek after the outward and literal meaning of the law"—a code for interpreting in a Jewish manner—"or, rather, they give way to their own desires." Apocalyptic texts might indeed *seem* to speak of earthly and bodily resurrection, Origen conceded, but the force of such scriptures "must be spiritual and figurative" (*On First Principles* 2.11.2).

For proto-orthodox and, later, orthodox thinkers, the ancient Jewish prophecies of Isaiah, Ezekiel, and Daniel, which spoke of a coming end-time, could not be repudiated. At best, their problematic passages could be allegorized. The book of Revelation, however, was of uncertain authority. When a third-century Egyptian bishop, Nepos of Arsinoë, insisted in his treatise *On the Refutation of the Allegorists* on a more literal reading of the text, Origen's pupil Dionysius, bishop of Alexandria, debated with his followers for three full days. He then wrote his own refutation of Nepos, *On the Promises.* Subjecting Revelation to rigorous literary criticism, Dionysius concluded that John its author could not be the same man as John the apostle, the author of the gospel. The denial of apostolic authorship deprived Revelation of much of its authority. The canonical status of Revelation remained in play throughout the fourth and fifth centuries.

Christians—even those who were notionally within the same church—thus expressed a wide range of responses to the book of Revelation and to the message that it embodied. Some, spurred by immediate circumstances, actively anticipated the imminent arrival of an earthly kingdom. Others, like Justin, asserted that all scripture spoke of two comings of Jesus: the Christian awaited his second glorious manifestation, when he would gather the raised saints into an earthly Jerusalem for a thousand years. Others, generating learned chronologies, scientifically calculated the time of the Kingdom's arrival. Others—among the proto-orthodox, most notably Origen—radically allegorized John's apocalyptic text; others, like Dionysius and, following him, Eusebius, queried its apostolic authority. In their situation of continuing persecution, post-Constantine, the Donatists could carry on enacting and anticipating an earthly kingdom: they were, after all, the true heirs of the martyrs. Others, encouraged precisely by the benefits of imperial support, could conclude that the Kingdom was about to arrive because the gospel had reached the whole world.

It was with this unstable and destabilizing collection of behaviors and interpretations that Christians, anticipating the approach of the apocalyptic year 6000—the equivalent by our dating system of 500 CE—awaited the dawning of the reign of the saints.

Apocalypse Now

Between the years 389 and 420 CE, different disturbances beset the empire. Hail; earthquakes; a solar eclipse; famine and violent storms. Apocalyptic expectation transformed these events into prodigies. But none of these matched the trauma of 410, when the city of Rome fell to invading Goths.

Promoted during Augustus's principate as "the eternal city"—*Roma aeterna, aurea Roma*—Rome's tremendous cultural capital had transferred readily into Christian idioms as well. As much as persecution spurred negative associations—Rome as the apocalyptic Babylon; the emperor Nero as the ultimate anti-Christian persecutor and, indeed, as the Antichrist—so too did it give rise to positive ones. Rome became the city of the church's two chief, foundational apostles, Peter and Paul. Legend connected both saints to Rome, where (so the stories) both had been martyred under Nero, Peter by crucifixion, Paul by the sword. This meant that Rome housed the bodies of these two most prestigious figures. Their retrieved relics would encourage both local piety and pilgrimages. The more the city was associated with the memory of persecution—especially after Constantine—the more the number of its martyrs proliferated, congesting both the Christian city's landscape and its calendar.

Completing his seizure of western power in 312, Constantine had conquered Rome. He respected the city's pagan institutions while undertaking an ambitious building program that put specifically Christian sites on the urban map. Consolidating power in 324 in the East with his defeat of his rival emperor Licinius, Constantine in 330 then founded a new Rome, Constantinople, an eastern nerve center of political and military power. Both he and later emperors imported various relics to the new city, but these could never match the prestige of Peter's and Paul's. In the West, imperial courts and, thus, imperial clout concentrated in frontier capitals like Trier and Milan; in the East, Antioch remained an important seat of administration. Constantinople, however, repositioned the center of gravity, serving as the emperor's permanent residence. Yet the new city never undermined the cultural capital of the old. Rome continued to abide as the (imaginative) heart of the wide-flung empire, for Christians no less than for pagans—which is why its sack, in the year 410, came as such a shock.

We hear the loudest reverberations in Christian literature, because Christians had the most to answer for. When the old gods had been worshiped, Rome had thrived. Supplanted by the Christian god, their patronage and protection had ceased—and the Christian god, clearly, had not been up to the job. (The fact that the city had "fallen" to Christian invaders, Alaric and his Goths, was an added awkwardness.) These complaints called forth a huge response from Augustine, *The City of God against the Pagans*. But his bulky masterpiece was only partly directed at dismantling pagan criticisms. The entire final third speaks to—or rather, against—the millenarian expectations of Augustine's own church.

Underlying his response to both audiences, pagan and Christian, was the more fundamental issue of Christian triumphalism, the theological celebration of the empire's patronage of the church. Such triumphalism was undergirded by the assumption that biblical prophecy lined up with current history. To this way of thinking, the hand of God could be clearly discerned in contemporary events, which were transparent on biblical promises. Such prophetic decoding could convey both a positive message (the triumph of the church) and a negative one (disasters presaging the End).

Earlier Christian apologists—Melito, Origen—had argued that the empire and the church had been founded (nearly) simultaneously by divine providence: the order imposed by empire, they held, had facilitated the spread and the growth of the church. Constantine's surprising conversion in 312 then provided triumphalism with history's pole star. Commenting on the emperor's ambitious building projects in Jerusalem, Eusebius had rhapsodized that it seemed as if divine glory had at last returned to its ancient seat. "Perhaps *this* is the new Jerusalem announced in the prophetic oracles" (*Life of Constantine* 3.33.2). Politics recast prophecy: through the *pax Romana Christiana*, a (nonapocalyptic) holy kingdom had been established on earth.

Augustine himself had similarly celebrated imperial legislation that, in 399, had ordered the closure of some pagan temples in Carthage. But the fall of Rome in 410 for him began to close the window of prophetic transparency that the antipagan imperial laws of 399 had thrown open. In *City of God*, his certainty about the eschatological value of current events gave way to an abiding agnosticism. Only in the period narrated in the Bible, he now insisted, *because* it was narrated in the Bible, could God's actions in history be clearly seen. With the close of the apostolic period—thus, of the New Testament canon—time, Augustine now asserted, had become eschatologically opaque. No event, whether positive (the destruction of idols; the universal proclamation of the gospel; the Christianization of government) or negative (famine, earthquake, foreign invasion) could reveal the shape of the divine plan. Extrabiblical time was thus radically secularized, as was human politics. The empire, neither demonic before 312 nor divine thereafter, simply did not figure as a marker or as a medium of revelation. The fall of Rome therefore, urged Augustine, revealed nothing about God's timetable for history's end.

What, then, about the promises of the book of Revelation? In the closing books of the *City of God*, Augustine argued that these had already been realized. Christ's bodily Second Coming as the triumphant Son of Man? It had *already* occurred, through the coming of his "body," the church. The saints' reign with Christ on earth? They do so *already*, in the church, through their manifest presence at their tombs. And their thousand-year reign? "One thousand" is a number that indicates a quality ("the fullness of time," $10 \times 10 \times 10$) not a quantity ("one thousand years"). If the number is actually a symbol for perfection, then the saints' reign is of unknowable temporal duration. The binding of Satan? He has *already* been bound, that is, his power, through the church, was now bridled. Satan was thus bound until, not at, the end of the age. Given that all these prophecies have already been fulfilled, Augustine urges, Christians should stop looking at current events—like the fall of Rome—through an apocalyptic lens. No one knows when the End will come, and Revelation cannot help with any such calculus.

What then about feasting, drinking, terrestrial plentitude, all those great eschatological promises anticipated in the celebrations around martyrs' tombs? The fleshly body will be raised spiritual, Augustine insists, agreeing with Paul's statement in 1 Corinthians 15.50. "Flesh and blood cannot inherit the Kingdom of God." But "spiritual," he explains, refers to the body's moral orientation, not to its substance. The raised body, he insists, will have corporeal substance. It will even have gender. (The question had clearly been debated.) But the raised body will not dwell on a transformed earth. Rather, insists Augustine, defying the scientific thinking of his day, these spiritually oriented fleshly bodies will—paradoxically—dwell in heaven, where saints will stand in chaste and comradely contemplation of the beatific vision of God. No food, sex, or social relations in the Kingdom. As for the millennial seventh day of the cosmic week, the eschatological Kingdom—that, says Augustine, is the saints themselves. "After the present age God will rest, as it were, on the seventh day; and he will cause us, *who are the seventh day*, to find our rest in him" (*City of God* 22.30).

Augustine's arguments established a plumb line for all later learned orthodox readings of Revelation. Contemporaries, however, were less convinced. Events combined with long tradition to undermine the persuasiveness of a nonapocalyptic understanding of current history. Thanks to the Vandal invasions of the western empire in the mid-fifth century, Augustine's world very nearly did "end" on time. One North African chronicler, in 452, divined that the name of the Vandal king Geiseric, if decoded, revealed the number of the apocalyptic Beast of the book of Revelation, 666. Another North African—Quodvultdeus, Augustine's own younger colleague—argued strenuously that the apocalyptic signs of the approaching end-time were currently being fulfilled: the barbarian tribes of the Getas and the Massagetas, he held, were none other than the long-foretold forces of Gog and Magog.

The year 500/6000 slipped past, but Western chronographers continued to recast their timetables. Famine, earthquakes, plague, assorted terrestrial and celestial disturbances—all continued to send people into panic, from late antiquity through the high Middle Ages and beyond. Eventually, religiously inflected dating systems shifted from counting by the ages of the world to counting *anno domini*, from the Incarnation. This calendrical change in turn highlighted the apocalyptic possibilities of the year 1000—as also of the year 2000. Repeatedly disconfirmed but

never discredited, the expectation of the approaching Kingdom continues evergreen in Christian proclamation.

Different Endings: Heaven and Hell

Christ as redeemer had a double function in Christian traditions. By his
death, he saved from sin; by his resurrection, he saved from death. The
believer in this life could participate in the work of redemption through
moral effort (ascetic supererogation, support for the poor) and by penitential actions. Redemption from death, for the proto-orthodox, had to
wait for time's end and the corporate event of the resurrection of the dead.

As the End oscillated between "soon" and "later," eschatology—
theology about final things—developed in different ways. The redeemed Christian was promised eternal life, but if the establishment of
the venue of eternal life, God's kingdom, was indefinitely postponed,
what happened in the meanwhile? With the separation of soul from
body, where did the postmortem individual go? Was there life after
death before Christ's Second Coming, or simply some quiescent state
of "sleeping"? Where, and how, was life after death lived? On these questions, we see the development of two different kinds of eschatological
real estate: heaven, and hell.

Christian concepts about the afterlife had precedents in both pagan
and Jewish culture. Homer's *Odyssey* and Virgil's *Aeneid* had featured
their hero's descent into the underworld, to converse with the shades of
the dead. Hades itself was conceived as subdivided into two zones,
pleasant (Elysium, abode of the few) and radically unpleasant (Tartarus, much more populated with tormented shades). For philosophers
of Platonic and Neopythagorean bent, the soul was the self, and it was
immortal. Flesh, clearly, was not. For them, the ultimate abode of the
soul was with the stars: the individual soul, free of the body, would ascend into the heavens, *ad astra*. Afterlife is lived by the soul, not by the
soul reunited with the body.

Concern about afterlife, however, did not dominate most ancient
Mediterranean religions. "Ancestral practices" focused primarily on how
to live one's present life, not on what might happen in some postmortem

future life. Philosophers and members of mystery cults might focus on afterlives; but did other people? Some common funeral inscriptions gestured toward annihilation ("I was not, I was, I am not, I care not"). Others bequeathed the person's shade to the "infernal gods," *dis manibus*: the abbreviation D.M. is so formulaic, like our R.I.P., that it is found even on Jewish and Christian tombstones.

Jewish biblical texts are famously vague about the conditions of individuals after death. In the late Second Temple period, however, afterlife begins to be linked to ideas about resurrection. "Enoch," for example, a biblical figure from before the Flood (Genesis 5.21–24), sometime in the third or second century BCE was given a tour of postmortem territories assigned to different sorts of human souls, righteous and (varying degrees of) unrighteous: the latter would endure punishments eternally. The blessed, Enoch saw, will inherit a fecund, peaceful earth (1 Enoch 10.18–19) and, ultimately, will shine like the luminaries of heaven (104.2). Daniel 12 spoke of the dead "awakening from sleep," some to everlasting life, others to eternal contempt; the righteous would be "like the stars." Second Maccabees linked martyrdom and the suffering of the righteous explicitly to a postmortem restoration of the fleshly body: "The king of the universe will raise us up to an everlasting renewal of life, because we have died for his laws" (7.9).

In gospel traditions, Jesus tells of the soul of poor Lazarus after death. Lazarus is borne by angels to the "bosom of Abraham," while the rich man who ignored him in life spends eternity in Hades, across an unbridgeable space, in burning torment (Luke 16.19–31). The fires of Gehenna are unquenchable (Mark 9.48). The torment of the wicked precedes the day of judgment: souls alone, minus their bodies, can feel thirst and pain. What about the fate of the redeemed? Contesting with Sadducees, Jesus speaks of the postresurrected state of the saved as being angelic: those who rise from the dead "neither marry nor are given in marriage" (Mark 12.18–27). In the Gospel of John, Jesus speaks elliptically of his followers' gaining eternal life as a present condition as well as a future one: his own resurrection guarantees that his followers "will live also" (John 14.19). Paul, too, talks of eternal life, teaching that the bodies of believers whether living or dead will be transformed into bodies of *pneuma*, material spirit—very fine stuff, not not-stuff—fit to dwell in the realm above the moon once Christ returns. All those who worship images, however—that is, in Paul's day, most of humankind—will be the objects of "the wrath that is coming" (1 Thessalonians 1.10). Yet in his final letter, Romans, Paul seems to speak of a universal redemption: "the fullness of the nations" and "all Israel" will be secured for the celestial Kingdom (Romans 11.25–26).

In these afterlife traditions, the ultimate destination of the (un)dead was calibrated according to behavior in this life. This conviction gives us a glimpse of the ideas both about universal justice and about ethics, what counts as wrong behavior, what as good. Afterlife provides a belated opportunity for justice, when the righteous are rewarded and the wicked punished. In some apocalypses, angels are judged as well as humans.

The Christian tours of heaven and hell that begin to accrue in the early second century wax especially articulate about what constitutes sin—and about the torments that await sinners.

The *Apocalypse of Peter*, an early second-century text, opens by praising divine mercy, though very little mercy is shown to those considered wrongdoers, who are subject to the "judgement of wrath." Once judged by Christ at his Second Coming, the newly (re)embodied will suffer, in quite precise ways, for all eternity. Blasphemers will hang by their tongues. Women who tempted men to fornicate will hang by their hair; their male partners, by their genitals in a "place of fire." Murderers will burn forever in the sight of their victims (*Peter* 7). Women who aborted pregnancies will sink in pain and excrement up to their necks, their breasts oozing congealed milk that turns into flesh-eating beasts. "God wills it so" (8). Slanderers gnaw endlessly on their own tongues; the deceitful have their lips cut off; those who trusted in wealth will be tormented in filthy garments (9). Other afflictions beset usurers, idol worshippers, those disrespectful to parents, lapsed virgins, disobedient slaves, and practitioners of sorcery (10–11). Torments notwithstanding, these sinners will acknowledge that their (perpetual) punishments are just.

About the redeemed, *Peter* has much less to say. Moses, Elijah, the patriarchs, and the righteous, as well as those who have been persecuted for Jesus's sake will stand in a great garden (16), much like the venue anticipated in some pagan traditions. The author scarcely speaks about the upside of final judgment; his energies and attention focus primarily on the eternally damned. After a few brief remarks on the destiny of the saved, "Peter" ends by praising God for preserving the names of the righteous in the book of life (17). Redemption wrought through Christ, for this author, is clearly not universal.

Later apocalypses and other early church fathers express variations on these themes. And afterlife itself begins to monopolize Christian sensibility: this life becomes a prelude for the individual's ultimate eternal life, whether in heaven or in hell. What determines who goes where? In the view of some, salvation is limited to membership in the right Christian community, marked by baptism. *Extra ecclesiam nulla salus* was taught by the bishop Cyprian mid-third century: outside of the church there is no salvation. In this view, the vast majority of humankind is doomed to unending torment; the few, the happy few, to eternal bliss.

But church membership (and membership in the right church, meaning the church of the author) was itself no guarantee of heaven either. The *Apocalypse of Paul*, a later text derived partly from the *Apocalypse of Peter*, features a tour of a hell occupied predominately by failed Christians. Besides the (usual) fallen virgins, "Paul" sees a fornicating presbyter in a river of fire, tortured by angels; a lector who did not practice what he read standing in a fiery river while a red-hot razor slices his lips and tongue; ascetics who failed to love their neighbor and care for the stranger suffer burning pitch and sulfur; those whose theological opinions on Christ, Mary, and the eucharist differ from the author's own are encased in a stench-filled well. The redeemed, meanwhile— their virtue calibrated by levels of sexual continence—ascend to a Paradise in the "third heaven," to live with Christ for a thousand years in a place of superabundant richness. Higher achievers pass to a beautiful city (the heavenly Jerusalem?), their zone of residence again tied to their levels of piety in their former life.

If Christ is the sole pathway to salvation, what then of all those generations born before his coming? What kind of divine justice would account them as doomed? The *Acts of Pilate*, a fifth-century text, answered

these questions. It developed an idea present *in nuce* in a canonical letter, 1 Peter 3.19, which claimed that Christ after his death but before his
resurrection "made a proclamation to the spirits in prison"—meaning
to those souls in hell. *Pilate* described the postmortem Christ's rescue
mission to the underworld. Confronting Hades, binding Satan, Christ
liberates the dead ("all you who have died through the tree which
[Adam] touched," 8.24, 1), paying special attention to the saints of the
Old Testament: Adam, the prophets, and the patriarchs, as well as
the (pre-Christian) martyrs. All these proceed to Paradise as a group—
spirits still, not yet reembodied. Presumably, at the final resurrection,
they would resume their bodies, and the final judgment would occur.
Through Christ, these pre-Christian saints had already been redeemed, to live their afterlives prior to the Second Coming.

Ideas about heaven and hell reflect ideas about the character of God.
The biblical god is praised for being both just and merciful. But in what
proportions? Does his mercy extend to all his creation? In the End,
would all be saved to life eternal? Origen thought so. Anything less, he
taught, would undermine the grace and omnipotence of God, and diminish the scope of Christ's mission of salvation. But majority opinion
tilted in the other direction. God, or Jesus, assumed the stern features
of a late Roman imperial magistrate, justly punishing—though for
eternity—those who violated divine law. Some apocalypses softened
this sentence with an idea of mitigated mercy. In traditions about Mary's
descent into hell—she is horrified and grieved by the suffering that she
sees—she negotiates a release of nine hours every Sunday. *The Apocalypse of Paul* envisions Sunday as a full day of rest; other texts name the
period of respite as lasting for the fifty days between Easter and Pentecost. Eternal just punishment would be leavened by periodic mercy.

What is the purpose of hell: punishment, or rehabilitation? Is eschatological suffering purgative or punitive? Answers varied. Those "com-
passionate Christians" who urged that hell would not last forever were the
targets of Augustine's closing arguments in his *City of God*, a defining
master work of late Latin theology. He urged a type of eschatological
symmetry: if saintly beatitude were eternal, he explained, then the suf-
ferings of the damned had to be eternal too. The effectiveness of saintly

intercession, he further held, had its limits: no martyr patron could guarantee salvation.

Further, Augustine taught, people would suffer in hell not only for their own sins, but also because of the inherited stain of original sin, which stemmed from Adam's insubordination. Even babies, if dying before baptism, were irredeemable on account of original sin. *All* humanity after Adam, he urged, was justly condemned as a *massa damnata*. Even membership within the true church (that is, Augustine's church) was no guarantee of salvation. Given that humanity was universally marked by Adam's sin, what required explanation was not God's just condemnation of the many, but rather his merciful decision to remit punishment to the few. Why are the damned damned? In order to demonstrate God's justice. Why are the saved saved? In order to demonstrate God's mercy. "Many more are condemned by vengeance than are released by mercy" (*City of God* 21.12).

At the final resurrection, Augustine explained, fleshly body and spiritual soul for both populations, the saved and the damned, would be eternally reunited. But the nature of flesh will have changed. For the saints, flesh will be entirely and effortlessly under the control of spirit. For the damned, flesh will be so configured that it will be capable of sustaining fire and pain eternally, inescapably. Whereas in this life death could mean a release from pain, in the afterlife, even that avenue of escape was foreclosed. After the resurrection, for all humanity, death will be no more—to the detriment, even the regret, of those in hell.

The flesh of the saints, too, will have undergone eschatological transformation, not only moral but also physical. The resurrected body will conform to a certain aesthetic. Men's breasts, for example, would still have nipples, despite their serving no purpose other than ornamentation. All the saved—even infants and children, Augustine speculated—would be raised in their prime, at the same age as Christ was when raised (that is, around the age of thirty). The body would be perfected and beautiful. Amputees would have their limbs restored. The saint would be neither overweight nor underweight. Physical defects will have no place in heaven. The only exception would be the scars of the martyrs, which will abide—as did Christ's wounds, after his resurrection—as (beautiful) signs of their righteous valor. And somehow, the embodied saints will be able to see the nonembodied God (*City of God* 22.29).

All forms of Christianity proffered a vision of redemption. Teachings about the afterlife as the realm of that redemption obliquely defined how the faithful should act, and what they should believe, in this life. Narratives of heaven, teaching about the retrieval of the heroes of the Old Testament, made a theological point: these people had in effect been Christians before Christ. The Old Testament really was a preparation for the New Testament, the old Israel a prelude to the new. Narratives of hell taught about the hazards of sin, the particular sin linked with its own particular punishment. Eternity held out the promise of condemnation as well as of salvation.

How much of this stern and frightening message accounted for the spread of the Christian movement(s)? A lot, opined the late second-century pagan critic Celsus. Christians, he said, invented terrors by their teaching about everlasting punishments (*Against Celsus* 3.16). Hell was part of the hard sell. This, despite the repugnance and incoherence of Christian teachings about the resurrected body—apparently, in Celsus's view, another loud part of the missionary pitch.

It is foolish of them also to suppose that, when God applies fire (like a cook!), all the rest of mankind will be thoroughly roasted and that they alone will survive, not merely those who are alive at the time but also those long dead who will rise up from the earth possessing the same bodies as before. This is simply the hope of worms. For what sort of soul would have any further desire for a body that has rotted? The fact that this doctrine is not shared by some of you [Jews] and by some Christians shows its utter repulsiveness, and that it is both revolting and impossible. For what sort of body, after being entirely corrupted, could return to its original nature and that same condition which it had before it was dissolved? As they have nothing to say in reply, they escape to a most outrageous refuge by saying that "anything is possible to God." (*Against Celsus* 5.14)

Celsus goes on to argue that the idea of physical resurrection offends against right reason. Eternal soul is reasonable; eternal flesh is not. Origen, critiquing Celsus in turn, concedes that this doctrine of physical resurrection is preached in the churches, but "it is more clearly understood by the intelligent" (5.18). The dead are not given back their same bodies, he urges. Rather, deferring to Paul's statements about flesh, blood, and spiritual body in 1 Corinthians 15, the eschatological body will be constituted of spirit—or so, says Origen, do the more "intelligent" understand. By implication, the majority do not.

It is against Origen's position that Augustine taught: fleshly body's nature, he insisted, is changed morally, but not physically. People rise in their "same" bodies, though for the saved, these bodies will be ethically and aesthetically reformatted for eternal beatitude. And by insisting that such bodies will abide "in heaven," Augustine literally cut the ground out from under terrestrial visions of a kingdom of God on earth. In this way, Augustine united two originally different end-time visions, one celestial ("up there," in heaven), one terrestrial (down here, on earth, for the embodied saints' thousand-year reign). Eschatological flesh will dwell in heaven. More of it, though, will burn forever in hell.

In Christian stories and apocryphal apostles' acts, hellfire often seems to have been more consistently emphasized than were visions of heaven. Here pagan, Jewish, and Christian conceptualizations converged. Tartarus (with its population of tormented shades), Gehenna (a place of "unquenchable fire where the worm never dies," Mark 9.48), and hell together formed a culturally coherent whole.

Eternal pain for moral malfeasance, howsoever conceived, spoke in a readily comprehended cultural vernacular, one that conveyed positive moral and theological teachings while articulating the dangers of defiance. Christ may have come the first time in order to bring redemption; at his Second Coming, Christ the judge would bring just condemnation as well. Heaven and hell served both as the end points of the individual's life, and as the final point on the arc of history. In this way and for these reasons, the message of damnation assumed a prime place in the Christian message of salvation.

5

CHRIST AND EMPIRE

To the Emperor Caesar, God, Son of God, Augustus.

ROMAN IMPERIAL INSCRIPTION

Lord Jesus Christ . . . Son of God . . . begotten, not made.

NICENE CREED

Give me, emperor, the earth cleansed of heretics, and I will
give you Heaven in return. Help me eliminate the heretics,
and I will help you eliminate the Persians!

BISHOP NESTORIUS TO EMPEROR THEODOSIUS II

*Ideas about God were embedded in biblical narrative, but theologians parsed
them by the criteria of philosophy. Ideas about Jesus as Christ were embedded in New Testament writings but also parsed by the criteria of philosophy.
What was the status of Christ, as God's son, relative to God himself? How
divine could Christ be before monotheism—belief in one single, supreme
god—was compromised? How human could Christ be, without compromising his divinity? With Constantine's conversion in 312, all these questions
were amplified, the stakes raised. Imperial politics would have a determinative effect on the creeds and councils of the imperial church.*

+ + +

Theology

What is a god?

In Roman antiquity, different literatures provided different answers. Myths, stories about the gods, presented superhumans whose emotional lives were all too human. Gods contested with each other, married and mated with each other, and favored particular locales and peoples. They consorted variously with humans, by whom they might have offspring. They were beautiful, powerful, and immortal. They could at any time manifest in dreams, in visions, through sacred statuary, or by immediate epiphany. They could direct events on earth and were susceptible to persuasion. And they were generally invested in how they were treated. Cult thus formed the glue of divine/human relationship. Showing piety toward the god could elicit divine benefaction: long life, children, well-being, wisdom. Failure to do so could elicit divine anger.

The Jewish god was also a narrative character, mediated through scriptural story. He too had personality and emotions. He loved; he hated; he battled other, lesser gods. He forgot and remembered, made choices, grew angry, punished and forgave. He gave laws. He guided history. Occasionally biblical texts suggest that God had a body: he formed humans in his image; his footfall warned Adam of his coming; he shielded Moses with his hand, revealing only his back; he dined with Abraham. Without sexual partners, he had sons, who were also superhuman (so Genesis 6.2). He stood in a paternal relationship with Israel, his "first born son," and especially with the kings of David's line. He conversed with other divine beings and with humans. Like most ancient gods, he was particularly present at his altar and, once it was built, in his temple. Being faithful to his ordinances resulted in benefaction: long life, children, well-being, wisdom. Failure to do so could elicit divine anger.

Philosophy offered a very different discourse about "god." Its categories were generated not from ancient narratives but from intellectual propositions. In its Platonic forms, theology—philosophy specifically about divinity—held that the highest god was all good, radically transcendent, immaterial, unchanging, perfect. In its Stoic forms, theology held that god was the immanent, rational, organizing power of the universe. For both schools of thought, the mind was the highest, most divine part of human being. As an intellectual discipline, theology coordinated these definitions of divinity and of humanity with other key elements of philosophy: matter, cosmos, time, soul, ethics. The way to apprehend god, for the philosopher, was through the mind.

Allegory could retrieve the ancient narratives, enabling them to speak philosophical truths. Through allegory—*allos* (other) *agorein* (to speak): "other-speak"—the enlightened reader could see through the surface meaning of the text to the intellectual depths that the narrative level concealed. Odysseus sleeping in the cave of the nymphs might seem a tale of a homesick hero. Understood allegorically, the scene depicted the way that the soul yearns to leave the physical body and return to its true home in the upper cosmos. The serpent deceiving the first woman who then gets her husband to eat the forbidden fruit might seem like the story of a primal fall. Understood allegorically, the story relates how the senses ("Eve"), if turned toward lower things ("the serpent"), can distract even the mind ("Adam") from its pursuit of divine truth.

Theology as a form of discourse was intrinsically the preserve of a tiny intellectual elite. Only they had the education and the ability to think in this way. Most of the issues, the concerns, and even the vocabulary used for expressing philosophical ideas lay well beyond the grasp of the vast majority of ancient people. Yet theology came to assume an outsized role in Christian culture, hotly contested. Its talking points were distilled in sermons, in song, in prayers, and eventually in summary statements, "creeds." By the fourth century, these creeds, framed by bishops, were promulgated by state-supported councils. Creeds functioned as statements of political allegiance as well as distillations of theology.

Christianity inherited all the complications of Hellenistic Jewish theology, which had blazed the trail for reading biblical narrative in Greek through a philosophical lens. Divine attributes, like God's word or reason (Logos) or wisdom (Sophia) or power (*dynamis*) could be personified, adding another dimension to interpreting scriptural texts, easing them toward philosophical interpretation. In the first century, Philo had deployed God's Word in this way, as the agent in creation. God's Logos, he said, was a "second god" and God's "Image," through whom sonship could be conferred to virtuous humans. "For if we have not yet become sons of God," he says in one treatise, "yet we may be sons of his invisible image, the most holy Logos" (*On the Confusion of Languages* 147). Elsewhere he refers to God's Logos as his "first-born son."

Philo's Logos thus functioned as a mediator not only between God and cosmos/creation, but also and specifically between God and humanity. Though he too was divine, he was also clearly subordinate. Mediation assumes three parties: first, God; second, the mediating figure; third, the object of mediation, be it creation writ large or humanity in particular. The mediating figure may be divine, may indeed be designated [a] "god"; but for mediation, logically, to work, the mediating figure cannot be the same as either pole of what he mediates. He is a go-between.

Paul, much less systematically than Philo, expresses this same pattern of subordinate mediation. God's messiah is other than God himself: he is that god's "son." Sons are subordinate to fathers (especially in Mediterranean antiquity). Paul can refer to both God and Christ as "Lord," but that word, *kyrios*, while used of various divine entities, was also a mode of address to any superior: calling both God and Christ "lord" implies no confusion. (Paul calls pagan deities "lords" as well, 1 Corinthians 8.5.) Christ, says Paul, is his father's "image" (2 Corinthians 4.4): an image is derivative of or contingent on an original. Christ, God's preexistent agent in creation (as was Philo's Logos), was "in the form of god"—"god-form," meaning with a body made of pneuma (material "spirit")—until his descent into "slave-form," that is, human likeness (Philippians 2.6–8). Christ's flesh enabled him to die. Death preceded the glorious resurrection, which in turn presaged Christ's triumphant return.

One place where Paul might seem to tip over from being a late Second Temple Jew to being a fourth-century Christian comes in his letter to the Romans 9.5. In English, this passage could read: "of their people [meaning Paul's fellow Jews] according to the flesh is the Christ. God, who is over all, be blessed forever!" Or it could read: "of their people according to the flesh is the Christ, who is God over all, blessed forever!" The English translation depends on how the sentence is punctuated, with or without a full stop after "Christ."

On this issue, there are several things to bear in mind. The first is that Paul's original letter had neither punctuation nor even space between the letters. Modern readers are the ones whose punctuation shapes Paul's sentences. Second, given that Christ has a plenipotentiary role in Paul's story of redemption, he *could* be the "god over all who is blessed forever," without confusing him or identifying him with God the Father. "God" in antiquity was a very elastic term. Third, the identification of Christ with God the Father, the claim that he was equally as divine as the Father, took until the imperially sponsored councils of the fourth and fifth centuries to formulate. Were Paul identifying Christ with God in the mid-first century, it was a point that eluded theologians for the next three hundred years.

By the late second century, proto-orthodox Christian theologians also had the four (not-yet-canonical) gospel narratives to consider, which further complicated theological reflection. The three seen-together or "synoptic" Gospels, Mark, Matthew, and Luke, relate the public actions of Jesus of Nazareth: there is no cosmic back story. In Mark, Jesus simply appears as an adult, declared by God as his son at baptism, and again, later, at his transfiguration. The original ending of Mark has no resurrection scene, just an empty tomb. This gospel, in comparison with the others, is theologically spare.

John, by contrast, prefaces his account with an elaborate theological prologue: Christ is the Logos of God. He takes on flesh. (John does not say how: he has no birth narrative.) He comes down to the lower realm and then goes back up, above, to the Father. In English, the prologue reads, "And the Logos was God." Again, punctuation and capitalization, both modern conventions, can distort the Greek. Translated clunkily but literally, John's text reads: "In the beginning was the Logos, and the Logos was with the God, and the Logos was god." For the claim—incoherent by the canons of ancient thought—that the Logos was the same entity as the high god, the article should be repeated before the second *theos*, "god." Thus, "*the* God was *the* Logos." The prologue claims high divinity for the Logos, God's Son, Jesus Christ, the only one who has seen the Father. (How anyone sees the invisible God is another question that will preoccupy theologians.) The Johannine

Logos preexists his becoming flesh. Still subordinate, then, though highly divine—indeed, as with Philo, John's Logos is the next most divine being to God himself.

Matthew and Luke each have birth narratives, though these differ between them. In both, Jesus is born in the messianically correct town, Bethlehem, David's natal city. In both, Jesus is conceived of a virgin by means of holy spirit. Virgin mothers are a trope for the birth of heroes in Greek mythology, but the evangelists are thinking with the Greek of Isaiah 7.14: "A virgin will conceive and bear a son, and he will be called Immanuel," Hebrew for "God-with-us." Through story-telling, these evangelists teach that Jesus is both the son of God—literally—and the messiah. If John's, like Paul's, is a "high" Christology, and Mark's by comparison a "low" one, the Christology of the later two synoptics seems "medium."

Divine Sonship

Later Christian theologians, reflecting back on Paul's letters and the gospel stories as well as on the vast bulk of the Septuagint, sought to explain with precision both Christ's divinity (how he related to God the Father) and Christ's humanity (how a divine figure was also human). Those who focused on Mark's gospel favored an idea labeled "adoptionism": Jesus began life as a mortal, and was "adopted" son of God at his baptism. Adoption still conferred divinity.

This idea was abroad in majority culture. The son of god in the Roman world was no less a figure than the emperor. Augustus stands as the font of this imperial ideology. His adoptive father, Julius Caesar, had claimed divine descent from Venus. Deified after his own death, Julius conferred his divinity on his adopted son Augustus: "god from god," as one papyrus proclaimed. Each succeeding emperor—Tiberius, Caligula, Claudius, Nero—was adopted as his predecessor's son. Each was divine.

Augustus was not *genealogically* the divine Julius's son. That is, he was not a begotten son, but rather a man "made" divine son through the mechanism of adoption. In statuary, on coins, in inscriptions, and on monuments, through cult, Augustus's divinity was everywhere proclaimed. Though unquestionably human, Augustus, in a world where divinity traveled along a cosmic gradient from greater to lesser, was unquestionably divine as well. In a culture that teemed with gods, Rome ultimately would proclaim only two universal deities: the emperor, and Jesus.

Adoptionism, however, in the view of some, did not speak adequately to claims for Jesus's preexistence. John had identified Jesus as God's Logos. Paul had imputed both a historical and a heavenly preexistence to Christ. Christ, said Paul, was the rock from whom the children of Israel had drunk in the desert; Christ was the "man from Heaven" who had had a god form before assuming human likeness. These claims still subordinated Christ to God, as indeed did all the Christological titles: Word, Son, Messiah, Image. Divine subordination still protected ancient "monotheism," since one sole divinity, God the Father, stood at power's pinnacle. "Logos Christology," as seen in the work of Justin Martyr, conforms to this idea. The Logos may be "another god," a *heteros theos*, as Justin says; but he is still a lower god.

Still, some later theologians, uncomfortable with this divine superfluity, sought to bolster monotheism by speaking of Father, Son, and Holy Spirit as different modalities of the same divinity, with function conferring identity. God as Father was one mode; God as Son—suffering, dying, rising—was another; God as Holy Spirit—inspiring, sanctifying—a third: but all were the same, single god, a "monarch." Called "Sabellianism" in the East and "Patripassianism" (Father-suffering) in the West, Monarchianism was condemned by other theologians as heretical. It came too close to claiming that God the Father had suffered on the cross.

How, then, to articulate the distinctions between these two entities (or three, including Spirit)? Combatting Monarchian theology, Tertullian proposed that God be envisaged as "one *substantia* in three *personae*." This formula would come into Greek as one *ousia* (which means "being" or "essence") in three *hypostases* (individuated entities or *prosōpa*, "persons"). The insistence on one ousia protected the singleness and simplicity of the ultimate God against any charge of tritheism; the invocation of three separate prosōpa protected against modalist Sabellianism. Christology, indeed, theology, had clearly entered into a reactive phase: ideas were formulated against others, which then came to be considered, for various reasons, inadequate or offensive.

Middle Platonic cosmology further complicated Christian theology. Earlier formulations, whether pagan or Christian (as we see with Justin) had held that hylē, unformed matter, had preexisted along with theos, the high god. Cosmos, the ordered material universe, was in turn eternally generated through the mediation of the demiurge, a lower divine power. The coeternity of all these dimensions of reality insulated God from any imputation of change: changelessness was an essential aspect of his perfection.

As the metaphysical opposite of theos, hylē represented imperfection and change. Despite the impress of divine forms, primal matter could communicate its intrinsic deficiencies to cosmos, especially in the sublunar realm. Hylē thus provided this system with a ready explanation for the problem of evil: unformed matter, not the perfect god, was the ultimate source of the world's imperfections. In the crucible of developing second-century Christianities, however, various theologians fretted over this idea. Did preexistent matter imply some kind of limit on God? Why would the good God pronounce creation "good" if it were based in and on deficient matter? And to what degree would matter imply or enact a cosmic realm independent of God? It was in these circumstances, as a battle between Christian intellectuals over the moral status of matter, that the (counterintuitive) idea of creation ex nihilo, out of nothing, eventually took hold.

Creation ex nihilo drove the arguments fueling later Christologies. If only God was God, and if he "created" out of nothing, then was anything not-God by definition part of his creation? To which pole of this binary should Christ be assigned? Theologically (thus, philosophically) the issue was contingency. Was the Son independently God? If so, was that not ditheism? If not, was that then Sabellianism, a too-close identification of Father and Son? Was Christ, as Son, not contingent on the Father? Simple vocabulary pulled in one direction: contingency. But concerns about the goodness of creation, the mechanisms of salvation, and the oneness of God pulled in another direction: equality. The Son, some theologians began to insist, was "begotten" of the Father, not—as by adoption or by creation—"made." By being divinely "begotten," the Son shared in the Father's ousia.

It took the genius of Origen, in the early third century, to frame a Christology that was both radically egalitarian and subordinationist at the same time. Origen distinguished between God and everything else in terms of "body" and in terms of contingency. Only the triune God, he taught, was completely self-generated, and only God was absolutely without body of any sort. The inner dynamics of the triune God, however, accommodated distinction, the scope for God the Father being unrestricted; for the Son, involved with secondary, temporal, material creation; for the Holy Spirit, restricted to the (true) church.

A century later, Alexandria would be convulsed over these questions, the battle lines drawn between the bishop, Alexander, and a priest, Arius. According to one version of the story, Alexander preached on the unity of the Trinity. His presbyter, Arius, hearing Alexander's speech as an endorsement of Sabellianism, took Origen's ideas in another direction: the only-begotten Son was contingent on the father, he taught, though timelessly generated by him. In the sense of contingency, not of time, Christ had a "beginning." Christ was still divine, just not as divine as the Father. But contingency, to Arius's enemies, implied creation, "creature-liness." The claim seemed to diminish Christ's godhead.

Alexander and Arius communicated their disagreement to other bishops in the East, who promptly got swept up in the argument. Arius amassed considerable support with two bishops in other important cities—Eusebius of Nicomedia (an eastern capital), and the church historian Eusebius of Caesarea (an administrative node of the empire). Antioch's bishop sided with Alexander. Then suddenly, in 324, the dynamics of the controversy altered dramatically. The emperor, Constantine, weighed in.

Constantine, Nicaea, and After

To the reigning imperial powers, Constantine seemed an imperial interloper. But he was also an effective general. Once his troops, in 306, declared him Augustus, he made a sweep of the West, conquering territories and amassing power. The last western city to fall to him, in 312, was Rome. As was usual in antiquity, he felt that his victory had been aided by a god. But the god in question was a relative newcomer: Christ.

Controversy continues to swirl around the issue of Constantine's conversion. The definitive point of dramatic reversal narrated by Lactantius and by Eusebius does not correspond to Constantine's actions. Even after the formation of his new allegiance in 312, he continued as pontifex maximus, the imperial overseer of traditional Roman cults. His coins bore images of the sun god, Sol Invictus. The Chi-Rho symbol of Christianity appears on them only belatedly. Pagans continued to dominate his court, his civil apparatus, and his army. He closed only a limited number of pagan sites, while countenancing the building of new ones. He was not baptized until on his deathbed. The idea of a single, dramatic moment of conversion, which both Lactantius and Eusebius claim he narrated to them, could well be a creation of his own retrospect. His active involvement with Christians, when he suspended the imperial directives of Diocletian's persecution in 306, had begun six years prior to his victory at the Milvian bridge.

In the event, after his 312 triumph at Rome, Constantine handsomely repaid Christ's favor, becoming an enthusiastic patron of Christian assemblies. He involved himself deeply in complex theological disputes. He worked hard to bring some sort of concord and unity to his chosen community. His commitment to Christianity seems unambiguous. His problem initially may have been identifying which Christian church to support.

There were many different Christian communities, of widely variant theologies, when Constantine experienced the power of the Christian god. Valentinians and Marcionites still assembled. The Montanists of the "New Prophecy" prevailed in Phrygia in Asia Minor. Manichaeism, Diocletian's suppression notwithstanding, spread from one end of the empire to the other, and beyond. In the wake of the imperial persecutions, more new communions, like that of the rigorist Novatianists, the Melitians, and the Donatists had formed. So why did Constantine sponsor the particular group that he did? Perhaps he had been influenced through his prior contact with Lactantius, whom he had chosen to be a tutor for one of his sons. Perhaps he was influenced by his mother Helena, who may (or may not) have been Christian herself at this point. Perhaps he was already in sympathy with Ossius, the western bishop who would later serve as his episcopal emissary. The simplest explanation is that he chose the church that he happened to be already familiar with, perhaps through an earlier, covert affiliation.

Constantine's personal religious motives to one side, his new choice of sponsorship had practical benefits as well. Christians of all sorts concentrated in cities. (The term for non-Christian gentiles, *pagani* or "country dwellers," was coined later in this period.) And cities were themselves nodal points within the power network constructed by empire, centers through which emperors could exercise local control through provincial governors and collect the all-important taxes that supported the army.

The Christian communities that Constantine chose to sponsor were especially characterized by strong institutional organization, which mimicked the Roman provincial one. They were headed by a monarchical bishop, an "overseer" with a lifetime appointment. The origins and evolution of this ecclesiastical position, the ways that it developed into a signature church office, are obscure: in the late first and early second centuries, prophets, wandering teachers, charismatic intellectuals (like Origen in the third century), and wonder-workers all wielded authority together with local "presidents" or bishops and presbyters. But by the mid-third century, (male) bishops emerge at the apex of stable (and salaried) hierarchies of presbyters, deacons, readers, and exorcists. Sometimes, elevation to the office depended on family connections: sons of bishops became bishops themselves. Sometimes the bishop was chosen by acclamation: the congregation would shout out their choice, which could lead to congregations split between favored candidates. Sometimes the presbyters chose a bishop from among themselves, though the candidate was ordained—infused with holy spirit—by other bishops.

Their duties were both pastoral and administrative. Bishops interpreted scriptures, expounded doctrine, and presided over liturgies, especially for initiation (baptism) and for the celebration of the community ritual of the eucharist. Importantly, they were invested with the authority to forgive sins. Locally, and no less importantly, bishops mediated charity, controlling welfare distributions to church dependents and to the urban poor.

Assertions of episcopal authority began to grow in the second century. *First Clement* held that the apostles themselves had established the rules for the orderly appointment of church leaders. According to Ignatius of Antioch, the bishop "presides in the place of God" (*Letter to the Magnesians* 6.1), a view repeated in the later *Didascalia Apostolorum* ("Teaching of the Apostles," preserving early third-century traditions). The *Didachē*, a manual of Christian discipline (early second century?), while acknowledging the authority of wandering apostles and prophets, also upheld that of the stationary "overseers" and deacons. Irenaeus, late in the second century, presented bishops and "true presbyters" as the sole guardians of apostolic teaching (*Against Heresies* 4.26, 2). Tertullian, in the early third century, argued that the original bishops of the empire's major cities had all been appointed by the apostles (*Prescription against Heretics* 32). By the mid-third century, the apostles had become bishops themselves.

As a loose federation of scattered communities, these monarchical churches sought to align on issues of doctrine and discipline across vast distances. Bishops attempted, through regional councils and through correspondence, to stay coordinated with each other—another testament to their administrative organization. Letters threaded independent churches together. A papyrus fragment reveals that Irenaeus's work against heresies, written in Lyon in the 180s, had already made its way to Egypt by the turn of the century. Regional synods convened to coordinate responses to various challenges. In 250, some sixty bishops gathered in Rome against the rigorist Novatian, divided over policy for reintegrating the lapsed back into community; in the 260s, three large synods repudiated the teachings of the bishop of Antioch, Paul of Samosata. Prestige, and property bequeathed by the faithful, accrued to bishops, especially in the wealthy major cities. As dispensers of charity, bishops functioned as local patrons with considerable clout, commanding the loyalty of their urban base. Besides setting calendars, serving as conduits of Spirit through sacraments, forgiving sins, ordaining priests, and consecrating other bishops, they exercised juridical roles within their own churches, settling internal disputes.

These bishops, in short, represented—and offered—an empire-wide network of influence and support. Constantine's patronage would amplify what these bishops were already doing in their communities. The bishops, in turn, offered him a talent pool for a new kind of magistrate.

Already in 260, the emperor Gallienus issued edicts ending his father Valerian's persecution of Christians. And in 311, the Christian god had been eased into Rome's pantheon by the eastern emperor, Galerius, when he ended Diocletian's persecution and exhorted Christians to pray to their god for the safety of the res publica and of the emperor (Lactantius, *On the Deaths of the Persecutors* 34.5). But Constantine, in 312, made a singular commitment. The Christian god had aided his ascendancy. He would repay. While maintaining the imperial role of pontifex maximus over traditional cults, Constantine also assumed personal responsibility for the proper worship of the Christian deity as well.

For this reason, the discord of the North African church, which embroiled him almost immediately, commandeered Constantine's attention. Inheriting from the Second Sophistic an emphasis on homodoxia and homonoia, unanimity of thought, prelates urged that proper religio should be unanimous, the identity and unity of the true church unambiguous. Constantine agreed, for reasons that were doubly practical. First, only right religio could guarantee the security of the empire. And, second, the emperor had to know which bishops to sponsor. It was in the course of his attempts to resolve North Africa's Donatist conflict that Constantine set an important precedent. With the failure of a commissioned episcopal council to produce a satisfactory result, he had gone on to convene, in Arles in 314, an episcopal synod overseen by himself.

In 313, together with the eastern emperor Licinius, Constantine issued a declaration formally establishing freedom of practice for all inhabitants of the empire, specifically mentioning Christians, the so-called Edict of Milan. Once he consolidated power over the East in 324, however, Constantine positioned himself specifically as Christianity's champion. He then met with another unhappy surprise: his newly unified empire was once again riven by disunity within his favored church. He tasked his episcopal adviser, Ossius of Cordova, with quieting the discord. Arriving in Alexandria, Ossius sided with his fellow bishop Alexander against the presbyter Arius. The council that he subsequently called in Antioch ended with provisional excommunications, including that of Eusebius of Caesarea—another unhappy result. Constantine then took matters into his own hands once again. He called for an "ecumenical"—that is, an empire-wide—episcopal council, to be held under imperial sponsorship at Nicaea in 325. And he himself would be present, to ensure the result he sought: concord.

More than two hundred bishops—the number is uncertain—assembled at Nicaea. The vast majority were from the East, only a handful from the West. (The Roman bishop, Silvester, did not attend but sent two presbyters to represent him.) A clogged agenda confronted them: not only deciding on the nature of Christ, thus of God, but also fixing the date of Easter, which wandered between lunar (thus, Jewish) and solar dates in different communities. They had to sort out a policy for episcopal jurisdictions, which imitated imperial provincial organization. Over what extraprovincial territories would each metropolitan bishop exercise authority? What was to be done about the disciplinary schisms over how to reintegrate those who had lapsed, which followed in the wake of the first imperial persecution (the Novatianists, in Rome) and the last (the Melitians, in Egypt)? What was the status of clerical marriage?

The decisions of the council, ultimately, could not be enforced. Positions identified with Arius long prevailed; Easter calendars continued to differ; episcopal jurisdictions were continuously contested; the Melitians and Novatianists perdured; the issue of clerical marriages was left unsettled. But the rewards of imperial support encouraged cooperation. Only those who obliged the emperor could expect his benefactions.

One lasting result of the Nicene council was its movement toward a creed that, by the end of the century—and only by the end of the century—would serve as the touchstone for imperially recognized orthodoxy. Despite his own shaky grasp of the finer points of theological dispute—a quarrel "over small and quite minute points," as he complained to Alexander and Arius (Eusebius, *Life of Constantine* 2.68.2; 71.1)—Constantine had insisted on the use of *homoousios*, "of one substance."

This term would define imperial orthodox theology about Christ. It was interpretable enough to wrest the consent of those, like Eusebius of Caesarea and Eusebius of Nicomedia, who inclined toward Arius. Eventually, by 328, Arius himself would be reconciled, too, to the imperial church. Christ was now, by decision of the council, fully God. A corollary question—if so, then how fully human?—remained contested for another century and never met with unanimity.

Constantine effected a phase change in Christianity. For the first time, the idea of "orthodoxy" had serious social purchase. Only the churches that he recognized would receive the benefits that obliging him and his quest for concord could bestow. And those benefits were considerable. Constantine transferred huge amounts of wealth to the "universal and orthodox" church via its bishops. He did so by confiscating the holdings of some temples, stripping them of their gold and silver ornamentation and melting down cultic statuary. In some instances, he redistributed funds by transferring the revenue-producing estates supporting the temple cults to his own purse (the *res privata*) or to that of the local bishop. He sometimes did the same with the revenues of civic estates. By despoiling the temples he accomplished two goals: building up the churches (and tying its bishops to himself in effect as his clients) and compromising public pagan cult.

Constantine also ordered provincial governors to provide annual grain distributions for church personnel and dependents (virgins, widows, orphans, the poor). These grain rations were channeled through the bishops. He sponsored the development of monumental Christian architecture, erecting huge basilicas and encouraging bishops, enriched from the res privata, to do the same. The upkeep of these buildings and provision of their sumptuous furnishings were likewise underwritten by the government.

And Constantine transferred more than wealth. He thereby also transferred power. Grain distributions enhanced the status of bishops as important local *patroni* in their own cities. Further, bishops could now adjudicate civil cases and call on imperial authorities to enforce their decisions. Their authority to oversee the manumission of slaves was affirmed. Bishops could legally receive bequests. They could travel at public expense, by the imperial posting system. And they were excused from the onerous and expensive service to city councils (*curiae*). Episcopal office, with its tax exemptions, local power, and juridical authority, became an attractive career choice for men with talent and ambition.

But Constantine's largesse came at a cost. Failure to cooperate had more than financial consequences, considerable though those were. Only clergy who obliged him would keep their sees: exile, with Constantine, became a tool for enforcing party discipline. It was one that he did not hesitate to use. The prelate who exemplifies the application, and the failure, of this means of control was Athanasius of Alexandria, who succeeded Bishop Alexander in 328.

Constantine sought concord. Athanasius had his own ideas. Implacably opposed to Arius, he refused to receive the latter back into communion, even though Arius had himself reconciled with the emperor. Worse: Athanasius also had little truck with receiving rigorist Melitian prelates back into the fold. Constantine summoned him to yet another council in Tyre in 335, where the powerful Eusebius of Nicomedia arranged for his excommunication and deposition. Not only were Athanasius's means of policing orthodoxy in Alexandria violent, Eusebius charged; he had also threatened to inhibit the transfer of Egyptian grain from the port city to the new eastern capital, Constantinople. Off went Athanasius to Gaul. The contacts that he made in the West would serve him well in this protracted battle of wills.

Recalled to Alexandria in 337 with Constantine's death, Athanasius was soon pushed into exile again by Constantine's son and eastern successor, Constantius II. The bishop refused to ratify a compromise creed favored by the new emperor. (A creed, however much it represented a credo, functioned as well and not least as a public declaration of political fealty.) In 339, consequentially, Athanasius found refuge in Rome, within the independent territories of Constantius's brother. The bishop of Rome received Athanasius in defiance of his excommunication in the East—an assertion of authority that only deepened the ecclesiastical split growing along the political fault line between Constantine's heirs.

Compounding these troubles was a power vacuum that developed suddenly within the church at Constantinople. Eusebius of Nicomedia,

Arius's old ally and Athanasius's nemesis, had assumed the see of Constantine's new city; but late in 341, Eusebius died. Contested between
two prelates, the position's power was compromised, hampering the
eastern bishops' political effectiveness. Empire-wide schism loomed.
The attempt to head it off, at a council in Serdica (342–43), only made
matters worse: eastern and western bishops split into two separate con-
claves. Finally, Constantius blinked and allowed Athanasius to return to
Alexandria in 345.

Power politics in their imperial inflection were no less troubled. In the
West, Constantius's brothers, Constantine II and Constans, fought with
each other, with Constans emerging victorious. Then Constans fell to a
usurper, whom Constantius overcame in turn. The empire was now reunited under a single monarch, diminishing the scope for ecclesiastical
maneuverings. Constantius exploited his opportunity, arranging for Athanasius's condemnation by two councils in Arles and in Milan. Noncompliant western bishops, including the bishop of Rome, were duly exiled, as
was Athanasius once more, ousted by military force in 356. This time the
recalcitrant bishop stayed closer to home, fleeing to hide with monks in
the nearby desert and maintaining communication with his base back
in the city. His replacement was an Arian sympathizer, George.

Christology churned these waters even more. If *homoousia*, "of the
same essence" or "being" as the Father, staked too much on divine identity, could one say that Christ expressed *homoiousia*, "similarity of essence" with the Father, as some Homoian prelates ventured to pose?
Or—so George of Alexandria—was Christ's essence utterly unlike that
of the absolutely unique Father, a position labeled "Anomian," "dissimi-
lar"? The homousian theologians, with the fierce Athanasius as their
champion, brooked no compromise. One of Athanasius's exiled western
defenders, Hilary of Poitiers, appropriating the discourse of martyrdom, roundly reviled the Christian Constantius as Nero, Decius, and
Antichrist, persecutors all of the true church. In Hilary's view, Constantius was on the wrong side of the Christological debate.

Christological controversy generated more heat than light. It articulated battle lines drawn over the issue of authority. Who was in charge,
the emperor or the bishops? The bishop of Rome or, independently, the

metropolitan bishops? The individual bishop in his own district, or the majority of a translocal synod? As for Christology itself, earlier doctrine provided little guidance. The rhetoric of apostolic tradition notwithstanding, definitions of orthodoxy had long outgrown their New Testament sources: none of those authors had been thinking, or teaching, in terms of ousia. The content of orthodoxy in this period was itself under construction. The prerogative to decide which definition of "orthodoxy" would prevail was no less contested. The question had practical consequences: decisions determined who received imperial sanction, who support.

Suddenly, in 361, everything changed again. Constantius died. Athanasius returned to Alexandria in 362, local mobs having murdered George in an ugly urban riot. Athanasius would continue in his seat of power, interrupted by two more brief exiles, until his own death in 373. By then, he and all his episcopal colleagues, of whatever Christological persuasion, had lived through a shocking reversal of fortune. Constantius had been succeeded by his younger cousin, Julian, who in turn became sole emperor. With his rise to power, the new Roman ruler openly declared his own religious allegiance. Julian worshiped the old gods.

Julian

A cradle Christian, baptized in his youth, Julian was also a survivor. In 337 his Christian cousins, Constantine's sons and heirs, had slaughtered all the ancillary males of the family, including Julian's father. Too many family members, they felt, might muddy the waters of dynastic inheritance. The young Julian and his half brother, Gallus, were allowed to survive (though Constantius executed the unhappy Gallus in 354). Julian was even permitted to go to Athens to pursue his studies in philosophy. Making contact with pagan Neoplatonists, Julian covertly redirected his religious allegiances.

Julian was called from his studies suddenly in 355, when Constantius appointed him Caesar and tasked him with shoring up the Rhine border. Surprisingly, Julian demonstrated so much military talent that, in early 360, his enthused troops—resisting Constantius's order to relocate further east—acclaimed him Augustus. Only Constantius's death in 361 averted a brewing civil war. Julian was free to worship the gods.

How daring was his decision? Even after Constantine's conversion, and his championing of his favored church, the vast majority of the army had remained pagan, with little effort on the part of Christian emperors to affect a religious reorientation. The Roman senate had also remained overwhelmingly pagan, despite some Christian inroads under the Constantinian regimes. Pagans had served in prominent positions in the courts of Constantine and his sons. Civic celebrations and spectacles had all continued, though in principle decoupled from the animal offerings that the emperor had found so distasteful. And Constantine himself, his personal enthusiasms notwithstanding, had continued as pontifex maximus to oversee traditional cults. In the 330s, he even approved the establishment of cults to his own family, the *gens Flavia*, complete with priesthoods, theatrical performances, and gladiatorial combats (but no blood sacrifices), for a town in Italy (Hispellum) and a province of Africa. Imperial cult had remained a coin of privilege, and a means to garner imperial patronage and, thus, benefactions (such as immunity from curial service for imperial priests). Notwithstanding the triumphalist rhetoric of his two publicists, Lactantius and Eusebius, Constantine's kingdom had retained a pagan majority.

Julian's regime immediately affected the churches: he shut off the financial spigot and ended clerical privileges. Knowing well the Christian ideology of martyrdom, he also avoided any use of coercive force. His means of undermining the churches was more subtle: he would use tolerance. "I had imagined that the prelates of the Galileans were under greater obligations to me than to my predecessor," he wrote in a published letter, "for in his reign many of them were banished, persecuted and imprisoned, and many of the so-called heretics were executed." Julian would have none of it. "All this has been reversed in my reign. The banished are allowed to return, and confiscated goods have all been restored to their owners" (*Letter 52*). Back came the heretical leaders and exiled bishops, back came the Christological contestants. Left to their own devices, Julian was sure, and now completely free to be out in the open, Christians would claw each other to pieces.

Cannily, too, Julian determined to rebuild the temple of the Jewish god in Jerusalem. In Constantine's newly Christian city, the church of the Holy Sepulcher, lauded by Eusebius as a new temple on the order of Solomon's, loomed over the wasted mesa of the old temple site. Julian knew his New Testament, and the adversus Iudaeos traditions, which had made so much of the temple's destruction in 70 as a permanent sign of God's repudiation of the Jews and, specifically, of blood sacrifices. But Julian vigorously championed blood sacrifices for traditional cult (to an excessive degree, some pagan courtiers felt). Jews sacrificed to the highest god, he stated—though he also noted that, oddly, they sacrificed to none others. No matter. He would restore this sacred site to Jewish worshipers, to perform rites that Julian felt to be honorable, ancient, and correct.

The depth of Julian's Christian formation was evident in another regard: the ways in which he determined to revivify and restore traditional cults. These really amounted to a reform built on an ecclesiastical template. Traditional cults had formed no "ism": they had always been multivocal, locally specific, independent, uncoordinated, and energetically various. Julian now envisaged a sort of central administration, an organized pagan "church." High priests would exercise jurisdiction on the model of metropolitan bishops. The imperial treasury would support standing priesthoods and pagan charities for the poor, this last self-consciously modeled on Jewish and Christian philanthropy.

Finally, and most controversially, Julian ruled that Christians could no longer serve as teachers. The curriculum of the schools—for grammar, for rhetoric, for philosophy—had always been crammed with gods, and so it had remained, since the days when Alexander the Great had widely exported it. For this reason, the ideologically fastidious Tertullian had urged Christian teachers, a century and a half before Julian, to quit their posts (*On Idolatry* 10). What did a Christian have to do with pagan gods? Julian asked the same question and came to the same answer. Hellenistic Jews and, later, educated Christians had driven a wedge between pagan religiousness and pagan learned culture, appropriating the latter for their own ends. Julian insisted on closing that gap. His edict effectively cut the ground out from under Christian learning, infuriating classically trained Christian intellectuals, who claimed paideia for themselves.

All these projects came to naught with Julian's early death in 363, on campaign against Persia. With Julian, the Constantinian dynasty came to its close. A Christian successor, Jovian, was declared in the field. He ended Julian's initiatives. Church benefactions, however, would be restored to only a fraction of their previous levels: Constantine's generosity had proved unsustainable. But both in practice and in principle, the questions thrown into sharp relief with Constantine's sponsorship remained. Who was in charge? Who was in, and who was out? Which was the orthodox and universal church? And what was orthodoxy?

Continuing Controversies

Jovian died in less than a year. His successor, a military officer, Valentinian I, again split the empire East and West, handing the East to his brother, Valens. Neither brother, like Jovian before them, concerned himself with Christological niceties, perhaps as a matter of political pragmatism: the ongoing theological controversies, seeping downward to urban populations through sermons, song, and sloganeering, destabilized public peace. Taking a stand would compromise the imperial newcomers' neutrality and potentially alienate different contestants and their urban bases. In the view of the Homousians, however, this neutrality made Valens into an "Arian."

Both brothers died in office, Valentinian in 375, Valens, in a harrowing military encounter with Goths, in 378. Gratian, Valentinian's young son, briefly succeeded him in the West: it was Gratian who disavowed the old imperial title of pontifex. In the East, a nondynastic choice fell on another military man, Theodosius I (379–95). A fervent adherent of the Nicene position, Theodosius together with Gratian issued the Edict of Thessalonica in 380, establishing Nicaea as the empire-wide standard of orthodoxy:

We desire that all the peoples who are ruled by the guidance of our clemency should be versed in that religion which it is evident that the divine apostle Peter handed down to the Romans, and which the pope Damasus and Peter, Bishop of Alexandria, a man of apostolic

sanctity, adhere to. . . . We command that those persons who follow
this rule shall have the name of catholic ["universal"] Christians. The
rest, however, whom we judge to be demented and insane, shall sus-
tain the infamy of heretical dogmas, their meeting places shall not
receive the name of churches, and they shall be smitten, first, by divine vengeance and, secondly, by the retribution of our own initiative,
which we shall assume in accordance with divine judgement. (*Theodosian Code* 16.1.2)

Perhaps Theodosius thought that broadcasting his preference would
bully the various outliers into compliance. No less important, perhaps
he thought that it would quiet the raging factionalism of the eastern bishops. The stratagem might have worked, had it not been for a subsequent
canon promulgated at a council that he convened in Constantinople in
381. Under his supervision, the council championed Constantinople's
authority as second only to Rome's. Theodosius thereby alienated Alexandria, which had long regarded itself as the eastern empire's preeminent
see. Intercity and intracity contests over authority and prestige would
continue to be expressed in a theological key well into the fifth century,
as Alexandria, Antioch, and Constantinople faced off over teachings
about the nature of the Trinity and about the person of Christ.

The seesaw of imperial power and episcopal authority is nowhere
better expressed than in the relationship between imperial figures and
the bishop of Milan, the imperious Ambrose. The latter, an aristocrat of
senatorial rank, was serving as regional governor when he was called by
lay acclamation to serve as the city's bishop. Ambrose was first baptized,
then eight days later ordained. The exercise of authority, with its impli-
cations of power, came easily to him. An implacable foe of Arianism and
of traditional Roman religions, as well as an adamant supersessionist as
regards Judaism, Ambrose had no trouble facing down imperial power.
He may well have relished it.

One test came in 386, when the widow of Valentinian I and regent of
the adolescent Valentinian II, the empress Justina, required one of Milan's
cathedrals to be made available for the army's Gothic troops, who were
(or were labeled as) "Arian." Justina's and Valentinian's own sympathies

lay in that direction. Ambrose resolutely refused, mobilizing popular sentiment against Justina and invoking the language of martyrdom: he would give up his life before a Nicene building would be ceded. He and his people staged a sit-down strike within the contested basilica, refusing to yield to imperial troops. In the end, Justina backed down.

A second incident involved the emperor Theodosius. It concerned a synagogue in Callinicum, on the eastern edge of the empire. In 388, the bishop there had incited a Christian mob to burn down the building, an act that was both patently illegal and plainly disruptive. (A local Valentinian chapel met with a similar fate.) Theodosius ordered the perpetrators punished and directed the bishop to restore the structure out of his own funds. Learning of this, Ambrose refused to continue with a eucharistic service when Theodosius was present until and unless Theodosius rescinded his directive. Resistant, the importuned Theodosius finally acquiesced.

A third incident, two years later, occurred when Ambrose threatened the emperor with excommunication. The sources for this are late and conflicting, but at issue seems to have been Theodosius's handling of an urban rebellion in Thessalonica. Residents had murdered the presiding Roman military official, evidently for ordering the arrest of a popular charioteer. In response, the army was said to have massacred thousands. Ambrose demanded that Theodosius do public penance for his role, whether in ordering or in countenancing the slaughter. According to these later sources, Theodosius complied. His status as a baptized layman complicated his relation to episcopal authority. The emperor was still unquestionably supreme: he controlled the army and had a monopoly on coercive force. Equally unquestionably, however, the bishops as urban powerbrokers with their bases of popular support exercised local clout.

Theological contestations, meanwhile, continued apace. At issue now was the Holy Spirit's relation to God the Father and the Son. Were they all of the same ousia (essence)? If so, how were they to be distinguished? Were they all one *hypostasis* (an independently existent entity) or three hypostases in one ousia? Communities split over the argument: at one point, Antioch had three different claimants to the episcopal see, the contestants ranging across the interpretive options, each with the popular backing of his own violent urban faction. Again, the fight was parsed in terms of "Arianism," by this point more a slogan than a description. Politicking between Alexandria and Rome over Antioch finally led to a resolution, and two of Antioch's contestants were sent packing.

Ultimately, the work of the Cappadocian Fathers—Basil of Caesarea, his brother Gregory of Nyssa, and their friend Gregory of Nazianzus—quieted some of the turmoil by arguing that the Trinity represented three hypostases in one ousia. The Son was "begotten" of the Father; the Spirit "proceeds" from the Father. Liturgical tradition—baptism in the name of the Father, the Son, and Holy Spirit—unobtrusively supported their formulation. This satisfied some and not others. High theology continued to steer between the Scylla of Sabellianism and the Charybdis of tritheism. Biblical language could not oblige the ambitions of late Roman theology: theologians were stuck with terms set by philosophy.

Fissures also appeared in theological constructions of Christ. The question of his divinity, for the Nicenes, being settled at Nicaea, another remained: how human was he? And in what way? Apollonaris of Laodicea urged that divine Logos had replaced human mind: as a unified person, Christ had to have had but a single nature, which clearly had to be his divine one. And since Christ was truly God, his mother, Mary, could be rightly acclaimed *Theotokos*, "God-bearer." Against this position, Theodore of Mopsuestia urged that the union of Jesus and God was one of will. Christ, he insisted, had *two* natures, one fully divine, the other fully human. Only a full assumption of human nature, argued Theodore, could effect salvation.

The contest dragged on, reaching a continuous boil from the 420s through the 450s, during the reign of Theodosius II. The two primary contestants were Nestorius of Constantinople, a student of Theodore's, and Cyril of Alexandria. Alexandria, proud heir to Athanasian Christology, emphasized Christ's divinity. (The standing competition for prestige and authority between the two cities did not calm the conflict.) High divinity, Cyril insisted, made Mary—the cult of whom was energetically developing in this period—the "God-bearer," *Theotokos*, a word long sanctioned by liturgical use. Christ's two aspects, divine and human, were merged into one hypostasis: Christ had a single, divine nature (*physis*, thus a "miaphysist" position). Nestorius, shoring up the idea of Christ's humanity and deploring the earlier formulations of Apollonaris, rejected the term in favor of *Christotokos*, "Christ-bearer." This seemed to the Alexandrians to diminish Christ's divinity. Argument continued unabated.

Finally, through a series of slick political maneuverings and outright bribes, Cyril prevailed: Nestorius was deposed and exiled. A pro-Nestorian council of bishops in turn pronounced Cyril deposed. Theodosius, hesitating, eventually acquiesced to Nestorius's fate while withdrawing his confirmation of Cyril's deposition. But the emperor could not indefinitely tolerate a standing schism: that might alienate heaven, and thereby threaten the security of the empire. It also confused imperial administration. And it unsettled public peace, since cities split between contesting bishops were wracked by urban violence. A compromise was patched together, affirming Cyril's position but repeating many of the phrases amenable to the Nestorian-leaning sympathies of Antioch.

The compromise was unstable. Conflict again broke out shortly after Cyril's death in 444, when Antiochene loyalists attacked the Alexandrian formulations as denying the true humanity of Christ. Everyone jumped into the ensuing fray: the emperor's powerful sister, Pulcheria; the western emperor's regent, Galla Placidia; the bishops of Alexandria, of Constantinople, and of Rome. The Second Council of Ephesus, convened by the emperor (449), satisfied nobody. And then, compounding the controversies and confusions, in 450 Theodosius II suddenly died. A new emperor, Marcian, reinforced the legitimacy of his appointment by marrying Pulcheria. They insisted on convening yet another council at Chalcedon (451).

Some five hundred and twenty bishops, mostly from the East, now met at Chalcedon. Marcian and Pulcheria, hailed respectively as a "new Constantine" and a "new Helena," attended only one of the meetings, but their agents ensured that the program remained on track toward some sort of stable compromise. The bishop of Alexandria was condemned and deposed, the Antiochene position of "two natures"— amenable to Pope Leo of Rome—affirmed. Christ was proclaimed "truly

God and truly man," two natures "without confusion, change, division or separation," coming together in one hypostasis. Paradox was as much clarity as the Christological conundrum could achieve.

Marcian declared contention at an end. It was not. Christological controversies divided even this one notionally unified community: Christians in Egypt, in Syria, and in Palestine immediately rejected Chalcedon. Their separate communions persist to this day.

The Imperial Church

How did Christianity affect empire? And how did empire affect Christianity?

In terms of the personal behaviors of the chief secular power players, Christianity seems to have had small effect. Constantine eliminated Licinius and his nine-year-old son as soon as he took over the eastern half of the empire in 324. The deaths of his own son Crispus and wife, Faustina, were laid at his door. Rule was bloody business: Constantine's decision to be baptized only when near death showed practical prudence. His surviving sons murdered nine of their other close male relatives as they, in turn, consolidated their imperial inheritance. No late Roman ruler hesitated to use coercive force, including murder, whether to police cooperation with imperial policy (seen as the enforcement of "orthodoxy") or to clarify any ambiguities around power.

What of orthodoxy's outliers? How did Christian imperial power affect them? Constantine's patronage had its first and harshest effects on other Christians, now officially branded as "heretics." Their persecution continued, if anything more pointedly since they could be targeted by their local competitors, those bishops now empowered by the state. Christian diversity was in effect criminalized, though as with the earlier anti-Christian persecutions, so now: enactment according to the wish of the bishops depended on the sporadic cooperation of governors and local elites.

Pagans fared better. Some practices were abridged, though the army remained overwhelmingly pagan, as did the empire's total population, most of which (perhaps 80 percent?) lived in the countryside. Pagan cults would not be proactively legislated against until the reigns of Gratian and of Theodosius I in the 380s. Their efforts, too, met with uneven results. But empowered bishops and emboldened monks could initiate local exercises of coercive force. In 391, the bishop Theophilus oversaw the destruction of Alexandria's famous Serapeum; in 415, when the city was convulsed in an urban riot orchestrated by Bishop Cyril of Alexandria, the pagan philosopher Hypatia was torn limb from limb.

Jews, finally, the perennial outliers, were reviled at the Council of Nicaea, but this was because some churches—against Constantine's wishes—continued to observe Easter according to the Jewish calendar's designation of Passover. Imperial law in fact affirmed Jewish freedom of practice for Jews; and the Jewish patriarch in Tiberias retained his own prestige, another power player of the late empire. But again, belligerent initiatives could disrupt social peace. In 388, Callinicum's bishop spurred a Christian mob's destruction of a synagogue; on Minorca in 418, another bishop spurred the destruction of the synagogue and forced conversion of the island's Jews; in the mid-fifth century, the infamous Barsauma and his monks ravaged Jewish sites in Roman Palestine.

Constantine's personal enthusiasm for and vigorous favoritism toward one Christian denomination flooded the designated churches with economic benefits, greatly enhancing the bishops' position where it mattered most, at the local level. Exempt from taxation and curial duties, bishops—distributing grain, supporting church dependents, adjudicating civil cases—became major urban powerbrokers, relentless ecclesiastical politicians, and indefatigable combat theologians. But what they gained in power, they lost in doctrinal independence: theology, at least in principle, had to coordinate both with episcopal consensus and with imperial policy. Creeds—simplified statements of complex theological positions—became a mechanism of this coordination.

Yet bishops could also push back, especially by using their local base, becoming masters at orchestrating urban riots and imposing their views against rivals by force. City populations were radicalized, often to the point of violence. In the East, militant monks became part of the mix, a potent force readily mobilized by belligerent bishops resisting imperial replacements. By exercising coercive force, monks legitimized it.

This phase in the development of imperial orthodoxy is largely a tale of bishops, emperors, and theologians struggling to assert authority, often through muscular means. And the intellectual wrangling over issues Trinitarian and Christological can seem like the theological equivalent of particle physics. Ousia, prosopon, hypostasis, physis: how was the vast majority of the faithful ever and even involved?

Gregory of Nyssa, commenting on the atmosphere in Antioch, observed, "If you ask for your change, someone philosophizes to you on the Begotten and the Unbegotten. If you ask the price of bread, you are told, 'The Father is greater and the Son inferior.' If you ask, 'Is the bath ready?' someone answers, 'The Son was created from nothing'" (*On the Deity of the Son*). As much as he exaggerates for comic effect, Gregory also reveals an intriguing level of downward penetration of these lofty concepts. Through sloganeering, song, sermons, and liturgy—as well as through civic patriotism and loyalty to their local *patronus*, the bishop—masses who had no means of grasping the fine points of theological dispute were socialized into having a place in the fight. The emperor had his army, but the bishop, through the lumpen laity and local monks, in effect had his own militia.

"Arianism" was originally only a schismatic position: in terms of sacred texts, liturgical calendar, and sacraments, Arius and Alexander stood in communion. Arius's position became an "ism" and subsequentially a "heresy" because of the imperialization of the church. Other eastern bishops had so energetically waded into the controversy that Constantine, walking in a few years later, had to oblige: concord between bishops mattered for concord between heaven and earth.

This moment in the history of Christianity is invariably analyzed in terms of politics and—or versus—theology. These are the terms we think with. But the two were never distinct and separate realms in Roman antiquity: what *we* think of as "politics" and what *we* think of as "religion" were eternally wed. We draw a distinction that would not have been all that evident to contemporaries.

The intimate linkage, or synonymity, of religion and politics is best illustrated by the fate of Rome, both the city and the empire, in the West. Under Constantius II, a bishop Ufilas had missionized tribes of

Goths at the edges of empire. Ufilas had espoused a gospel-based message against the philosophizing homoousian Christology of the Nicenes. The Goths probably thought that they were affiliating with Roman religion. Once inside of Rome's borders, they discovered that they were "heretics." Rome looked down on Goths as "barbarians." Doctrinal difference underscored ethnic difference. If to be Roman was to be "Nicene," then clearly these tribes were "Arian." It is doubtful that resistance to homoousia as anything other than a slogan fed mainstream Gothic identity.

In an odd way, the "Arianizing" of these tribes, the Goths and ultimately the Vandals, worked to strengthen the claims to hegemony of the bishop of Rome. The central government of the western empire crumbled in the mid-fifth century as these tribes, originally mobilized as troops for various Roman strongmen, settled permanently within the empire: in Italy, in Provence, in Spain, and ultimately—shockingly—by conquest, in North Africa as well. Romans expressed resentment by doubly repudiating the newcomers as "barbarians" and as "heretics." Once again, the rhetoric of martyrdom sounded. When Christian Vandals disenfranchised catholic prelates in North Africa, to be replaced by their own clergy—ironically, by appeal to laws that the catholics themselves had framed against Donatists—catholics hailed their actions as "persecution." "I am a Christian! I am a Christian! By Saint Stephen [the protomartyr], I am a Christian!" a catholic child asserts in a tale of Vandal aggressions, sounding the rhetoric of martyrdom, casting Christian Vandals as pagan persecutors. To be catholic was to be ("really") Roman; to be Roman was to be catholic; and to be catholic and Roman, insisted Rome's bishop, was to be loyal to the directives and decisions of Rome. Out of loyalty perhaps not unmixed with nostalgia, western Christians would look to Rome, the see of the apostle Peter, its first bishop.

But what the papacy gained in the West it lost in the East. Rome pressed for recognition of primacy vis-à-vis Constantinople. At the Council of Chalcedon (451), this was and was not affirmed. Canon 28 read, "Primacy and exceptional honor shall be preserved for the most God-beloved archbishop of Senior Rome according to the canons." And then the shoe dropped. "But the most sacred archbishop of imperial

Constantinople, New Rome, is to enjoy the same privileges and honor." Given that no effective emperor ruled in the splintering West, Constantinople could well afford to be both gracious and independent: there was little chance of repeating the charged situation that had threatened to break into doctrinally augmented civil war between Constans and Constantius II back in 345.

The emperor Zeno's best efforts to achieve doctrinal concord, in 482, only led to further fracturing. Zeno had tried to find a way to knit together the pro- and anti-Chalcedonians by issuing, on his own authority, a unifying doctrinal teaching called the *Henotikon*. It both condemned Nestorians and endorsed Cyril, made no reference to two natures, and deliberately avoided all mention of Chalcedon. It thereby inflamed urban violence in Jerusalem and Ashkelon (where pro-Miaphysite crowds drove court-appointed Chalcedonian bishops from their sees), and in Scythopolis, Alexandria, and Antioch (where Chalcedonian bishops were lynched). Rome, staunchly Chalcedonian, broke with the eastern church. Schism perdured for more than thirty years.

"Christianization" and "Romanization" were never discrete processes: what became the imperial church had formed within the matrix of Roman culture and power politics. Well before Constantine, both Melito of Sardis and, later, Origen had argued that the empire, under Augustus, and Christianity, with Christ's incarnation, had been coordinated by divine providence: the pax Romana had facilitated the spread of the gospel (Eusebius, *Church History* 4.26.7–8; *Against Celsus* 2.30). Eusebius repeated the lesson. Constantine, in reuniting the empire, he proclaimed, had overseen the triumph of the church. Monarchy recapitulated monotheism: as one god ruled in heaven, so too his viceroy, the emperor, ruled on earth.

In its institutional structures, in its province-wide organization, in its concentration of authority in its bishops (especially in metropolitan sees), the church endorsed by Constantine was already "Romanized." Constantine's lavish patronage and the bishops' subsequent and unhesitating embrace of coercive force only made it more so. And in his politics if not in his personal conduct, the emperor became "Christianized," assuming a role within the church functionally analogous to that of pontifex maximus. Imperial concern for doctrinal concord was genuinely motivated, indeed galvanized, by concern for the well-being of the state. Bishops reinforced that mentality. "The fides of the emperor," intoned Ambrose, "produces strength in his soldiers" (*On the Death of Theodosius* 6).

A sixth-century baptistry in Ravenna displays a mosaic image of a beautiful young man. He is dressed as a Roman army officer, perhaps as an emperor. The open codex that he holds proclaims "I am the Way, the Truth and the Life." This is a portrait of Christ, drawing on the Gospel of John. The death of Jesus of Nazareth in this mosaic is referenced only gently by a small cross-bar on the staff borne over the figure's armored shoulder. Dressing a god in Roman military garb was a traditional means of naturalizing foreign deities: the Egyptian gods Apis, Horus, and Anubis had been presented in this way. We see another naturalization here. In this figure of the Roman Christ, his two natures, that of church and of empire, truly do come together as one.

6

THE REDEMPTION
OF THE FLESH

It is sown a soulish body; it is raised a spiritual body. . . . I tell you this,
brothers: flesh and blood cannot inherit the Kingdom of God.

PAUL ON THE RESURRECTED BODY, 1 CORINTHIANS 15.44, 50

How wonderful will be that body which will be completely subdued to
the spirit! . . . It will not be a soulish body. It will be a spiritual body,
possessing the substance of flesh, but untainted by carnal corruption.

AUGUSTINE ON THE RESURRECTED BODY, *CITY OF GOD* 22.24

*Ascetic practices had roots in both pagan and Jewish cultures, but over the
course of the second through fifth centuries, Christianity developed these
practices in new ways. Voluntary poverty, fasting, and especially sexual renunciation became premier expressions of Christian spirituality. The value
of marriage was heatedly debated, while sensational acts of self-denial commanded attention, admiration, and respect. This promotion of the ideal of
virginity and celibacy put the question, What was the relation of the body to
the self? And what was the role of the body in final redemption?*

+ + +

Ascetic Preludes

Rome's vestal virgins, chosen as children, were vowed to celibacy for thirty years while they tended the perpetual sacred flame at Vesta's hearth on behalf of the city. Throughout the Mediterranean, worshipers abstained from certain foods and from sexual activity to be in a state of ritual purity when approaching the altar of some sanctuary or shrine. Bodily disciplines informed ritual protocols of purification. And, for practical reasons (according to ancient medical science), athletes were known to avoid intercourse before participating in competitions. Indeed, the word "ascetic" rests on the Greek *askēsis* ("discipline, training"), drawn from the world of Greek athletics.

On a more theoretical level, Platonic philosophers conceived a body/soul dichotomy: the true self was the immaterial, immortal soul, which housed the rational mind. The soul (*psychē*) had "cooled" (*psychesthai*) in its contemplation of the divine, and so fallen into flesh. Flesh thus served as the soul's inconvenient vehicle as it sojourned in the realm below the moon: it was, in this sense, not the soul's native home. The goal of this philosophy was the return of the soul to the divine, an effort that was aided through physical self-control.

Stoics theorized body differently—it was diffused with material spirit, they said—but their ethics were no less austere. They too urged lives of self-discipline. Sexual activity should be confined to marriage, strictly and (urged Plutarch) solely for the purpose of begetting children. Cynics, meanwhile, flamboyantly countercultural, renounced possessions, embraced radical poverty, and lived lives minimally attached to the structures of civic society. Both for cultic reasons (as with the Vestals) having to do with purity, and for philosophical ones, then, pagan culture expressed a range of ascetic behaviors.

Regular periodic abstinence from sex informed Jewish marital custom: spouses were to refrain from intercourse during the wife's menstrual period. Priests at service were not to engage in sexual activity: they had to be in a state of ritual purity, as indeed did the person bringing the sacrifice. Food disciplines—most famously, avoidance of pork, or of meat retaining blood—were part of Jewish praxis. The Jewish year was punctuated with fast days. The book of Numbers chapter 6 describes ancient protocols to be followed by someone (whether male or female) who for a limited period consecrated him- or herself to God as a Nazarite: refraining from impurities, abstaining from wine, and not cutting hair for the duration of the vow. Periodic asceticism, both for priests and for lay Israelites, in short, was part and parcel of Jewish tradition.

In Roman-period late Second Temple Judaism, ascetic communities begin to appear. Philo speaks of a mixed group of celibate men and women, the Therapeutae, living communally outside of Alexandria. (Whether they were an actual community or Philo's idealization of one is up for debate.) According to Philo, they were dedicated to intensive philosophical study of Jewish scriptures in Greek. The Essenes, too, formed their own groups, predominantly male, both within towns and also by the Dead Sea; according to Philo, Josephus, and Pliny the Elder, they practiced celibacy. Essenes also communalized property and focused intensively on text study. Proliferating purity rules structured communal life.

The ascetic lifestyle of the Therapeutae, Philo claimed, was motivated by a philosophically informed quest for wisdom: disciplining the flesh freed the mind to concentrate on higher things. The Essenes, by contrast, were committed to an apocalyptic revelation of the approaching messianic end-time. It was this conviction that supported and informed their vigilance around issues of purity: they lived with angels in the foreshortened period before the final battle between the forces of good and of evil.

The missions of John the Baptizer, Jesus of Nazareth, and the apostle Paul, themselves (so far as we know) celibate males, evince a similar sensibility. The approach of the coming Kingdom called for preparedness. Repentance; immersion for purification; renunciation of wealth, of ties to family, and of sexual activity: these behaviors are promoted in traditions ascribed to John and to Jesus, and some appear in Paul's letters.

Paul's ascetic teachings especially cluster in chapter 7 of his first letter to his gentile assembly in Corinth. He ties them explicitly to his expectation of the travails to proceed Christ's return and the establishment of God's kingdom—"in view of the impending distress"; "the appointed time has grown very short." He teaches his ex-pagan community that "it is well for a man not to touch a woman." Yet, because of temptation, better that husband and wife live mutually in "marital debt," though if both partners agree, Paul adds, they can temporarily abstain from sexual activity to devote themselves to prayer. The apostle frankly admits that he says this "by way of concession, not of command. I wish that all were as I myself am"—that is, celibate. The unmarried and the widows are to remain as they are unless they cannot exercise self-control. Repeating a teaching that will appear attributed to Jesus in the later gospels, Paul says further that a wife should not separate from her husband, nor should a husband divorce his wife.

Paul goes on to speak, on his own authority, of a special female category, the "virgins." "Are you bound to a wife? Do not seek to be free. Are you free of a wife? Do not seek a wife. But if you marry, you do not sin; and if the virgin marries, she does not sin." Paul is reserved in this advice: marriage brings "worldly troubles," and he would prefer that his hearers be spared those. He ties this immediately to the urgency of the hour. "The time has grown very short. From now on, let those who have wives live as if they do not; let those who mourn as though they were not mourning, those who rejoice as if they were not rejoicing ... for the form of this world is passing away." The unmarried can concentrate on the Lord; the married have divided attentions. Paul's priority is to secure his people's focused devotion in the brief period remaining before Christ returns. But "if anyone thinks that he is behaving dishonorably toward his virgin," Paul continues, they may go ahead and marry; "it is no sin." If the man is firm in his self-control, however, he should resist, resolved to keep her as his virgin. He who marries his virgin does well, and he who does not marry does better.

Traditions ascribed to Jesus in the Gospels likewise convey ascetic teachings. Jesus himself renounces family and advises those who follow him to do the same. Both he and his disciples are depicted as wandering from place to place, minimally prepared for "tomorrow," proclaiming the gospel of the coming Kingdom. Interdicting divorce (to his disciples' dismay), Jesus in the Gospel of Matthew continues, "There are eunuchs who have been eunuchs from birth, and eunuchs who have been made eunuchs by men, and there are eunuchs who have made themselves eunuchs for the sake of the kingdom of heaven. He who is able to receive this, let him receive it" (Matthew 19.12). Elsewhere, Jesus teaches that marriage will have no place in the resurrected state, for the raised will be "like angels"—presumably not nongendered (since Jewish angels were usually gendered male), but not sexually active. Finally, when a rich man asks Jesus what he should do to inherit eternal life, Jesus first recites some of the Ten Commandments, and then finally advises, "Go, sell what you have, give to the poor, and you will have treasure in Heaven, and come, follow me."

Apocalyptic expectation informed these Jewish ascetic teachings preserved in these writings, Paul's letters, and the Gospels. Their foreshortened time frame accounts for their extreme quality. In the second century, these teachings shifted from ways to prepare for the Kingdom's imminent arrival to timeless stand-alone dicta, authorized by their evolving status as Christian scriptures. Various enactments interpreted the meaning of this heritage in changed circumstances, as the question of how to treat the body immediately impacted the issue of how to redeem the body—or, rather, the issue of what "redemption" itself meant. The result was a period of centuries-long experimentation, both individual and communal, in how to live a Christian life and, thus, in how to win eternal life.

The Ascetic Laboratory

The second through fifth centuries marked a period of widest, and wildest, Christian interpretation of these ascetic traditions, wherein pagan and Jewish practices and texts converged and merged with new concerns. The philosophical predisposition to see fleshly body as nonnative to the soul came together in the early second century with those forms of Christianity that saw the creator god of Genesis as other than the father of Christ. To escape the bonds of the flesh, which was the medium of the lower, creator god, celibacy was promoted and encouraged.

With Marcion, textual interpretation (the repudiation of Jewish scriptures; the prioritization of Paul's letters) and a cultural/philosophical predisposition (flesh as other than self, which was identified as soul or spirit) contributed to the formation of a coherent community ethic: the baptized member of Marcion's church, whether male or female, was vowed to celibacy. Marriage was a second-grade condition. (Marcion certainly had Paul on his side in support of this position.) Given how wide-flung and successful Marcion's church was, we can only surmise that this perfectionist ethic did not impede membership. Indeed, this two-tiered model—a celibate elite sitting on top of a married (and sexually active) majority—would unevenly characterize those churches that emerged, after Constantine, as "orthodox."

To make progress intellectually, ethically, or spiritually, the fleshly body had to be disciplined: that much would have seemed uncontroversial to any ancient person. But what was the empirical status of eschatological body? On this question—again, if we can trust their ecclesiastical opponents—both Valentinus and Marcion drew a consistent conclusion. Flesh was not saved; only spirit was. The redeemed "heretical" believer, according to Justin, expected to ascend individually up past the spheres of the material universe to his or her spiritual homeland above the realm of the fixed stars. Redemption *from* the flesh, not *of* the flesh.

Then to what end had Christ come, if not to redeem flesh? This question propelled the proto-orthodox rhetoric of "docetic"—that is, "appearance"—Christology. Heretics, said Tertullian, held that the Incarnation was a sham, thus the crucifixion a charade: Christ had not truly had a body, therefore he had not truly suffered on the cross. Tertullian's concept of redemption disallowed such a construal of Christian tradition. But Marcionite and Valentinian Christology emphasized a different aspect of the Christian message: not Christ as sacrifice, but Christ as redeeming revealer. In bringing the good news of the purely good god, the god above (the Jewish, demiurgical) god, Christ brought the knowledge of salvation to those with ears to hear.

Marcionite asceticism particularly irritated Tertullian. Despite the routine rhetoric of abuse leveled at the ethics of Christian competitors— that seeming ascetics were actually libertines, or that docetic Christology undermined the entire idea of salvation—Tertullian had to grudgingly acknowledge Marcionite Christians' practice of celibacy. Tertullian accordingly complained that Marcionite ethical behavior was itself intellectually inconsistent. If they worship a god of love, he opined, then they do not fear him. But why act ethically, if not fearing punishment? The highest god's moral law is unstable, Tertullian insisted, if not reinforced through fear. "If you decline to fear your god because he is good," he complained, "what keeps you from bubbling into all manner of vice?" (*Against Marcion* 1.27). Concealed in Tertullian's invective is his description of Marcionite ethics: they were not bubbling into all manner of vice but were living according to the ascetic ethics they heard in their gospel, and in the letters of Paul.

The opponents of these repudiated Christians were no less focused on sexual renunciation. Justin in his *Second Apology*, mid-second century, approvingly spoke of a woman who, without her husband's consent, decided to live a life of continence. (Paul had enjoined mutual consent.) And in his *First Apology*, he reported—again, approvingly—that a young man in Alexandria had recently petitioned the Roman governor for permission to be castrated by a physician. This enthusiast took literally Jesus's clarion to those who would make themselves eunuchs for the sake of the kingdom of heaven. (Origen, later Christians accused, had himself interpreted this verse in Matthew literally.) As the procedure was prohibited by Roman law, the governor forbade it; and so, Justin continued, the young man, refusing marriage, lived a life of continence. Two centuries later, the Council of Nicaea would move to discourage similar enactments of the gospel's call to make oneself a eunuch for heaven's sake.

Tatian, a Syrian student of Justin's, also focused on the ascetic message embedded in Paul's letters and the Gospels. He too, like Marcion, advocated celibacy as a condition for baptism—an opinion that earned him a label as "heretic" by the late second-century writer Irenaeus. He also advocated celibacy within marriage and, according to his critics, the avoidance of meat and of wine. Seeing Tatian past the blur of later orthodox accusations is difficult. He decamped from Rome after Justin's death (ca. 165) and returned to the Syriac-speaking East, where he became an influential figure. As author of the *Diatessaron*, a harmony of the four Gospels, he created a New Testament text that would remain the standard in Syria until the fifth century. Tatian's influence might also be seen in the wealth of apocryphal "Acts" of various apostles—Judas, Thomas, Paul, Peter—that retailed a message of extreme asceticism. To be a true Christian, proclaimed these stories, was to renounce social and sexual conventions, marriage in particular. The true Christian was the ascetic Christian.

The Acts of Paul and Thecla, a late second-century narrative, is a pristine example of this sensibility. The story evinces familiarity with the Gospel of Matthew: "Paul" preaches an asceticized version of Jesus's Beatitudes, particularly extolling virginity as the Christian virtue par excellence. "Blessed are those who have kept the flesh chaste, for they shall become a temple of God. Blessed are the continent, for God shall speak with them. . . . Blessed are those who have wives as not having them"—a reference to marriage partners who have disavowed marital relations—"for they shall experience God. . . . Blessed are the bodies of virgins, for they shall be well pleasing to God, and shall not lose the reward of their chastity."

Thecla is an ascetic Christian iteration of the Greco-Roman novel. The heroine, "a certain virgin named Thecla . . . betrothed to a man named Thamyris" is sitting by her window when she hears Paul speak. She "listened day and night to the discourse on virginity as proclaimed by Paul," noting the many women and virgins who heard him. Thecla does not *see* Paul—breaking the romantic convention of love at first sight—but *hears* his logos/word. It is enough to convert her to a life of radical lifetime renunciation. To her fiancé's fury, she breaks off her engagement. The enraged Thamyris speaks with two men who tell him that Paul "deprives husbands of wives and maidens of husbands, saying 'There is for you no resurrection unless you remain chaste and do not pollute the flesh.'" The author disavows this last message—the two speakers have been introduced as "full of hypocrisy"—but the kernel is the case: Thecla will not marry Thamyris, or anyone else.

The story bumps along as Thecla goes in search of Paul. She confronts hostile crowds, sustains the antagonism of her hometown, faces off with another importuning suitor (this one in Antioch), defeats wild beasts in the arena, baptizes herself, and is released by the governor. She then assumes male dress, acquires a band of male and female followers, and eventually finds Paul, who commissions her to "go and teach the word of God." Returning to Iconium, she finds Thamyris conveniently dead, and witnesses to her (previously alienated) mother. The story ends with Thecla on the road, enlightening "many with the word of God," and finally resting "in a glorious sleep."

Thecla and her *Acts* attained a remarkable and wide-flung popularity. Her cult flourished especially in the fourth and fifth centuries, but her story—and example—were already unsettling Tertullian in the early third. He objected particularly to the idea that women could teach and baptize. Undermining the authority of the text, Tertullian argued that Thecla's story was "wrongly inscribed with Paul's name." *Thecla* was the product of "a presbyter in Asia who put together that book, heaping up a narrative as it were from his own materials under Paul's name when, after conviction, he confessed that he had done it from love of Paul" (*On Baptism* 1.17). Female prominence, Tertullian claimed, was characteristic of heretical sects.

The social pattern that *Thecla* presents—wandering charismatic celibate teachers, often accompanied by a retinue of other virgins and renunciants—did indeed exist in real life, up through at least the fifth century, especially in Iberia (with the hapless Spanish ascetic Priscillian), in Syria, and in parts of Asia Minor. Various Christian texts advised communities how to test for the real thing (if an itinerant stayed longer than three days, he was an imposter), or how to comport oneself properly if coming into a new village (males were not to sleep over in a household occupied solely by female Christians).

Such ascetic volunteerism could pose a problem for bishops: these charismatic figures, outside of episcopal jurisdiction, were a challenge to episcopal authority. Vowed to celibacy but circulating in mixed company, such groups were easy targets for accusations of covert promiscuity—as, indeed, the heresy-hunting bishop Epiphanius leveled against them. A notable example of scandal occurred in 374, when a certain Glycerius, ordained a deacon by no less a figure than Gregory of Nazianzus, collected a group of virgins around himself and began to wander about in Cappadocia. During a saint's feast day, Glycerius shocked spectators by displaying his virgins as a kind of dancing troupe. Thereafter, he and his mixed assembly of vowed celibates dispersed into the countryside, Gregory's requests for their return and promise of amnesty notwithstanding. These charismatics, women and men, remained independent of ecclesiastical authority.

Glycerius may have used his dancing virgins as a source of revenue, presumably for their support. Other itinerants, however, embraced radical poverty as well as celibacy. According to Epiphanius, they wandered, slept in public places, alternately fasting and begging for food—like Jesus's original disciples, making no preparations for the morrow. In the mid-fourth century, Eustathius, son of a bishop and himself a monk, was credited with settling these groups into mixed monasteries; but this more stable social formation did little to diminish the radical nature of his ascetic commitments. According to the canons of the Council of Gangra (ca. 355?), Eustathius condemned marriage as closing off the path to salvation, a teaching that encouraged spouses (especially wives) to separate from their partners. He also proscribed eating meat, refused sacraments from married priests, and denied distinctions between slave and free, and between male and female (reinforced by these women's practice of cutting off their hair). Condemnation did not hamper his ecclesiastical career: despite his entanglements with doctrinal controversies, the extremism of his teachings, and the abiding scandal of his mixed communities of male and female celibates, Eustathius was later elected a bishop himself.

Ascetic Alternatives

Paul's letter to Corinth had already mentioned "virgins" and "widows." His condensed time frame spared him the necessity of establishing any long-term mechanisms for their support. He does not reveal how these women would have been maintained, whether by their own means, by family members, or by the community at large. The deutero-Pauline pastoral Epistles—1 and 2 Timothy and Titus—filled in the gap. Irenaeus, in the late second century, was the first to refer to these letters, which may have been composed specifically with Marcion in mind. Against any compounding of asceticism with authority, they make marriage a fundamental criterion for the man who would be *episcopos*, "overseer." The letters promote a vision of the Christian assembly as an orderly, settled "household of God," hierarchically organized, with women submissive to male authority, whether of "bishops" or of husbands. Women may not presume to teach or to have authority over men, though they may serve the community in the role of an assisting deacon. Widows are to be "enrolled" if they have been married only once, and are at least sixty years of age: ideally, though, they should be supported by their own families. Those who deny them such support are "worse than unbelievers." Younger widows, more subject to passions, are enjoined to remarry and to establish their own households. Despite the sin of Eve, teaches the writer, women can be redeemed through bearing children.

The "apostle" warns throughout against false teachers who forbid marriage and advocate abstention from foods. Perhaps these other Christians also avoided wine, since "Paul" advises "Timothy" to drink it in moderation for reasons of health. Believers are not to engage in godless chatter with such teachers, that is, with those Christians who hold these other views. And, as usual, women are presented as the weak chink in the community's defenses: they listen to anybody, says the author, especially to those who "make their way into households and capture weak women." Women, thus unmoored, "can never arrive at a knowledge of the truth." These deutero-Pauline letters, in brief, by conjuring a Pauline persona, tamp down the opportunities for charismatic ascetic volunteerism and implicit egalitarianism that could so easily be derived from Paul's own teachings.

Both widows and virgins as paragons of lived holiness would have a place within (and, to the irritation of some bishops, also without) organizing ecclesiastical structures. Were these women disproportionately represented among church dependents? By the year 251, the Roman church was supporting fifteen hundred widows and poor people. Some fifty years later, church goods seized during Diocletian's persecution included eighty-two women's tunics and thirty-eight veils, but only sixteen items of men's clothing: perhaps these proportions hint at demography. John Chrysostom claimed that his church in Antioch sponsored some three thousand widows and virgins. Female dependents, vowed to celibacy, made up a visible population within Christian communities.

Not all were indigent. Women could own property. Absent immediate heirs—the case certainly with virgins—women could leave bequests to the bishop. Female celibates, in short, also represented a financial resource. The wealthier the widow or virgin, the more prestige she might enjoy. This was certainly the case with the enormously wealthy elite women we hear of in the late fourth and early fifth centuries, women like the Roman widow Marcella (who convened a community of celibate women in her stately home), Macrina the virgin sister of Basil and Gregory (who did the same), the elder and younger Melanias (who gave extravagant endowments), Chrysostom's patron Olympias, and Jerome's Paula. These women were themselves highly educated. They sponsored controversial scholars and established celibate communities, whether in their own homes or by constructing common housing. They donated conspicuously to their churches and undertook significant building projects. Some traveled broadly. By cutting themselves out of the traditional social fabric of class and family, they had considerably more scope for enacting their own initiatives. They certainly received public and well-publicized praise from their erudite male admirers (and beneficiaries).

But there were many other arrangements. Perhaps the most sensational (and sensationalized) of these was the practice of "spiritual marriage," individual women and men intimately cohabiting in the same household though vowed to continence. Arising from Paul's discussion of virgins in 1 Corinthians 7, spiritual marriage had practical advantages: it provided the woman with stable social and financial support, while benefitting the man with domestic (if not sexual) services. Churchmen complained about the potential for scandal—Gregory of Nazianzus objected that such behavior oscillated between marriage and prostitution—yet the practice echoed the sort of domestic celibacy enjoined on married couples once past child-bearing, and on imperial clergy who, as married householders, were encouraged to live celibately with their wives once attaining higher office. No less a figure (and power player) than Pulcheria, the sister of Theodosius II and coconvener of the Council of Chalcedon, lived in such an arrangement with Theodosius's imperial successor, Marcian. Such practices were seen, by those who supported them, as laudable acts of spiritual supererogation, a way for the individual to participate proactively in the process of redemption.

Outside of the individual family household, ascetics also clustered in mixed groups of men and women. While some were peripatetic, eventually others settled into organized, urban communities, where they often took part in theological and ecclesiastical controversies (such as contested episcopal elections). Indeed, their role in these controversies put the bishops in an awkward situation: to criticize or to attempt to regulate the ascetics was to risk alienating their support. Eventually, Basil of Caesarea stabilized arrangements in Asia Minor by establishing double monasteries, wherein male and female celibates no longer cohabited but lived in separate quarters. And by moving these settlements outside of the city, Basil muffled their potential as lobbying groups.

Egypt also proved fertile ground for experiments with asceticism, both in the city and in the desert. In Alexandria, virgins and celibates lived individually in private households and together in mixed groups. In the early 300s, they became actively involved in both sides of the Arian controversy. Some seven hundred female virgins, a later church historian reports, actively supported their teacher, the presbyter Arius. These women, complained Bishop Alexander and his successor, Athanasius, comported themselves in public, insulted their opponents, and vocally promoted their own theological position. Other Egyptian Christians gathered around the learned teacher Hieracas, who organized a mixed monastery ("a great crowd") of celibates—virgins, monks, widows, people vowed to continence—in Leontopolis. He, not Athanasius, was the community's ultimate authority, which doubtless accounts for the ultimate destruction of his scholarship and his condemnation as a heretic. Athanasius would advocate a different model of urban female celibacy, one that required withdrawal (including from the public baths), strict separation from males, and principled seclusion. Such a lifestyle would domesticate these women's role in urban church politics: they would be under the direction of the bishop.

Athanasius himself is a bridge figure to a more radical form of ascetic solitude, the monks of the desert. Already in the late third century, men and women were withdrawing from city and villages to live in isolation in the wilderness, in caves or tombs or huts. Some lived as hermits (anchorites); others gathered in small groups (cenobites). Their isolation was not absolute: these people lived often on the edges of villages, which would supply them with their requirements for subsistence. Extreme fasting, minimal sleep, prayer, meditation on scripture, constant penitential self-reflection, wrestling with demons both external and internal: such were their prolonged labors.

The paradigmatic figure of the heroic solitary monk was Anthony (251–356), the subject of a famous *Vita* by Athanasius. As a young man, Anthony embraced radical poverty upon hearing Jesus's injunction in Matthew 19.21: "Go, sell all you have, give to the poor, and come, follow me." Repairing to the desert, Anthony brought the cosmic battle between good and evil into an intimate struggle, a personal contest with demons. "Without a doubt," he taught, "demons are afraid of ascetic practices," which he then itemized: fasting, keeping vigils, prayers, gentleness, tranquility, poverty, moderation, humility, love of the poor, almsgiving, the absence of anger, and devotion to Christ (*Life of Anthony* 30). Anthony was one of the great heroes of desert spirituality.

Other monks lived in semi-isolation, gathering periodically for worship or (scant) shared meals. Much larger and well-organized institutions evolved out of this movement. A federation of desert monasteries (some for women) organized under a rule, with thousands of members, flourished under Pachomius, an important founder figure. Under Shenoute the White Monastery thrived: one ancient source gives a figure of twenty-two hundred monks and eighteen hundred nuns. People would come to these charismatic figures for advice, for exorcisms, for prophecies, for divination, for cures. (Consulting rooms and halls for visitors sprang up to accommodate this foot traffic.) Again, the charismatic authority of these desert ascetics could pose a problem for the bishops. Athanasius wrote his way around the problem. The Anthony of Athanasius's *Life of Anthony* served as a spokesman for Athanasian theology: the monk's prestige bolstered that of his "biographer."

Stories of these ascetic volunteers, gathered by outside admirers, circulated and were preserved in collections. More than monks inhabited the desert, as these tales make clear: so, too, did demons. Extreme fasting and sleep deprivation led to visions, which had to be tested: demons might be their source. One semihermitic monk, Valens, saw Christ accompanied by angels. When he subsequently boasted to his fellows, "I have no use for communion, because I saw Christ this day," the vision was unmasked as demonic. Valens was brought around by being put in irons for a year. Another monk, Heron, resisting instruction, was likewise put in irons when he refused to partake of sacraments. Sacraments were administered by priests. They represented a way to coordinate desert spirituality with church institutions. To refuse sacraments was more than prideful. It represented an intolerable degree of independence—something that heroic individualism might too easily sponsor. As the *amma* ("mother") Syncletica taught, "While a person is in a monastery, obedience is preferred to ascetic practice. The former teaches humility, the latter teaches pride."

Despite the development of monastic communities, spectacular individual acts of asceticism continued. In the case of the stylite saints—men who perched on the head of columns for years at a time—such was literally the case: they provided spectacle. Simeon, the famous mid-fifth-century Syrian holy man, was a star of the genre. He began life as a monk, then later became a hermit. He was bothered by so many pilgrims and visitors that he retreated to a column north of Aleppo, where he spent his next thirty-some years. He only attracted more attention. Eventually, a sizable community of admirers and fellow ascetics gathered at the column's base, while petitioners and admirers were allowed to scale its side in order to put questions and requests. Simeon dispensed advice, gave opinions on theological issues, and mediated local disputes. His correspondents included the emperor Theodosius II and also the bishop of Rome, Leo. Later hagiographers depicted Simeon as acknowledging and acquiescing to monastic and episcopal authority. Isolated visually and physically, Simeon lived within a web of social and ecclesiastical relationships.

All these various acts of ascetic volunteerism were broadly publicized. Elite female asceticism was publicly mentored and broadcast.

Letters—like Jerome's to Paula's virgin daughter Eustochium, and to Paula's sister-in-law Laeta, and like Pelagius's to the consecrated virgin Anicia Demetrias—were meant to be circulated. Such acts commanded respect and admiration—except when they did not. Nonorthodox groups were routinely reviled, the bona fides of their continence questioned. Those within the fold were eventually policed not only by bishops but, after Constantine, by emperors. One imperial law ordered that men who used monasticism as a way to dodge their public duties "under the pretext of religion" were to be rooted out and returned to service; refusal meant loss of family property (*Theodosian Code* 12.1.63). Another forbade ascetic women from shaving their heads: such behavior was "contrary to divine and human laws." Women who did so were to be kept away from the churches and forbidden access to "the consecrated mysteries"—in effect, by order of the emperor, excommunicated. Bishops who permitted such behavior were to be expelled from office (16.2.27).

Another means of controlling ascetics was to label their behavior intrinsically heretical. Male Christian leaders who attracted female followers, who disavowed personal property, and who embraced physical disciplines such as celibacy and extreme fasting risked being labeled by rivals as "Manichaeans" (another church, much influenced by Marcion, that had a celibate elite and a sexually active laity) or as "Priscillianists." (The ascetic Priscillian, though himself a bishop, had been fatally accused by rival bishops of Manichaeism and magic.) The trouble was, of course, that such behaviors were more or less practiced within the imperial church as well. As with "orthodoxy," so too with "holiness": both concepts, ideologically and socially, remained under construction throughout this period and beyond, weaponized as necessary. What was laudable when speaking of one's own group was damnable when speaking of another.

Western monasticism tended to be more regulated, less extreme than those of the Egyptian and Syrian deserts that were its inspiration. Perhaps this was owed to elite Roman traditions of philosophical retirement, *otium liberale*: withdrawal to a country estate (for those who had the leisure and the property) to study and to read. In 386, having decided to join the Nicene church in Milan under Ambrose, Augustine engaged in such a retreat, repairing to a friend's country estate at Cassiciacum. Later, he would found his own monastic community within the North African city of Hippo. In the following century, John Cassian, himself a tourist to Egyptian sites, established separate monasteries for both men and women in Gaul. His model would eventually influence the discipline of Benedictine monks.

The call of the wild, nonetheless, was still heard in the West. Gregory of Tours (538–93) relates the travails of a sixth-century would-be stylite who stood exposed to the elements in Trier. At the order of local bishops, this man descended from his column, which was then unceremoniously knocked down. The bishops—men of the residual senatorial aristocracy—would carry the day in the post-Roman West.

Marriage, Celibacy, and Virginity

In Genesis 1, God creates humanity male and female and blesses them with the command to be fruitful and multiply. In Genesis 2, he is a divine matchmaker, bringing Eve to Adam. The heroes of Jewish tradition—Abraham, Isaac, Jacob, Joseph, Moses, David, Solomon—were all married. In the New Testament, so were Mary and Joseph, who have children other than Jesus: James, Joses, Judas, and Simeon, as well as at least two daughters (Mark 6.6). So was Peter and, according to Paul, a number of other apostles. How was this literary legacy read in a period that prioritized virginity and celibacy?

Some Christians who, like Marcion, identified the Jewish god as a lower and lesser demiurge had no problem repudiating marriage and sexual activity as well. Indeed, as we have seen, Marcionite churches had a two-tier structure, with only the celibate receiving baptism. Manichaean Christians, much influenced by Marcion, likewise built their communities around a celibate (and mendicant, and abstemious) elite, the "elect," and a broader community of supportive "hearers," such as Augustine himself had been for ten years in his early adulthood. They associated the Jewish deity with the forces of evil and denied any positive standing to Jewish scriptures. Marriage, sexual activity, and procreation, accordingly, were seen as the works of this lower god. The married patriarchs of the Old Testament, they urged, should command only contempt:

> We are not the ones who wrote that Abraham, enflamed by his frantic craving for children, did not fully trust God's promise that Sara his wife would conceive ... [but] rolled around with a mistress [Hagar].... And what about Lot ... who lay with his own two daughters? ... And Isaac, ... who shamefully passed off his wife Rebecca as his sister? ... And Jacob, Isaac's son, who had four wives and who rutted around like a goat among them? ... And Judah his son, who slept with his own daughter-in-law Tamar? ... And David, who seduced the wife of his own soldier Uriah, while arranging for him to be killed in battle? ... Solomon, with his three hundred wives and seven hundred concubines? ... The prophet Hosea, who married a prostitute? ... Either these stories are false, or the crimes that they relate are real. Choose whichever option you please. Both are detestable. (*Against Faustus* 22.5)

Thus wrote Faustus, a Manichaean *electus* and a former teacher of Augustine's. Faustus's polemic made two points clear. First, the Jewish texts were in no way serviceable as Christian scripture; and second, Old Testament figures could in no way serve as models of Christian morality. Small wonder, then, that the Manichees also favored the stories of extreme celibacy promoted in the apocryphal acts of the apostles—to the point where some catholic prelates discouraged reading these popular texts aloud in church assemblies.

The proto-orthodox of the second and third centuries, the orthodox of the fourth and fifth, were in a genuinely difficult position. They condemned the asceticism of their Christian rivals—Valentinians, Marcionites, the followers of Tatian and, eventually, of Mani—and especially their repudiation of marriage; but they also esteemed and emulated the same ascetic ideals. How, then, to find a place for Christian marriage?

The author of the Pauline Pastorals, as we have seen, simply advocated marriage for Christian leaders and laity both. The well-ordered, hierarchical episcopal household was the model for the well-ordered, hierarchically organized church. These marriages, however, were to be "chaste." Justin, mid-second century, echoing a pagan philosophical ideal, emphasized that the sole purpose of marriage was for the production of children. Clement of Alexandria, a generation later, not only repeated Justin's justification of marriage—a wonderful arena for the practice of self-control—but added that, since the good God created the universe, to participate in procreation was to cooperate with God's work of creation. Further, he argued, Jesus's prohibition of divorce demonstrated his support of marriage. And Jesus's own birth proved that there was nothing reprehensible about the process itself.

Celibacy, said proto-orthodox thinkers, while encouraged, could not be required. But it was the higher path. Sexuality as now experienced, taught Cyprian, was tangled up in the sin of Adam (which, as Tertullian had emphasized, was really the fault of Eve, the devil's "gateway"). The virgin clearly had the better prospect: her spouse, immortal, was Christ. Her choice enabled her to live already, in the time before the resurrection, like the angels of heaven. Besides, Cyprian observed, while being fruitful may have been incumbent on humanity in the days of the Old Testament, it was clear that "now" (ca. 250) the world's population was more than large enough. After the martyr, he said, the virgin will receive the next greatest reward of grace in heaven, superior to that of her married coreligionists. Around the same period, Origen of Alexandria, looking to Paul's instructions in 1 Corinthians, emphasized the importance of sexual abstention as preparation for prayer. And, pointing to the protocols of ritual purity in the Old Testament, Origen also taught that one should abstain before reception of the Eucharist. True for the laity receiving the bread of life; true, also, for the married cleric who consecrates it.

The Body, the Soul, and the Flesh

Compounding the problem of articulating a coherent ethic of sexuality were the questions that swirled around the issue of the origins of the soul and the theological status of flesh. The great Origen (187–254), in the early third century, had addressed these questions—and answered them—in the first work of systematic theology, *On First Principles*. Drawing deeply on Platonic philosophy, reading closely in both the Old and the New Testaments, Origen sought to understand in a coherent and coordinated way the full span of God's saving activity, from the first fall to final redemption. The key concept of Origen's system was the body.

Origen began with the standard Platonic definition of God: all good, all powerful, perfect, beyond time and matter, free from change. And God, Origen emphasized, is also radically, uniquely *un*embodied. True, stories in the Bible speak as though God had a body, but those passages invite the learned to investigate with spiritual understanding: they are metaphors and figures for aspects of the highest divinity, not simple descriptions of him.

But how, if creation is the work of God, can he be beyond time and change? What indeed is God's relationship to matter? Here Origen draws on the idea of eternal generation. Without matter, there is no time. "Creation" therefore refers first of all to God's timeless generation of *non*material creation, a universe of rational beings who had free will. These individual beings, said Origen, existed in what Paul had called "spiritual" bodies. In the eternal realm, spiritual body distinguished one rational being from another and distinguished all contingent beings from the nonembodied, self-existing godhead. This universe of rational, spiritually embodied beings had always existed together with the changeless God.

And these spiritually embodied rational souls had originally and appropriately concentrated their love on God. But then, says Origen, the soul (psychē) began to "cool" (psychesthai)—the old Platonic play on words. These souls' attention wandered, turning from God. All but one soul fell away. (Again, this spatial language is metaphorical: absent matter, there is no space, just as there is no time.) One soul continued so intensely in its love of God that it fused with the divine Logos, the unembodied son. It would later enter history, assuming flesh, as Jesus. Other souls slipped away, catching their falls from God at various "distances" from him. The souls of Satan and his minions fell maximally.

It was in this circumstance that God the Father, through the Son, called matter into being from absolutely nothing. Creatio ex nihilo was a secondary order, and an act love: matter, thus time, would provide the fallen soul with the means to learn from its earlier, prematerial mistakes. The diversity of fallen souls explained the physical structure of the universe: some fell to a lesser degree and were embodied as stars or as planets; others became human; others, lower still, became demons. A beneficent God placed each soul in precisely the right physical pedagogical environment wherein it could learn from its mistakes, repent of its former error, and turn once again in love to God. Once it does so, shedding its body of flesh, the soul will ascend in its spiritual body back out of the material cosmos to its true immaterial home, with God. God is both just and merciful; he loves all his creation equally; in his infinite wisdom, his divine providence places each soul in exactly the material body it needs in order, ultimately, to choose the good. Eventually, taught Origen, the whole cosmos will be redeemed. Even Satan will be saved.

Origen's system clearly resonated with certain aspects of Valentinian cosmology. For both Alexandrians, the material realm was not the native home of the preexistent (and immortal) soul. Both took seriously Paul's teaching in 1 Corinthians 15.50: flesh and blood cannot inherit the Kingdom. The raised body is a spiritual body. But for Valentinians, matter was a negative impediment to the soul's progress, the unfortunate result of a cosmic mistake. For Origen, matter was a gracious act of divine providence: the entire physical cosmos was structured as a school for souls. Of course, in the meanwhile, celibacy was preferable to sexual activity. But ultimately, all ways led back to God.

By the late fourth century, more than 150 years after his death, Origen's soaring speculations had come to seem uncomfortably close to heresy. Orthodox theologians were reading Genesis more literally. Adam and Eve were no longer metaphors, but enfleshed historical persons whose fall had affected all later generations with the punitive effects of sin and death. Resurrection of the body—of Christ and of the individual believer—had shifted to resurrection of the flesh. Hell was a place of permanent perdition, not (as for Origen) a metaphor for the soul's alienation from and difficulties in turning to God. And no one wanted Satan to be saved.

This focus on the primal parents in turn put new emphasis on the sexual act. Were Adam and Eve to have remained virgins? Were they sexually active only after the Fall—and, if so, was sin not inescapably linked to sexual activity? Was the sinfulness of sex not the reason why Jesus had been born of a virgin?

All these questions swirled around Marian piety, which reached a new pitch in the fourth century. The late first-century Gospels of Matthew and Luke had originally presented Mary's virginity as the fulfillment of a prophecy they saw in Isaiah 7.14. Second-century biblical apocrypha had embroidered the tradition enormously. The folkloric elements of the *Protoevangelium of James*—Mary's consecration to God as a three-year-old; her being raised in the temple by priests; her wedding the much older Joseph with both vowed to continence—undergirded the text's essential message: Mary had remained *ever* virgin, including during and after the (painless) birth of Jesus.

Many theologians rejected these ideas as too close to repudiated heretical teachings. Many who accepted Mary's postpartum virginity hesitated to affirm that she had remained intact during the holy birth as well. If Jesus did not have a normal human birth, where did this leave the doctrine of the Incarnation? But the fashion of female virginity, cresting in the late fourth century, elevated Mary as its prime symbol. Bishop Ambrose of Milan was one of its most fervent spokesmen. Mary's virginity not only modeled the life of the church's consecrated virgins, he insisted; it also modeled the sacred integrity of the (orthodox) church herself. Not coincidentally, this imagery likewise bolstered the status of the bishop, who functioned more or less as the church's guardian, much as Joseph had for Mary. And as impresario of the new ritual of the "veiling" of the virgin, Ambrose stood in the place of the paterfamilias, handing his virgin "daughter" over to her immortal—and virgin— bridegroom, Christ.

Other churchmen, themselves sworn celibates and monks, objected to this idea that marriage was a poor second to sexual continence. That position, they held, was tainted with at least implicit Manichaeism. These men defended marriage as equal in dignity and value for Christian life. God himself was the author of marriage, they said. He himself had enjoined fertility and childbearing on humanity. The saints of the Old Testament had had wives and children; so too, in the present, did many Christian clerics. While the extremist Jerome urged that humanity's original state had been virginal, that to be sexually active was in some sense to recapitulate Adam and Eve's fall from grace, and that monks, vowed to celibacy, were superior to married clerics, others, like Jovinian, insisted that sex was morally neutral, neither the cause nor the effect of an original sin whose punishment, rather, had been mortality. Christ had come to redeem humanity not from sex, but from death. Babies were born innocent of Adam's transgression. Sin was a freely willed individual decision, not a standing and global condition.

All these arguments were complicated by the Origenist controversy, which burst on—and blew apart—the pan-Mediterranean community of orthodox theologians in the 390s and early 400s. A century and some after his death, Origen's huge body of work, and the sensibility informing it, was regarded with suspicion, if not open hostility.

For Origen, souls had had no single ancestor in Adam. All had preexisted in eternity; all had, individually, sinned; all would freely choose, ultimately, to turn back to God. Spiritual body was redeemed; flesh, conjured to serve as a learning experience and as a temporary environment for the soul, would finally sink back into the nothingness from which it had been summoned. Flesh was not an essential part of the person. Later Latin thinkers, though, regarded the figure of Adam not as a metaphor, but as a historically existing person. He had been created body and soul, flesh and spirit, together. The body was as much a part of the person as was the soul. Adam as a historical actor served as the discrete point of origin for human flesh and for human soul both. Thus he was, as well, the historical origin of human sin and, thus, of human mortality.

Flesh came from flesh, these later theologians agreed. But did soul come from soul? Or was soul created afresh in every child? These were the only two options left, once the soul's preexistence, thanks to the controversy over Origen, was off the table as an option for orthodoxy. But how then, in either case, was Adam's sin inherited? Did sin not inhere in flesh and soul together? And if sin were inherited, how then was God just, to inflict the penalty of sin on unborn generations who had not sinned themselves?

These questions stood at the heart of the so-called Pelagian controversy, the prolonged face-off between Pelagius, an ascetic reformer and teacher in Rome, and Augustine, the North African bishop of Hippo. Pelagius, like Origen before him, emphasized divine justice and human free will. But unlike Origen, Pelagius saw Adam as the primal ancestor of humanity. Soul was meant to be embodied. Thus, for Pelagius, while flesh after Adam was mortal, it was not intrinsically sinful. Each soul, born anew and originally blameless, was the source of the individual's sin, committed by the free choice of the will. The sexual act was natural, created by God, who commanded people to be fruitful and multiply: no divine command could be sinful. The just God in any case would not hold people culpable for what was theirs by nature: people were culpable only for that which they did by choice.

Pelagius and his followers were driven out of Italy to North Africa by Alaric's sack of Rome in 410. His way of thinking seemed foreign to the Carthaginian prelates, whose theories of the soul's origins, thanks to Tertullian and to Cyprian, presupposed that soul came from soul. Defenders of Pelagius argued against this position: if soul came from soul, then, logically, the offspring of baptized parents should be born with souls already regenerated. Infant baptism, by this North African logic, they observed, would not be necessary. And if inherited sin were identified primarily with flesh, which was unquestionably inherited, was that not Manichaeism, which regarded flesh as evil? The question had a polemical edge. Augustine, who led the charge against Pelagius, had advertised his own Manichaean past in the *Confessions*, in order to disown it. Pelagius's defenders, not so delicately, implied that Augustine, in terms of his theological instincts, had in fact not left his past so very far behind.

Was Augustine extremist, or simply original? Arguing earlier against the stridently ascetic Jerome, reading closely in Genesis, Augustine had held that God had created Adam and Eve with the specific intention that they would have had sex and, thus, that they would have procreated in Eden, had they not sinned. (Procreation was the whole point of sex. Had God not intended it, Augustine observed, he would have had no reason to create woman.) Now, against Pelagius and his advocates, Augustine refined his position and spelled it out particularly in *City of God*.

Three things had changed since Eden, Augustine insisted: the nature of the fleshly body, the soul's ability to choose to act rightly, and the relationship of fleshly body to soul. Before the Fall, Adam's flesh had been under the complete control of his will. This meant that the act of procreation, had Adam and Eve not sinned, would have been entirely volitional, under the right direction of the soul: flesh was entirely obedient to mind. Erection; the conjoining of male and female "seed"; conception itself: all would have been accomplished through unimpeded will. Eve's virginity, too, would have been preserved: "The male seed could have been dispatched into the womb with no loss of his wife's integrity, just as menstrual flux can now be produced from the womb of a virgin without loss of maidenhead" (*City of God* 14.26). Fleshly body—the original home of the human soul—would have been rationally directed by the soul, through a will that was entirely in control of itself.

But Adam sinned, disobeying the divine command. Primal disobedience changed everything. In punishment for disobedience, the will itself became disobedient, divided, wanting and not wanting the same thing at the same time. And the body no longer obeyed the commands of the will. This was clear from the immediate effects of Adam's disobedience. As soon as Adam sinned, Augustine explained, he had experienced an involuntary erection. This had caused him shame, precisely because it was involuntary—"the rebellion and disobedience of desire in his body." Worse: irrational, involuntary desire from that point onward was necessary for each subsequent act of procreation, throughout the generations. The soul, in short, was no longer in control of its own desires, which escaped the command of the mind. Accordingly and in punishment, the soul was no longer in control of its own body. After Adam's fall, enfleshed soul was importuned by disordered appetites. And flesh itself was doubly subject to involuntary insult: that of unwilled and uncontrolled carnal concupiscence; and that of death itself, which drove the soul, unwilling, from its corporeal native home.

Sex as now configured, Augustine concluded, was neither "natural" nor theologically neutral. On the contrary. As currently constituted, sexual procreation depended on this penal condition, carnal concupiscence. Adam's original sin was passed on to each generation by the very process of generation. Baptism relieved the individual of the *reatus*, the guilt of original sin, but not of its consequences. Damaged soul came from damaged soul, damaged flesh from damaged flesh. It was for *this* reason that Jesus had been conceived by a virgin. Untouched by original sin, he embodied what Adam should have embodied: flesh and will united, unconflicted, fully free of the disruptions of desire, rightly ordered, at peace.

Christ was the model of true moral freedom. He had indeed felt human emotions, but he had done so voluntarily, by a free act of will. He had truly died, but he had done so voluntarily, by a free act of will. And at the resurrection, his body reunited with his soul, Christ had enacted the salvation of all the redeemed: he had ascended in his sinless flesh, up past the sublunar realm, into heaven.

Flesh itself, Augustine thus insisted, would be saved. As we have already seen, he held that the saints—a fraction of humanity, mysteriously chosen by grace—would themselves rise in their fleshly bodies. But that fleshly body would then be "spiritual." Flesh would still be flesh, but it would no longer be "carnal," that is, predisposed to sin; rather, it would be under the complete command of the soul. And the soul would be in complete command of its self, no longer subject to irrational desires. Body and soul would together, finally, achieve a harmonious whole.

Further, these bodies of the saints would be like Christ's own body, raised as he was in his prime. The raised body would be physically perfect: people fat now will not be fat then, nor people thin now thin then. Amputees will have their limbs restored. Redeemed flesh would even have gender: women would be raised as women. And children would be raised as adults. But this communion of saints would be ranked. The highest rank was reserved for the martyrs; the next highest, for the virgins; then, thereafter, everyone else. The miracle would be that those lower than these exemplars of excellence would feel no envy toward the higher-ups.

Ideology and Identity, Rhetoric and Reality

Both pagan and Jewish cultures had made a place for ascetic practices and for periodic sexual renunciation. But Christian cultures developed an entire ideology of asceticism in new ways, ones that led to new social formations: groups of widows and virgins, supported variously; spectacular acts of self-denial, from those of impoverished Egyptian peasant renunciants to those of a cadre of wealthy aristocrats, especially women, both in the Latin West and in the Greek East; lifelong renunciants of both sexes; charismatic ascetics, whether wandering or stationary, solo or in groups, male or female; the astonishing evolution of the monastery, both male and female; the slow growth within orthodoxy of a celibate clergy. Virginity male and female was idolized, the examples of Jesus and of Mary held up for imitation. Whole literatures developed, expressing and popularizing these ideals: sermons, treatises, public letters, apocryphal acts, collections of sayings, and stories. The ideal was reinforced by ecclesiastical canon law.

How did these ideals impact the lives of most Christians? The canons of church councils and the complaints embedded in sermons give us a glimpse of a reality unanticipated, if we attend solely to the rich literature of ascetic achievement. On the evidence, most people—the "silent majority," as one historian has called them—continued to marry, to have children, and to acquire and hold property. They led normal social lives, consorting and occasionally religiously cocelebrating (to their bishops' irritation) with heretics, pagans, and Jews. They enlisted the help of nonecclesiastical ritual experts, availed themselves of amulets and astrology, sought out exorcisms and cures. They frequented the public baths. They enthusiastically attended the spectacles and gladiatorial contests that continued long after Constantine. Christian men, preachers thundered, had sex with prostitutes and, perhaps even more commonly, with their own slaves. ("Can't I do what I want in my own house?" complains a Christian head of household in Augustine's *Sermon* 224.3.)

The esteem with which voluntary poverty was lauded had little effect on moneyed Christians who, in sharing their wealth with bishops and with monasteries, became part of the elite power structure of the church. Wealthy ascetic women kept control of their resources, deploying them as they would—with notable independence—to promote their own programs, or those of the churchmen whom they sponsored. And they established their own celibate communities. Aristocratic largesse, a Christian iteration of classical *philotimia*, love of public honor garnered through acts of conspicuous philanthropy, continued to correspond to prestige.

Wealthy Christians, including bishops, paraded in cities with their retinues of clients and slaves. As the orthodox church continued in imperial favor—or, perhaps as accurately, as imperial favor continued to define orthodoxy—bishops increasingly accrued wealth, both through grants of land and through the direct bequests of the pious. Bishops did more than serve as urban magistrates: they acted like them, retaining enough control of funds at their discretion that their sons could sponsor public games. As John Chrysostom discovered, the ethic and aesthetic of asceticism had little purchase on the social functions that an imperial bishop was expected to perform. John was driven from his see in Constantinople in no small part for being too ascetic, to the point of alienating his own episcopal clientele and even the imperial family.

The ideology of asceticism dominates our sources in part because we are so dependent for this period on the writings of its spokesmen. The ethic of asceticism became a primary element in the articulation of high theology, especially over the questions of Christ's person that convulsed church councils. And in part, it leaned on and grew together with the development of the post-Constantinian discourse of martyrdom: the ascetic was like a martyr and would receive the same reward as the martyr. Both discourses nourished the formation of an idealized Christian identity.

And as with martyrs, so too with the ascetics: the nonheroic majority was prepared to admire, from a practical distance, the accomplishments of the heroic few. The heroic few, whether as "heretics" or as "orthodox," engaged energetically with asceticism's demands. In confronting demons, in defying societal norms, in proactively participating in their own redemption, in living out their vision of the *imitatio Christi*, ascetics left an indelible imprint on evolving Christian culture.

7

PAGAN AND CHRISTIAN

You must have no part in such doings. Taking the auspices,
divination, omens, amulets, writing on leaves, the use of charms
and other spells—such things are the devil's worship.

CYRIL OF JERUSALEM, *MYSTAGOGICAL CATECHESIS* 1.8

O God of our patron St. Philoxenus, if you command us to
bring Anoup to your hospital . . . let the message come forth.

CHRISTIAN ORACULAR TICKET, PAPYRUS OXYRINCHUS 1150

*"Pagan" was an invention of the fourth century, distinguishing Christian
gentiles from non-Christian others. "Paganism" is the abstraction that refers
to Mediterranean culture in general. In what ways, then, is "paganism" con-
tiguous with Christian culture, in what ways contrasting? What distinguishes
pagan "magic" from Christian sacrament? How did the pagan Rome of Nero
become the Christian Rome of Peter and Paul? How do pagan meals for the
dead differ from the Christian cult of the saints? As Christianity emerged
and developed within Mediterranean culture, what did it retain, what did it
alter, and what did it leave behind?*

+ + +

The Mediterranean Matrix

Mediterranean culture was the matrix that nourished all forms of religiousness in Roman antiquity. To call that culture "pagan" is to capitulate to the process of Christian identity formation that roars into its own in the course of the fourth century. That was when the word "pagan" in the sense of "non-Christian" came into use in the Latin West.

The word *paganus* predates this usage. It relates to the word *pagus*, meaning a locality or region, or sometimes the community inhabiting that region. Pagani were people who lived in a particular place. Contrasted with military personnel stationed there, a "pagan" might mean a civilian. Often, the term indicated a "country dweller." It might have had the connotation, originally, of "outsider" or of "nonparticipant." (The East already had such a term, "Hellene," meaning "Greek," to signal a non-Christian.) Perhaps fourth-century Latin Christians mobilized the term with specifically religious connotations because Christianity was itself such an urban movement: the "countryside" remained more traditional. Perhaps, in light of the urban and urbane fourth-century pagan intelligentsia that resisted the newer religion, "pagan" was usefully insulting. However obscure its origin, "pagan," in imperial law, came to stand for superstitio in contrast to "Roman religion," by which the emperors intended (Nicene) Christianity.

"Paganism" as a concept denoting religious allegiance produced difference and created boundaries. Conceptually and practically, it was necessary not least for legal reasons, a verbal technique of "othering" to identify and create a social category of persons who were neither Jews nor communicants of the correct sect of Christianity. "Pagan" as a discursive term, in other words—that is, as a linguistic strategy—facilitated the later fourth-century development of an institutionalized imperial Christianity promoted by the Roman state.

Unsurprisingly, real life eludes the clarity of classificatory systems, both antiquity's and (leaning on these) our own: "paganism," "Judaism," and "Christianity." Even speaking in terms of the porousness of

boundaries implies that such boundaries exist. They do, but as secondary categories—that is, as our own analytical devices. Moschos Ioudaios, in the third century BCE, placed a votive inscription in the
temple of the healing gods Amphiaraus and Hygeia. They had commanded him to do so in a dream. Did Moschos think of himself as
"assimilating to paganism"? He lived in the Peloponnese, where these
gods lived as well. His obedience to their command simply showed a
commonsense piety, respect for the gods—powers bigger than he was.
His act tells us nothing about how he worshiped his own god, but his
self-designation as "Ioudaios," meaning "Judean" or "Jew," shows that
his affiliation with the god of Judea mattered to him as well. Centuries
later, in Phrygia, another Jew, Glykon, lived according to two liturgical
calendars, both Jewish and Roman: his endowment was to mark the
holidays of Passover and Shavuot/Pentecost, as well as the Roman new
year. We identify him as living in both worlds, "pagan" and "Jewish."
Surely, he experienced them as one. An inscription honoring a local
North African grandee and imperial priest, in the year 347 CE, bore the
mark of the Christian Chi-Rho. Was the honoree "pagan" or "Christian"? The inscription is perfectly ambiguous—which is a datum in and
of itself.

Syncretism—the coming together of "Christianity" with other, prior
religious traditions—does not reflect a mix of two discreet and different
entities. Still less does syncretism suggest a compromise or corruption
of some pure and separate body of doctrine with "paganism"—though
that is the image that heresiologists and later theologians rhetorically
present. "Christianity" is under construction throughout Roman antiquity. "Christianization" proceeded precisely *by* syncretizing foregoing
and ubiquitous patterns of life and thought with elements of its message: true for high theology, which depended on philosophy to proceed;
true for practices, which drew on the familiar. What else was there to
draw on? The expressions of Christianity that resulted not only varied
locally between different communities. They also varied within the
same locale between different members of the notionally same
community—as the complaints of the bishops and the canons of church
councils tell us.

Demons, Rituals, and "Magic"

This internal variety is nowhere more visible than in Christian discourse about *mageia*, "magic." All our ancient people lived in the same social world, inhabited by superhuman powers. Everyone dealt with the problem of how to structure and to manage relations with these powers, how to solicit their advice and their protection, and—since they were more powerful than any human—how to stay on their good side. Our labels "pagan," "Jewish," and "Christian" inhibit us from seeing how much this superhuman world was common to all inhabitants of the empire, and how much the medium for engaging this world was ritual: a combination of performative utterances (words thought to have real effects) and choreographed motions or actions.

No one contested the existence of these beings, or their social agency. The question was always how to deal with them. Superhuman powers constantly intervened in daily life, solicited or not. Those persons who sought direct contact who could not go on pilgrimage to the great oracle sites, such as Delphi, had means closer to hand to garner advice and aid, to control events, or to divine the future. These forces spoke through visions and dreams. They manifested spontaneously. They sent signs to be interpreted, whether through the disposition of animal viscera or the flight of birds or the weather. Lot oracles, dice, numerological tables (*sortes*); dream interpretation (a profession, informed by handbooks); the positions of heavenly bodies (astrology); the prognostications of holy men and women: all these represented technologies of communication, whether the power sought after was a god, a demon, a spirit, or a saint.

Divinity came in many registers, spanning heaven and earth. Different peoples categorized these powers differently. Hellenistic Jews in particular regarded gentile gods as gods subordinate to their own, highest god. "The gods of the nations are daimonia" pronounced Psalm 95.5 in Greek—"godlings," lesser gods; "daimons" and not only, in the sense of our word now, "demons." Paul likewise held that there were "many gods and many lords." His god and his god's messiah, Christ, he insisted, were more powerful than these other supernumeraries and should be the sole objects of his hearers' devotions (1 Corinthians 8.5–6).

Paul named many other, lower divine entities throughout his letters: cosmic rulers, authorities, and powers; "the god of this age" (2 Corinthians 4.4); hostile angels; Satan; cosmic "elements"; spirits (whether good or evil: the community in Corinth was supposed to be able to discern between them; 1 Corinthians 12.10); beings "above the earth and upon the earth and below the earth" (Philippians 2.10). He attributed agency to them. These powers were real. By eating meat sacrificed to them, he taught, his people risked partnering with them—an unthinkable thought, since they had the spirit of Christ or of Paul's god "in" them already (1 Corinthians 10.20–21). All these cosmic forces, Paul proclaimed, were about to be subdued by the returning Christ. At that point, they too would acknowledge the sovereignty of Israel's god through the victory of God's messiah (Philippians 2.11).

Paul's apocalyptic mentality, in other words, textually frozen in later Christian collections of his writings, polarized the graduated cosmos of Roman antiquity: these powers, for him, all rested on the negative side of his cosmic ledger. Hostile daimones and spirits—our "demons"—could inflict madness, deception, disease. Worse, in the view of some bishops, they could also prophesy and heal. They might manifest spontaneously, framing much of the struggle that engaged desert ascetics, the demons especially of fornication and of pride. For (some) Christians, demons demarcated a front line in the cosmic battle between good and evil.

Other contemporaries, of all religious persuasions, including many Christians, took a different view. A daimon or spirit was a lesser divine force. It could inhabit the thick atmosphere between the earth and the moon, or haunt given earthly locales, or emerge from the world below. It could mediate between higher gods (or the highest god) and humans. In this sense, a daimon could also be regarded as a "messenger," an *angelos*. Solicited properly, daimones could serve as sources of healing, and of information about the future.

One way to activate communication was through sacrifice: the smoke and smell arising from the altar attracted daimonic attention. Pagan philosophers might dispute the probity of blood sacrifices—some held that offerings of cereals, incense, or wine were more fitting—but offerings (especially before divine images) were a normal way to achieve divine/human interaction. Later church fathers, following Paul, condemned this as the worship of false gods—false not because these gods did not exist, but because they were lower than, and rightly subordinate to, the high god. That high god, when invoked by magicians, was himself the force behind the most powerful spells, opined Origen. Magic/mageia—ritual efficacy enacted by spoken or written formulas, by gestures (such as signing the cross), or transmitted through material objects—provided an ecumenical opportunity:

> "The God of Abraham, the God of Isaac, the God or Jacob" is used not only by those of the Jewish nation in their prayers to God and when they exorcise daimons, but also by almost all those who deal in magic and spells. For in magical treatises it is often to be found that God is invoked by this formula, and that in spells against daimons his name is used in close connection with the names of these men. (*Against Celsus* 4.33)

God or gods or angels were often called on, but the daimon was the work horse of magical spells, summoned to get things done, whether cures or curses. Often, if malicious (thus, "demons" in our sense), they needed to be exorcised by a superior superhuman force, summoned by the "proper" ritual expert. This was a serious business: a roster of church offices from Rome for the mid-third century lists fifty-two exorcists among readers and doorkeepers. By comparison, this same list gives forty-six presbyters and seven deacons (Eusebius, *Church History* 6.43). Exorcism was a Christian specialty.

The etiquette for dealing with divine powers, whether hostile or benign, was also ecumenical. In Egypt, by the fourth century, a brisk trade in oracular "tickets" had sprung up around martyr shrines. These were provided by scribes and by shrine attendants. The devotee could then take the ticket home, for use as a protective amulet. The saint, not a god or a daimon, would be invoked, but the technology was identical to that of "pagan" oracles.

The operative category, here, is not "pagan" versus "Christian." Both ritual acts (whether soliciting a saint or a spirit) are equally "Egyptian." The telling difference, in Christian eyes, is that non-Christian adepts called on a different numinous workforce. By insisting that demons were pagan gods or local spirits, these Christian adepts, whether monks or scribes, could likewise insist on distinguishing themselves from local pagan priests, magicians, and healers, who both looked and functioned exactly as they did.

The Christian demotion of Mediterranean gods or local divine forces to the negative status of demons set their moral valence: demons were always bad. Their source was the angelic rebellion against God (an interpretation of Genesis 6.1–4, when the sons of God mated with human females). They hovered around traditional altars and frequented whatever civic venues held their images. They stood leagued with any imagined enemy: heretics, Jews, non-Christian gentiles. They inspired persecutions. They accounted for similarities between Christian prophecies, stories, and rituals and pagan ones: once well placed in heaven, these fallen angels had knowledge of what would one day be Christianity and so inspired demonic imitations of them within pagan cults, to confuse and confound the unconverted. According to Justin, demons were the root reason in the first place why God's Logos became incarnate as Jesus: "for the sake of believing men and women, and for the destruction of the demons" (2 *Apology* 6). The final victory would occur only at Christ's Second Coming; but meanwhile his power was manifest in Christian exorcists whose skills, Justin claimed, were superior to those of their pagan competitors. What *we* do is religion, said church fathers; what *they* do—Jews, heretics, pagans, astrologers, healers, interpreters of dreams—is "magic." Their rituals worked, too: again, this was not disputed. But their very efficacy, said their Christian critics, was proof that these competitors dealt with demons.

At issue was proper ritual expertise—and what was "proper" was in the eye of the beholder. Celsus, the late second-century pagan critic of Christianity, accused Jesus of performing his miracles through "magic," a charge that Origen, some seventy years later, would heatedly refute (*Against Celsus* 1.6). Christians too, Celsus said, currently worked through the manipulation of demons. Irenaeus leveled the same charge against other Christians whom he considered heretics. And Christian healers, exorcists, and other ritual experts who dealt in spells insisted that their powers were divine, not demonic. Simply the name of Jesus, perhaps combined with brief recitations about him and a performative action, the sign of the cross, was enough to control demons, said church fathers. Such simplicity, they insisted, contrasted with the more elaborate rituals of those they condemned as sorcerers who relied on lengthy incantations and various media. Simplicity suggested superior power.

Christian magical spells, however, surviving especially in Egypt, tell another story. Amulets frame Christian elements, like the name of Jesus, with series of vowels, magical words, esoteric signs, and a customary closing formula, "Now, now, quickly, quickly!"—all standard features of "magical" spells, part of the technical repertoire. We have complaints in Christian sources about monks who fashion amulets out of fox claws, crocodile teeth, and snakes' heads. The Council of Laodicea had to forbid priests from serving as such ritual experts, enchanters and astrologers, and from making and wearing amulets (canon 36). To Augustine's enormous irritation, the name of Christ was invoked in spells and amulets that he considered and condemned as "pagan." The client, and the adept, would presumably not see this as a problem: for all we know, both considered themselves good Christians. Christian grave finds reveal amulets calling on God to protect against malevolent forces, along with spells and curses mobilizing angels, called down on those who might violate the grave. Buried Christian lead tablets preserve curses and binding spells. All these attest to forms of piety that were not under the control of bishops and emperors. Incantations and amulets, long indigenous to Mediterranean culture, would seem to those who used them simply to be a neutral technology of communication with the superhuman world.

Christian "professionals" like bishops and intellectuals who condemned these ritual practices as mageia, illicit ritual practices, mobilized rhetoric already available in Roman law. Roman law had distinguished between religio (proper cult enacted in public) and superstitio (excessive religious credulity, which particularly characterized foreign cults).

After the fourth century, when Christianity moved into the public sphere and private pagan sacrifices were forbidden, Christianity (or the imperially recognized sect of Christianity) became religio, and private pagan sacrifice was deemed superstitio. Superstitio was rhetorically conflated with magical practices and illicit divination. Roman law had long forbidden certain activities: harmful spells and potions; divination of the future (especially if that involved questions about the sitting emperor). Eventually, legislation would name maleficia—rituals performed to harm people—as a crime only slightly lesser than treason and murder. Charges of mageia were trained not only against non-Christians but also against those Christians who were deemed heretical, such as Manichees, Priscillianists, even Nestorians. Accused of Manichaeism and magic both, Priscillian was executed on account of the latter indictment.

Like "heresy," in other words, "magic" became a weaponized discursive category, a way of speaking that delegitimized perceived rivals. The polemical use of the word masks how much the spread of Christianities proceeded precisely by ritual expertise—exorcisms, healings, divinatory possession, and also sacraments. Baptism, already by Tertullian's period (late second / early third century), was performed as a way to drive out demons. It was articulated through ritual gesture and performative utterance, as was the eucharist, it too a protective action and a medicine against demonic harm. The argument over rebaptism that so ripped apart Cyprian's mid-third-century North African church was a contest over whether the status of the ritual expert—in this case, the bishop—might compromise the efficacy of the sacramental ritual. Could a compromised cleric—someone in defiance of Cyprian—truly be a conduit of holy spirit? Cyprian said no.

Sacraments—rituals that churchmen regarded as legitimate—not only protected against demons. They also (magically?) policed the faithful. Cyprian reports the case of a young woman who lapsed during the troubles under Decius and who then partook of the eucharist before having been properly reconciled to the church. No sooner had she taken the sacrament than "she began to choke and, a victim now not of the persecution but of her own crime, she collapsed in tremors and convulsions" (*Concerning the Lapsed* 26). Taken improperly, the sacrament itself monitored behavior. "If she had deceived man, she was made to feel the punishing hand of God."

Eventually, bishops, acting in concert through councils, would deny sacraments to fellow Christians as a way to discipline, and thereby to control, the erring—indeed, to define what "erring" was. The Council of Elvira (early 300s, pre-Constantine) itemized such errors and penalties. Access to sacraments, for various sins, was denied for stipulated periods of time. Serious infringements, such as idol worship or participation in the imperial cult on the part of baptized men meant denial of sacraments even when death approached. (Consequences would be experienced in the afterlife.) Sacraments were denied, too, for the baptized man who kills another by sorcery—not because of the murder itself, but because that ritual act would have involved him with demons ("idolatry"). A baptized woman who "overcome with rage" beat her female slave to death was to be denied access for seven years if the act was deliberate, five if accidental. Parents who gave their daughters in marriage to Jews or to heretics were to be banned for five years. People who had Jews bless their fields, since this undermined the authority of the Christian ritual, were to be thrown out of the community entirely. Sacraments, in brief, were a controlling type of Christian mageia.

What we see here is evidence not only of a wide range of behaviors on the part of Christians notionally within the same community, but also of efforts on the part of the bishops to exercise control over that community. That means of control involved ritual expertise at every level. Legitimate ritual ("what we do") was sacramental; illegitimate ritual ("what they do") was "magic." The high intellectual discourse of theology that so dominates our literary sources cannot afford us a glimpse at this other social world. Some intellectuals—by definition, a small elite—may have joined various Christian communions because they were persuaded by philosophically informed arguments about the nature of the Trinity or the meaning of the Incarnation. Christianization on a large scale, post-Constantine, was encouraged by a multitude of factors: political (like the legal and financial advantages to clergy); social (like the strong webbing of ecclesiastical patronage, thus access to charity, enabled initially by imperial largesse); and what we might label "religious." Not least of these was the promise held out that, in Christ, the faithful could be released, both in this life and in the next, from the press of the power of demons.

Neutralizing Pagan Tradition

High Christian culture was accomplished by repurposing "pagan" ideas. It owed its success in no small part to the prior work of Hellenistic Jewish intellectuals in the period following the conquests of Alexander the Great. Hellenistic Jews, especially in Alexandria, had been the first to drive an ideological wedge between pagan religious culture and pagan paideia, intellectual culture: rhetoric, grammar, philology; philosophy; and techniques of textual interpretation such as allegory (the art of reading a text as saying one thing but as meaning another). The one (cultic practices directed to the gods) could be eschewed; the other (philosophical thought) could be embraced—indeed, said Philo, philosophy was already what the biblical texts declared, if one knew how to read them correctly, with true understanding. Paideia was thereby rendered culturally neutral, usable without qualm. Jews further claimed that what the Greeks got right, they got from the Jews anyway, a position later entirely adopted by Christian apologists. Plato owed his wisdom to Moses, who was older. It was Moses, according to Philo, who was rightly deemed "the philosopher."

Christian intellectuals who wanted to think philosophically about their convictions had only pagan philosophy to draw on: that was the culture that was. They were aided in their endeavors by the work of Philo, whose allegorizing commentaries on the Greek text of Jewish scriptures paved the way for later Christian thinkers like Justin, Clement of Alexandria, and, especially, Origen. Eusebius regarded Philo as all but Christian. In Philo's work, the biblical texts opened up in new ways to be appreciated in the categories of Greek paideia. He made biblical narrative rational, that is, interpretable as philosophically meaningful. Especially through his thinking on God's engagement with creation through his divine word, the Logos, Philo paved the way for later Christologies, which identified Christ, variously, as God's Word.

The categories of Christian anthropology drew from the same well. Humans were imagined as composed of three aspects: mind or spirit, soul, and fleshly body, which was bound to spirit through the intermediation of soul. Philo had argued that the human mind was made in the image of the Logos, the image of God: this template was taken over entirely by later Christian thinkers. To control the body by the mind was to exercise virtue, the pursuit of moral excellence. Later Christians, such as Augustine and Pelagius, might quarrel over the mechanisms of this control—for Augustine, it was most fundamentally a gift granted by God; for Pelagius, an act of free will aided by God—but their ultimate goal, apprehension of God through the mind, would have been entirely recognizable to Philo and, before him, to Plato. For all their strenuous insistence on newness and revelation (when they were not emphasizing continuity and antiquity!), Christian theologians can be regarded as expressing another phase in the development of classical thought.

Ideas about God were another area of convergence. Both at a popular cultic level and at a rarified intellectual one, some late Roman pagans were also "monotheists," believing in the supremacy of a single highest god behind the manifestations of divine many-ness at lower cosmic levels. Their universe was the same as the one occupied by their Christian counterparts: heaven was hierarchically organized, with one god highest on top. Local gods, the pagan author Celsus opined, were really like regional governors, all subordinate to the single divine ruler (*Against Celsus* 8.35). "Born of itself, untaught, without a mother, unshakeable, not contained in a name, known by many names, dwelling in fire, this is god," sang Apollo in hexameters in a fourth-century inscription in Oenoanda in Asia Minor. "We, his messengers [*angeloi*], are a small part of god." Preserving a known oracular passage (quoted by Lactantius in the 320s), the inscription seems linked to the worship of "the highest god," *theos hypsistos*, whose popular cult, expanded through Asia Minor, involved bloodless worship, prayer, and the lighting of lamps, receptacles of fire. The father of Gregory of Nazianzus, himself a bishop, had elided from hypsistarian worship to Christianity.

Christian rhetoric constructed "paganism" as a way to put distance between the church and this shared way of thinking. Sometimes, however, the closeness was acknowledged.

> If the Platonists prefer to call these "gods" rather than "demons" and to count them among those of whom their founder and master Plato writes that they are gods created by the highest God, let them say what they want. For one should not engage with them in a controversy about words. For if they say that they are not blessed by themselves, but by being attached to his who has created them, then they say precisely what we say, whichever word they may use for them.

Thus wrote Augustine, in *City of God* (9.23). The argument, he seems to admit here, is not over cosmology or theology per se. It is over vocabulary and, thus, over the status of these lower beings, especially on the question of whether they should receive cult. Some bishops said "no" and argued that invoking these powers for cures, or for learning of the future, was tantamount to worshiping them. Christian exorcists, healers, and those who consulted astrologers and ported amulets and availed themselves of "magic"—ritual practices deemed illegitimate by the bishops—were unpersuaded, hence the bishops' condemnation of these Christian practices as "pagan." But these repudiated Christians were simply doing in a lower register what the intellectuals were doing in a higher register: drawing on the cultural material that lay at hand in order to make sense of their world, and to exercise some control over it.

If the terms of biblical exegesis, constructive theology, and ritual practice leaned heavily on pre-Christian culture, so too did the rhythms of the urban calendar, punctuated as it was by sponsored festivals celebrated through theatrical performances, horse races, gladiatorial combats, wild animal spectacles, and public feasting—*pompa diaboli*, ceremonies of Satan, some churchmen lamented. Mediterranean cities had always been religious institutions: such activities were seen as honoring presiding deities, thus safeguarding the city. Traditional cult was deeply embedded in urban life. The conversion of Christianity into an arm of the late Roman state did little, initially, to change this, so interwoven was religious and civic life at every level.

Tertullian in the early third century had urged Carthaginian Christians to avoid these festivals, to stop attending the shows and the races and the competitions, to avoid public feasts: all such, he insisted, smacked of idolatry. Again, his polemic reveals the wide range of behaviors that other Christians within his community thought entirely permissible (up to and including the manufacture of cult images! See *On Idolatry* 6,2). Such civic activities, they pointed out, were nowhere prohibited in scripture. Still others held that false gods were in the eye of the beholder. "It isn't a god, it's the Genius of Carthage," protested another Christian, reproached for attending the public feast celebrating the presiding spirit of the city (so Augustine, *Sermon* 62.10). Augustine complained that "the demons delight . . . in the manifold indecencies of the theater, in the mad frenzy of chariot races, in the cruelty of the amphitheater," evidently to little avail (*Sermon* 198 Dolbeau). Ecclesiastical objections notwithstanding, Christians continued to observe (and continue to observe) the Roman New Year, January 1, celebrating, drinking, and exchanging gifts with neighbors. "But someone says, 'These are not practices of sacrilegious rites. These are vows of entertainment,'" preached Peter Chrysologus, giving voice to a layman's position. "And this merriment is for the new, not an error of the old. This is the beginning of the new year, not a pagan transgression'" (*Sermon* 155.5).

Top-down discouragement of traditional Mediterranean worship waxed muscular in the late fourth century—the withdrawal of public funding for these cults; the final removal of the Roman senate's altar to the goddess of victory in 382; the forbidding of public sacrifices for the city of Rome in the same year; the imperial order mandating the closing of Carthage's temple of Juno in 399. Imperial initiatives enforced Christianization, but only up to a point. The feasts and games, the emperors ruled, should continue, now that they had been stripped of the "paganism" of blood sacrifices. "According to ancient custom, amusements shall be furnished to the people, but without any sacrifice or any accursed superstition; and they shall be allowed to attend festival banquets, whenever public desire so demands" (*Theodosian Code* 16.10.17, in 399). Theater was also to continue, "lest sadness be produced" (15.6.2, also 399).

A similar accommodation of pre-Christian and Christian celebration is visible in an elaborate deluxe calendar, made for a Roman Christian aristocrat, for the year 354. This famously displays not only pagan feast days and games, celebrations of the imperial cult (for Constantine's dynasty), along with astrological signs, but also an Easter cycle, along with a list of the bishops of Rome, beginning with Peter. In this period, too, the birthday of Jesus (thus, the celebration of the Incarnation) was associated with the Roman celebration of the winter solstice, the birthday of the Sun, December 25. Time was arguably ecumenical—again, to the dislike of many bishops. Eventually, the feast days of the saints would reshape the civic year: in the fourth century, for the month of August alone, Carthage celebrated no fewer than nine saints. The old feasts nevertheless also continued to be observed for centuries, and some (again, like January 1) seem not to have ceased at all, or (like December 25) have continued in Christian guise.

Prying these festivals loose of their pagan matrix was a social feat analogous to the earlier intellectual one of prying paideia loose from the traditional gods. Their native resonance was in effect neutralized. And not all bishops were so particular. Bishop Pegasius of Troy, in the 360s, whether out of local patriotism or enthusiasm for paideia, revealed to Julian that he countenanced the performance of sacrifices at the shrines of the heroes of the Trojan War (Julian, *Letter* 19). Confronting a monk determined to shut down the local celebration of the Olympic Games in 434–35, the bishop of Chalcedon simply told him to go away: "As you are a monk, go and sit in your cell and let the matter rest. This is my affair" (*Life of Hypatius* 33).

The Christian Capital

Rome was sui generis. It was the eternal city of the empire, the traditional heart of imperial government, home to the storied senate. Yet Christians there claimed Rome for themselves as *the* Christian city par excellence: site of the martyrdoms and, thus, home to the relics of the two preeminent, foundational saints, Peter and Paul; site of Peter's "episcopacy," per reading of Matthew 16.18: "You are Peter, and upon this rock I shall build my church." Rome's traditional imperial hegemony ultimately combined with this Petrine tradition to add—at least in the eyes of Rome's bishops—to the prestige and authority of the Roman see. When amenable to their own purposes, other bishops would appeal to Rome's authority to bolster their own (as did Cyprian against his local competitors, following the events initiated by Decius in 250). When not amenable, Rome could be safely challenged or ignored (as did Cyprian, when he fell out over rebaptism with Rome's bishop, Stephen). But the idea of Rome as the premier see persisted, negotiated variously once imperial power (and a lot of hectic theological wrangling) gathered around Constantine's new Rome, Constantinople. Rome's cultural capital was nonpareil.

Christ-following assemblies, presumably a mix of Jews and gentiles, had existed in Rome in the mid-first century, on the evidence of Paul's letter to the community there. Tacitus, in the early second century, had famously described Nero as scapegoating Christians for the fire in 64. Nero's lurid reputation in later Christian circles made him into a premier persecutor, responsible for the executions of Peter and Paul, and thus for the legend that the city contained the relics of both. The author of the book of Revelation, sometime in the first century, had reviled the city as the Whore of Babylon—sitting on seven hills, fornicating with the kingdoms of the earth, drunk on the blood of the saints. Yet the status of the two apostles ultimately outweighed any ambivalence that Christians might have felt: at the end of the day, Rome was the city not of Nero, but of Peter and Paul.

Mid-second century, teachers of many stripes—Valentinus, Marcion, Justin, Ptolemy, Marcellina—had been drawn to the capital. Christians organized as various house churches and reading groups, and no central authority prevailed: certain teachers and groups, like those around Valentinus, seemed comfortable floating between these different assemblies. By the end of the century, partly to repudiate and exclude all this "heretical" variety, Irenaeus, in Lyon, generated a list of "apostolic succession," tracing Rome's bishopric backward from his own day to the heroic period under the two premier apostles (*Against Heresy* 3.3.2–3).

Roman ecclesiastical leadership, even once notionally centralized, could still be a source of division. In the early third century, the episcopacy of the proto-orthodox church was claimed by two contestants, Callistus and Hippolytus, their mutual antagonism expressed both doctrinally and personally. The community, rancorously divided, split. After the experience under Decius, Rome, like many cities, had multiple communities and bishops, divided along lines of church discipline, that is, on what to do with those who had lapsed. The quarrels between episcopal candidates with their respective partisans were so contentious that the pagan imperial authority, Maxentius, had to exile the three main contestants. Even after 312, when imperial patronage should have clarified such contestations, papal politics could be roiled, factions formed. A sharp rivalry between Ursinus and Damasus in 366 crested in a riot in a basilica, leaving 137 people dead. Damasus ultimately prevailed, though his efforts to brand local schismatics as heretics in order to prosecute them in a court of law failed. Later, when Ursinus continued to defy the authority of Damasus, a pagan urban prefect, Praetextatus, had to intervene.

Unable to unify Rome's Christians, Damasus ingratiated himself with the city's ruling elite, which was at this time a mix of pagan and Christian (sometimes within the same marriage). Constantine's patronage of the "universal" church had served to promote interest in Christianity among Roman aristocrats. This imperial patronage also elevated the status of Rome's bishops, likening them to the governing elite. They "are assured of rich gifts from ladies of quality," observed the pagan historian Ammianus Marcellinus. "They can ride in carriages, dress splendidly, and outdo kings in the lavishness of their table" (*Histories* 27.3.14). Damasus certainly played his role with aplomb, building Christian holy sites around the city, thereby changing its liturgical topography; writing Virgilian verses for the (proliferating) tombs of martyrs; collecting around himself an impressive retinue; garnering the support of wealthy Christian women. His public profile was noted by others. "Make me the bishop of Rome," Praetextatus quipped to Damasus, "and I will immediately become Christian" (Jerome, *Letter to Pammachius against John*, 8).

If the Roman aristocracy slowly became Christian, Roman Christianity in its upper social strata likewise became aristocratic. Already by the 350s, Christianity had made inroads among Rome's elite. Expensive

Christian sarcophagi begin to appear as, also, the fine calendar of 354. Great ladies, some vowed to ascetic celibacy, began to sponsor and to patronize the local (and competitive) Christian intelligentsia. Jerome, for a time in the 380s resident in the city, benefited significantly from such patronage, though he lambasted others who sought the same. Wealthy Christian widows, he acerbically complained, have houses "filled with flatterers and guests. The clergy . . . kiss these ladies on the forehead and, putting forth their hands (so that, if you knew no better, you might suppose them in the act of blessing), take wages for their visits" (*Letter* 22.16). This flow of wealth was enough of a problem that, already in 370, an imperial edict forbade such clerical solicitations, interdicting bequests as well as outright gifts. No cleric should accept anything from "women to whom they have attached themselves privately under the pretext of religion" (*Theodosian Code* 16.2.20). On the evidence, the edict had little effect. These women of independent means continued exercising traditional patronage, transposed to a new key.

Classical culture bound Christian and pagan aristocrats together. Classical literature's assimilation to a Christian framework is nowhere better illustrated than by the poem of Faltonia Betitia Proba. Taking each line of her *cento* from Virgil, Proba rearranged their sequence so that Virgil seemed to speak "in praise of Christ." Proba was the wife of a pagan husband who only belatedly joined her in the church. Her literary efforts, like those of Damasus himself, both effected and displayed the ways in which Christianity was rendered culturally respectable in the eyes of Roman elites. That respectability, combined with the imperial sponsorship of the church and the disestablishment of traditional Roman cults, added to the momentum of aristocratic conversion. The social profile and civic importance of the city's bishop accordingly increased as well.

Though the Greek East continued to be troubled by ancient intercity competitions, and though both Milan and Ravenna, seats of the imperial court, were nodes of political power, Rome had no real local rival for spiritual authority. Its apostolic foundation by Paul and especially by Peter put it in a class by itself. So too did Bishop Damasus, whose tasking Jerome to retranslate the Gospels from the Greek finally gained for the

West a single definitive Latin version of Christian scripture. Though often politely (if tacitly) ignored by the eastern churches, Rome—and, thus, its bishop—held an unimpeachable primacy in the West.

In the course of the fifth century, some things changed drastically, but others remained the same. One by one, Goths and Vandals peeled away the provinces of the West. Aristocratic Roman Christians and pagans (not least, those of Rome's senate) became absorbed in adjusting to the new realities of a ruling Arian military class. Rome's bishop played an ever increasing role in urban politics. Leo I, bishop from 440 to 461, even successfully deflected the attentions of Attila the Hun when the latter threatened the city in 452. Later tradition claimed that he assumed the old imperial title of pontifex maximus. By the end of the fifth century, emperors had disappeared from the western empire. But the city, the senate, the monarchical bishop, and even some of the old traditional ("pagan") spectacles perdured.

The "Second" Church

Imperial Christianity was a movement played out in many registers. The products of literate elites loom over our reconstructions but should not be allowed to dominate them. More than theologians, bishops, and emperors contributed to Christian formation. Few people had the education—or the leisure time—to acquaint themselves with the soaring theological speculations and bitter controversies that characterize these centuries of Christian development. What of the vast bulk of that population whose religious loyalties, by the fifth century, had aligned meaningfully around the idea of "Christian"? What—and how—can we know about them?

We are hampered first of all by a near complete absence of demographical data. We do not know how many people, in any given century, lived in the empire. We do not know, therefore, what percentage of the population, at any given time, identified as "Christian." We can chart neither a pattern of growth, nor a rate (though some have tried). One often sees cited the figure of 10 percent of the total population as Christian (of all stripes?) for the period of Constantine, and that population would be represented especially in the cities. But, again, this is a guess sanctioned chiefly by repetition. In fact, we do not know.

Archaeological data—the foundations of buildings; grave finds; inscriptions—can begin to fill this evidentiary void, though they complicate the picture as well. While there were public Christian buildings, such as the basilica near to Diocletian's palace, in the period before Constantine, small structures predominate. Remains of a house church in the frontier town of Dura-Europos in Syria for example, mid-third century, suggest a repurposed building that could accommodate no more than about seventy people. Scholars estimate that the city held perhaps between six thousand and eight thousand souls. Assuming that the total Christian population was larger than seventy persons (which would represent less than 1 percent of the town's inhabitants), where else and how else could they have gathered?

One answer is, out of doors. And the most likely outdoor meeting place would have been a cemetery. Cemeteries, usually built outside of and adjacent to settlements, were active social spaces in antiquity: families would gather periodically throughout the year to celebrate a commemorative meal (*refrigerium* in Latin: "refreshment") around and over the tomb of their dead. Often, cemeteries were outfitted with dining rooms, or tables on which to dine. The dead were included in these meals: libations were poured through a tube or hole through the coffin to the deceased. The dead were another generation of the family, somehow still sentient, present at their tombs. Such cemetery rituals effected a mode of continuing contact. This pre-Christian custom continued unabated, kept by Christians as well.

What happened after the Constantinian inflection point, when infusions of wealth led to a building boom of monumental basilicas? These could and did hold larger numbers than their earlier, more modest forerunners, though many structures continued to be moderate, capable of holding at the most a few hundred worshipers. These would have been that part of the community who would gather to receive the eucharist, and to hear the bishop's preaching. Again, this small number cannot reflect the actual size of the total local Christian community, nor in big cities like Carthage or Alexandria or Antioch would it represent a broad economic cross section. More of the faithful could gather out of doors, in celebrations that would not require the presence of clergy, though sometimes clergy participated, too. Again, the prime gathering place was the cemetery.

The cult of the saints with its *convivia*, the festal celebration of food and drink around the martyr's tomb, developed out of the family cult of the dead. Martyrs, though already ascended to heaven upon their death, were powerfully present at their burial site as well. Vows were taken there, in exchange for benefactions. The saint's charismatic presence worked cures and miracles, drove away demonic infestations, aided in knowing the future—all forms of divine assistance that, with the partitioning of the saint's body, were transferred to their relics as well.

Some bishops complained repeatedly of the unseemliness and the overenthusiasm of these celebrations and sought to manage them. There was, first of all, the danger of fraternizing with non-Christians. Death brought no distinctions: pagans, Jews, and Christians were all interred in the same locations. Families held grave banquets in the same places. People would visit with each other during their meals. Celebrations always brought with them a dangerous mixing—hence the complaints of the literate about Christians participating in the festivities of the city, in the convivialities of the January new year, in the celebration of urban spectacles, in the dancing with Jews in public spaces on their holidays (much lamented by Chrysostom). Mixing undermined efforts to construct an articulated, controlled and controllable, externally bounded community.

Worse yet, perhaps, because internal to the community, was the issue of behavior. At the festival of the saint's death day, people would gather the night before for the vigil. There, in mixed company, they sang, they danced, they drank, they ate, enjoying themselves too much and too indecorously for the tastes of some in the ecclesiastical establishment. The enthusiastic devotions of the laity were condemned by the learned as "pagan" and as flirting with improper ritual—dancing at martyrs' shrines, Augustine insisted, delighted demons. (Dancing had long been integrated into religious celebrations, pagan, Jewish, and Christian.) Such celebrations were something that Donatists did, he said, thus

something that catholics should not do. Ambrose forbade even symbolic eating and drinking within his churches. Councils issued canons
forbidding parties within churches, attempting to get at least the clergy
to cease such celebrations. "No bishops or clergy should have banquets
in churches," ruled the Council of Carthage in 397—churches were built
over graves; graves were eventually housed in churches—"and, so far as
it is possible, the people should be barred from such convivia" (canon 42).
The people's celebrations—evidently abetted, on occasion, by clergy
themselves—nevertheless continued.

Church structures could contain only a fraction of a community,
even allowing for the construction boom that followed in the wake of
Constantine's conversion. By the late fourth century, further, in urban
settings, those inside frequently constituted for the most part the better-
off economic stratum of the community: casual mentions of wealth, of
quality clothing, cosmetics, and jewelry, of the management of slaves
and of other property crop up easily in the sermons of an Augustine or
of a Chrysostom. The Christianity of those *inter muros* was (at least
theoretically) shaped by the bishops: orderly liturgy, regular sacraments, strict separation of sexes within the church, acquaintance with
disputed theological issues of the day and with the interpretation of the
approved texts of the church's writings.

What proportion of the total community of those who identified as
Christian did this group "within the walls" represent? One historian has
guesstimated perhaps 5 percent. But their spirituality could overlap
with that of the far greater number, the 95 percent (?) who in effect
constituted a "second" church. These people congregated mostly out of
doors, their venue of choice around the tombs of and memorials to the
special dead. This means that the cult of the saints was no curious side-
line of late Roman Christianity. It probably described the way that the
far greater number of Christians were "churched."

We hear in the bishops' laments the differences between the religion
of the literate authorities and the lived religion of people's practices,
though these could be observed by the wealthy and by some of the
clergy as well. Dancing, singing, drinking, and eating, along with prayer,
constituted their liturgical activity. "Martyrs represented that superhuman

power which was accessible to the mass of people in a way the Triune God was not." They managed demons through amulets, incantations, spells, and, when and where possible, through contact with the relics of the saints. Sometimes, they became possessed by spirits at these shrines, enabled thereby to divine the future. Did they also go to the church? Sometimes, yes. But the bishops began to go to them, preaching in the cemeteries at martyria where they could reach the largest numbers of the faithful, and dispensing the sacrament there. Other bishops continued to condemn the festive convivia as "pagan."

How do we regard these people, so quiet in our literary sources, so invisible in so many histories of the growth of Christianity? They make up an important sector of that population among whom Christianity grew.

This raises the question: How do we define "Christianity"? Was it a religion of doctrines about how God became incarnate; about how three divine persons constitute a single deity; about how the soul, after Adam, manifests sin? Or was it a religion of contested interpretations over how to read sacred texts? Or was it a religion of realpolitik, chosen by an emperor concerned to ally himself with a powerful god, to protect his empire? Or was it a religion of charismatic exorcisms and the defeat or domestication of demonic powers? Or was it a religion of bishops and councils, their disputes fought out between cities whose rivalries long preceded the empire's involvement in the church? Or was it a religion of extreme fasting and self-mortification, of heroic, even extravagant asceticism? Or was it a religion of effective ritual actions, amulets, spells, and incantations no less than of sacraments? Or a religion of dancing, feasting, and celebration over the graves of the charismatic dead?

Identities and Boundaries

The answer, of course, is that Christianity was all these things, because "Christianity" was never a single thing. All these factors must figure in our reconstructions. If the spread of Christianity had depended on the arguments of the theologians, its success really would have taken a miracle: very few people had the education to understand what all the arguing was about. Gods and demons, intellectuals and enthusiasts, sacraments and magic, interurban and intraurban politics, new disciplinary behaviors and social formations: all went into the mix.

People were won over in part because they were enabled to control the omnipresent demons. Also, the faithful could look forward to the rewards of a good afterlife, ensured in part by good relations with the very special dead. No less important, they were motivated in their loyalties by wanting to avoid the flames of hell. They were socialized into taking sides in theological disputes through sermons, liturgies, creeds, and popular songs that reduced complex theologies to talking points and slogans. To many of them, there would have been not an iota's worth of difference between homoousia and homoiousia. What mattered was loyalty to their prime urban patron, their bishop, and to what they were told was timeless tradition.

Some scholars have referred to these people as *incerti*; others, echoing the bishops, as "semipagans," people who had a foot in two different worlds. The problem with the first term, *incerti*, is that these people, when challenged, did not seem "uncertain" about their identities in the least. As they told criticizing clergy in no uncertain terms, they were Christian. And so they were.

The problem with the latter term, "semipagans," is that it masks the degree to which *all* Christian culture, high no less than low, was made up of elements from the world that everyone lived in. What was the option? From where else could building blocks be quarried? There was no view from nowhere, above and outside of the world one lived in, from which one could construct something untouched, bounded, and entirely new. "Paganism"—not an -ism, but simply majority Mediterranean culture—framed the whole.

We see this in the behaviors associated with the saints' cults. We see this in the evidence of Christian ritual expertise ("magic"). But dependence on majority culture is no less true of the intellectuals. Justin depended on Philo, and both depended on the good Greco-Roman education that they received. Disavowing rhetoric and philosophy, Tertullian artfully deployed both. Origen is impossible to imagine outside of the context of Roman-period Platonism. Augustine's profoundly original thought drew deeply on that of the pagan Plotinus and Porphyry, and all these thinkers drew from the philosophies of Plato and of the Stoa. In terms of depending on their surrounding culture to express their theologies, these men were no less "semipagan" than were the celebrants around martyr memorials. If "semipagan" is an unhelpful label for these elite theologians, then it is no less unhelpful for the cemetery's celebrants.

In dealing with the labels "pagan" and "Christian," we are dealing with a double problem of classification: first, how we identify these ancient people; and second, how they would have identified themselves. Pagans did not know that they were "pagans" until elite Christians told them that they were. The rhetoric of these ecclesiastical elites dominates our written evidence. They were also the ones to label the cult of the saints a "pagan" residuum; they were the ones who condemned recourse to unofficial ritual expertise as indulgence in "pagan" magic; they were the ones to complain that convivia were "pagan" excrescences. They were the ones, indeed, who invented and deployed the word "pagan" as a counterpoint and contrast to "Christian."

Their efforts paralleled and echoed the similar processes informing imperial law. Book 16 of the *Theodosian Code* did more than establish correct protocols for the imperial church—regulating priestly personnel, liturgical practices, financial arrangements, and so on. It also defined religious deviance. Heretics, apostates, Jews, and pagans were now situated as legal categories, hemmed in with legal disabilities. Religious difference was dangerous. It undermined public safety and the prosperity of the empire.

These new legal taxonomies of deviance both created and witnessed to the late empire's redefining of diplomatic relations between heaven and earth. The many-ness of traditional Mediterranean religions—the vibrant variety that denies an "-ism" status to "paganism"—was labeled as "other." To be a pagan—or a Jew, or a nonconforming Christian—was to be, in some essential way, not only un-Christian but also un-Roman.

But how did these so-called pagans—or paganizing Christians—identify themselves? Here we must attend to oblique evidence: the complaints that stand in the treatises and sermons of literate authorities. Those many Christians (including clerics) who honored Decius's mandate to perform a supplicatio to the gods may well have thought that they were simply fulfilling their duty as Romans. It was (some of) the bishops who told them that they were *lapsi,* "lapsed." (And some of the bishops were lapsi themselves.) Post-250, martyr narratives, starring unambiguous heroes, evolved specifically to counter this looser construction of Christianness. Astrologers, diviners, makers of amulets, healers, celebrants at martyrs' graves and at urban spectacles: the highbrow rebuffed all these Christians as "pagans." They answered back, "I am baptized, just as you are."

When ecclesiastical elites summoned the rhetoric of "paganism," they were not describing difference, but *making* it. These differences of practice were an intra-Christian issue. By deploying the word and the concept "pagan," churchmen were able to construct and to present these Christian practices that were beyond their control—and indifferent to their authority—as "other" than Christian; indeed, as essentially non-Christian. At stake was the concept of the church as a universal and uniform translocal entity—as, after Caracalla in 212, was the idea of Rome itself.

The very rhetoric of "paganism" when leveled at other Christians gives the measure of how fluid and multifaceted Christian identity could be.

CONCLUSION

"Christianity." "*The* faith." "*The* church." By using these terms in the singular, we repeat the rhetoric of the retrospectively "orthodox," and we obscure the vital variety that always characterized this protean movement.

As we know from Paul's letters, the message of imminent redemption in Christ was already multivocal in the mid-first century, when it was still a form of Second Temple Judaism. This variety never ceased. By the second century we see very disparate communities contesting with each other. What united them was the common conviction that "salvation" (itself variously defined) had been wrought through Christ.

But there agreement ended. Some Christians were recognizably sympathetic to Jewish practices, or indeed were Jews themselves. Others roundly repudiated Jewish texts and traditions, holding that the Jewish god was an unknowing, perhaps errant subordinate of a higher god who was the father of Christ. Still others, while rejecting Jewish practices, insisted on reading Jewish scriptures in Greek as prophecies of Christ and of their own gentile communities. Others celebrated Easter according to the Jewish date of Passover. Others continued to receive ever-refreshed revelations. Some still expected the imminent arrival of God's kingdom; others denounced such views as "Jewish." By the fourth century, imperial initiatives will attempt to suppress this variety. Yet even within the imperial church—as we see in the convulsions over Christology, in the condemnations of "magic," in the tensions around the cult of the martyrs, as well as in the continuing synagogue activities of some gentile Christians, including clerics—unanimity, though asserted, was never established.

Christian ideas about the body—its relation to spirit, thus to self; its relation to Christ, thus to redemption—particularly illustrate this absence of unanimity. Paul, like many ancient Mediterranean thinkers, had juxtaposed "flesh" to "spirit," and seen the transformation of the former into the later as the measure of final redemption. Through the spirit of Christ, the fleshly body at the End would become a body of spirit. The body was not shed, but changed, becoming like Christ's risen body, to take its place in the heavens, that is, among the stars. Later gospel writers, Luke and John, had on the contrary insisted on the fleshly physicality of Christ's risen body. This cohered with later visions of final redemption that anticipated the saved individual's physical body reuniting with its soul, to dwell for a thousand years on a transformed earth—a vision celebrated in the energetic cult of the martyr and in the transformative charisma of saints' relics.

What to do with the fleshly body itself in the meanwhile became a question. How could one best prepare it for redemption? Run a well-ordered household? Perform regular rituals of purification? Confession of sins? Ascetic withdrawal, fasting, abstention from sex? Joining a community dedicated to such disciplines? And what would happen to the soul while it awaited reunification with the body? Would it simply "sleep"? Would some souls, either immediately or eventually, ascend to the presence of God? Would others be tormented in hell, where they would remain for eternity thereafter? What, indeed, was the scope of salvation—for all (as Origen urged), for some (as imagined by the authors of apocryphal Acts), for few (so Augustine)? All these different ideas swirled around as various Christian traditions formed. Even on so fundamental an issue—the meaning of redemption in Christ—no single view ever prevailed.

Nor could Christians agree on the nature of the divine. Was God absolutely unique? How divine, in comparison with the Father, was the Son? If the Son were less than fully divine, how could he effect salvation? If he were less than fully human, how could he effect salvation? The higher the Son's divinity, the more tenuous his relation to humanity.

If he did assume flesh, was it the flesh common to all humanity? Or was it flesh of a unique and special sort? Theologians argued endlessly, councils convened, and eventually even imperial government weighed in. The divisions that arose from these questions shape modern Christian communities to this day. We have to bear all this diversity in mind when we speak of "the triumph of Christianity." The question remains: which Christianity?

The triumphant literature that emerges especially in the wake of imperial patronage speaks of the movement's spreading and growing with incredible speed. Modern historians often repeat the claim. But we know little about rates of growth, because we have no firm data to draw on. We do not know how many Christians of any and all sorts lived in the empire by the year 100. Nor do we have any figures for the years 200, or 300, or 400. Nor do we know how many people in general the empire held in any era, though numbers—fifty million? sixty million?—are frequently floated and repeated. With Manichaean Christianity, we can at least have a sense of speed. Mani died in Persia in 276; his church was already condemned in the West by Diocletian some two decades later. But Mani had a network of already-established Christian communities as a base to draw on.

How did these Christianities spread? How did churches—of all persuasions—come to be formed? After Paul's generation, for how long did associations (whether synagogue communities or professional groups) incubate these movements? Scholars speculate that networks, whether personal or professional, were major conduits. Individual households also played a key role. If a head of house joined the movement, presumably his whole household—wife, children, slaves, freedmen, clients—would join as well. Conversions in this way would branch. Outsiders in search of healing, exorcisms, and divining the future might frequent a Christian group and, if these needs were met, decide to affiliate. Perhaps the celebrations in cemeteries, replete with acts of charismatic healing, attracted outsider notice. Later, imperial sponsorship brought new incentives. Over the course of three centuries, clustering chiefly in cities, the numbers of affiliates of all sectarian persuasions clearly grew; the better the organizational infrastructure, especially as it formed around the figure of the monarchical bishop, the stronger the community, because the stronger and more organized the mechanisms of support. But (recalling Pliny's letter to Trajan) traffic went in both directions: Christians could become ex-Christians, too.

How did this apocalyptic Jewish messianic movement, with its odd outreach to pagans in the face of the world's imminent end, transmute within three centuries into an arm of the late Roman state? Or to phrase the question more traditionally: what accounts for the "triumph of Christianity"?

In chapter 15 of that masterpiece of Enlightenment historical writing, *Decline and Fall of the Roman Empire*, Edward Gibbon famously ventured five answers. First, he named the "inflexible and intolerant zeal of the early Christians," which he saw as derived from Judaism, now released from the limitations of ethnicity. Second, Christianity's doctrine of a future life. Third, the miraculous powers ascribed to the early church. Fourth, the pure and austere morals of the early Christians. And fifth, the union and discipline of the "Christian republic." To this list have been added the arguments that paganism was itself losing steam, dying a natural death; and that Judaism, after the unsuccessful Judaean revolts of 66–73 and 132–35, withdrew from the gentile world. Circumstances, in other words, conspired to neutralize these other religious options.

Our aerial tour of antiquity's historical terrain has called much of this reconstruction into question. Christians were not the only ones who conceived of an afterlife, though they did elaborately develop and narrativize their ideas about it. Pagans and Jews had their wonder-workers too—Apollonius of Tyana in the first instance, Honi the Circle-Drawer in the second—but their stories are unfamiliar because they are preserved in less mainstream writings. The "purity and austerity" of Christian morals was an ideal enunciated particularly in writings about martyrs, monks, and saints' lives, and in letters exhorting great ladies to an ascetic lifestyle. Sermons, conciliar canons, and contemporary histories, however, tell the quite different story of Christians acting pretty much like their non-Christian contemporaries: complying with imperial edicts; soliciting the services of astrologers and assorted ritual experts, especially healers; having sexual relations with prostitutes and slaves; beating their slaves; participating in imperial cult (whether pre-Constantine or post); attending gladiatorial contests, horse races, and other spectacles; prevailing through applications of coercive force. And especially after the great ecumenical councils, we see how factious the "orthodox" bishops and populations could be. Constantine may well have wished for the "union" and "discipline" of Gibbon's "Christian republic." But he wished, and worked, in vain.

What about the triumph over other religious options? Paganism would not have to have been so targeted by Christian legislation had it been quietly dying of its own accord. And, as we have seen, "paganism" was too amorphous a phenomenon to be restricted, or complaints about the Christian celebration of civic holidays and the Christian recourse to healers, astrologers, and ritual experts would not be so loud in the record. Jews in Roman antiquity, outside of the early generations of the Christ movement, had not run missions to convert gentiles; but they continued their close social interactions with them, continuing to take their place within majority culture. Jews erected large public buildings, where they welcomed non-Jewish patronage and involvement, and cocelebrated their holidays with non-Jews—much to the irritation of some Christian spokesmen and clerics. Christian Rome legislated against Jews, too, demanding that they be barred from positions in the military and in government service—which means that they were there. Conversions to Judaism were forbidden by imperial law, which implies that such conversions occurred. Legislation both ecclesiastical and secular aimed to isolate these communities, which suggests that they were not just fading away. On the evidence, both were too much part of the Mediterranean mix for such initiatives to entirely succeed.

What stands out in the process of Rome's Christianization, distinguishing one particular sort or sect of Christianity both from other sorts and from non-Christian communities, is the strong institutional organization, centered around the bishop, that emerges clearly by the mid-third century. It was the church of the bishops that captured Constantine's allegiance, his continuing supervision and toleration of traditional and imperial cults notwithstanding. Bishops by that point had weathered the storms of occasional state coercion, whether through resistance, subterfuge, or acquiescence. Despite the problems of discipline that always followed in the wake of the imperial persecutions, and the rigorist abreactions of the Novatianists, the Donatists, and the Melitians, communities continued to muster around their bishops, to receive both sacraments and the patronage of charity.

Originally chosen for their lifetime appointments by acclamation of the laity, bishops transitioned to being approved by other bishops and, in some cases, later, appointed by the emperor. They worked within structured translocal organizations that sought to coordinate doctrine, calendars, financial resources, community mores, and liturgical protocols. They served as urban patrons and, after Constantine, as local strongmen. Their authority was enhanced by their new relation to the state, by their monopolizing of local charity and (thanks to monks and "hospital workers," *parabalani*) by their mobilization of local muscle, by their influence that spread through an expanding web of relations to wealthy patrons, ascetics and monks, the poor and the almost poor. They were the executives of a movement, in short, that cultivated a broad social reach.

The roots of Constantine's personal piety trace back to his military victory in 312. The particular church that he ended up sponsoring had articulated institutional structures. How and why he made the specific choice that he did is less than clear, the dramatic clarity of later accounts of it notwithstanding. But if his decision was in part prompted by concern to unify a fractured empire, Constantine chose well: the bishops provided the emperor with an alternative and effective functioning magistracy, a more immediate foothold in the cities, a way (at least notionally) to bind together the empire. The emperor provided the bishops with new wealth and, thus, new power. It was a synergistic relationship, ultimately to the bishops' advantage: even once the empire dissolved in the West, the scaffolding of presiding bishops perdured.

Still, the question remains: Why did Christianity—that is, this particular Christianity—emerge as the *sole* official religion of the empire? Later emperors, though Christian, might have followed the earlier examples of Gallienus in 260 and Galerius in 311. They could have allowed all the various Christianities to take their place among the many other cults of the empire as, briefly, did Julian. A practical pluralism might once again have prevailed.

But it did not. Instead, emperors beginning with Constantine moved to suppress other kinds of Christians, qua heretics. They interfered with and impeded traditional cult practices. They cut funding to ancient cults. They singled out Jews and Judaism for special opprobrium. Why?

Here we need to consider what Gibbon identified as the "inflexible and intolerant zeal of the Christians." This in no small part sprang from and was undergirded by the rhetorical training of second- and third-century elite spokesmen. It manifests in the written record of the proto-orthodox of the second and third centuries, with their insistence on homonoia, unanimity, and their consequent vilification of Christian rivals, as well as of Jews and of pagans, which shaped so much of the ideological patrimony of imperial Christianity. Agonistic rhetoric polarized options, sweeping away the clutter of choice. Only one way—the speaker's way—could be the right way.

This rhetorical patrimony, and ideological inflexibility, in turn fed into two quite different concerns post-Constantine: the empire's perennial focus on right religio as a bulwark against catastrophe, and the bishops' commitment to a principled exclusivism—one that their own congregations very often did not share.

The focus on right religio, long traditional, protected against divine anger. This mentality had motivated Augustus to assume the priestly office of pontifex maximus in the dawning days of the empire. It motivated Theodosius II centuries later, when he convened an ecumenical council in 429: he acted, he said, so that the condition of the church might honor God and contribute to the safety of the empire. After 312, deity's identity may have changed, but this religious conceptualization of the celestial/terrestrial pax remained the same. Right religio pleased heaven, no matter what heaven's denomination. Christianization proceeded precisely because its impetus, from the government's side, was so Roman.

Christian exclusivism, on the other hand, the insistence on the worship of one god only, was indeed, as Gibbon charged, an inheritance from Judaism. But this insistence was specific to a particular mood of

Judaism. Israel's god had long demanded that he be the sole focus of his own people's piety. But other peoples had their gods—occasionally derided in Jewish texts as "godlings," daimonia, or as mere images—just as Israel had theirs. "Every people walks, each in the name of its god," the prophet Micah observed, "but we shall walk in the name of the Lord *our* god forever" (Micah 4.5). This "ecumenical" posture, variously expressed in Jewish scriptures and manifestly true in daily experience, allowed for the live-and-let-live ethic of the Diaspora, where synagogue communities accommodated the involvement and welcomed the patronage of interested pagans. In this view, other people's worship of other gods was entirely normal.

But Jewish apocalyptic eschatology—the motor of the earliest movement—universalized the exclusivism of Jewish traditions, holding up Israel's god as the final and sole deity of *all* peoples. At the end of days, so these traditions held, all nations would worship Israel's god alone. Foreign deities were to be demoted or denied. Even after Christianities outgrew their originary apocalypticism (and Judaism); even after they disagreed between themselves on the identity of the high god; even after they went their separate ways into different regional churches within the empire, this exclusivist, universalizing impulse remained. Ultimately, this exclusivism was supported by politics: One god, one church, one empire, one emperor.

In the fourth century, this exclusivism combined with the Roman dread of religious irregularity to produce the church of the state. Right religio was defined as only one type of Christianity ("orthodox"), and, especially after Theodosius I, as only one type of orthodox Christianity, namely Nicene Christianity. Suppression of religious difference ensured the common weal. This mentality combining concern for legitimate religion together with public safety had led to the sporadic persecution of Christians in the first three centuries. In the course of the fourth century, this very same mentality propelled imperial Christianity to its position as the defining religion of the empire.

ACKNOWLEDGMENTS

In the beginning there was Chadwick. Henry Chadwick's *The Early Church*—originally published in 1967; lightly revised in 1993—reigned for decades as a classroom classic for college courses on ancient Christianity. Combining great descriptive clarity with seemingly effortless explanation of doctrinal obscurities, *The Early Church* also served as a wonderful introduction to the topic for the interested outside reader.

But in the half-century plus since that book first appeared, a revolution has occurred in the study of ancient Christianity. Methods borrowed from other disciplines have breathed new life into old sources. Liberal arts faculties of religious studies now investigate Christian origins in comparative perspective. Roman social history, Jewish Studies, Women's Studies, social identity theory, cultural anthropology, and more: all these disciplines have reframed the topic.

The ancient Mediterranean, in short, is not the same place that it was in 1967. It was time, I thought, to retell the story of the early church. Though I followed Chadwick's lead in resisting the scaffolding of footnotes in order to concentrate on narrative, I have cited ancient texts when referring to ancient authors. The Supplementary Readings for each chapter will signal the modern authors with whom I am in dialogue.

Anyone who works in the area of Roman religions owes an incalculable debt to the scholarship of Peter Brown. His many writings mark milestones in the study of Roman late antiquity, now grown into its own field of specialization. Elizabeth A. Clark, Ramsay MacMullen, Robert Markus, Wayne Meeks, Ed Sanders, and Jonathan Z. Smith, nonpareil guides all, cut new pathways through this historical landscape. It is with profound gratitude that I acknowledge my indebtedness to them all.

In conversation and in writing, many colleagues have generously shared their time and learning with me. David Frankfurter and Ross Kraemer read and commented on those sections of my manuscript that depended on their expertise. Meghan Henning and Candida Moss, together with David, kindly shared their syllabi with me: their varied approaches to ancient Christianity helped me to conceptualize the book. Esther Chazon patiently oriented me in scholarship on the Dead Sea Scrolls. Troels Engberg-Pedersen pondered the opening line of John's gospel with me. Tina Shepardson illumined some of darkest corners of the Miaphysite controversy. Éric Fournier graciously read and commented on my entire manuscript, fortifying both my arguments and my bibliography. Continuing conversations with Margaret M. Mitchell and with Adele Reinhartz have ever enriched my thinking. To all these good friends, my heartfelt appreciation and thanks.

As I was completing this project, several lectureships gave me the opportunity to present my ideas before audiences both academic and lay. I thank the faculty of Yale University's Divinity School for their invitation to give the 2020 Shaeffer Lectures ("Christian Identity, Paul's Letters, and 'Thinking with Jews'") and the faculty of Saint Catherine's University in Minneapolis, for their invitation to give the 2022 Goodman Lecture ("Mediterranean Mixing: Pagans, Jews and Christians in Roman Antiquity"). Daniel Boyarin and Erich Gruen kindly welcomed me to Berkeley to give the 2022 Taubman Lectures at the University of California ("Jewish Romans and the Rise of Christianity"). A plenary lecture at the 2022 meeting of the North American Patristics Society, at the invitation of Andrew Jacobs, provided the occasion to think together with colleagues about problems of evidence and interpretation ("The Subject Vanishes: Jews, Heretics and Martyrs after the 'Linguistic Turn'"). Again, to all, my thanks.

Since 2020, along with colleagues Matthew Novenson (Princeton Theological Seminary) and James B. Rives (University of North Carolina), I have served as a series editor for the Edinburgh Studies in Religion in Antiquity. Interacting with my co-editors has been enormously stimulating and educative, as has reading and responding to the various excellent manuscripts submitted to the series. Our work together has sharpened my sensitivity to the historical sources while increasing my methodological peripheral vision. I am deeply grateful for the learning opportunity that ESRA, and the Edinburgh University Press, have given me.

My husband, Fred Tauber, listened patiently while I struggled out loud with shaping the story of these first five centuries. He also served as my first reader, astutely marking up my manuscript and showing me where my presentation needed further work. His continuing support made all the difference. Sandra Dijkstra, literary agent *extraordinaire*, offered unstinting encouragement. The generous comments and criticisms of two anonymous colleagues helped me greatly to improve the manuscript. Fred Appel, my editor at Princeton University Press, waited patiently while my text changed and grew. I thank him, and all the others of the Press's production team, for their help in bringing this book into print.

Much of the research upon which the current study rests was completed in Israel where, since 2010, I was privileged to teach as Distinguished Visiting Professor in the Department of Comparative Religion at the Hebrew University of Jerusalem. Conversations with departmental colleagues there added immeasurably to my efforts: I thank especially fellow Christianists Brouria Bitton-Ashkelony and Yonatan Moss. At Scopus every spring, together with Oded Irshai, professor of Jewish history, I offered a graduate seminar focusing on the interactions of pagans, Jews, and Christians in Roman antiquity. Oded brought to our classroom his astonishing command of rabbinic sources, Greek patristic authors and historians, and archaeological data. He contributed as much to my own education as he did to that of our students. If the past is a foreign country, then Oded is the ultimate guide. With thanks for all the times we worked and taught and laughed together, Oded, I dedicate this book to you.

TIMELINE

Before the Common Era (BCE)

Circa 1000 David consolidates cult in Jerusalem. His son Solomon
builds the First Temple.

586 Babylon conquers Jerusalem, destroys the First Temple;
some Judaeans deported to Babylonian territories (= the
First Exile).

530s Persia conquers Babylon. Some Judaeans return from
exile. Construction of Second Temple gets underway,
completed in 519.

332 Alexander the Great conquers the region of the eastern
Mediterranean up to the edges of Afghanistan. Dissemination of Greek language and culture in his territories
("Hellenism"). Spread and settlement of Jewish populations throughout Mediterranean regions.

Circa 200 Completion of translation of Hebrew scriptures into
Greek (the Septuagint).

166 Maccabean Revolt against Hellenizing policies of Antio-
chus IV of Syria. Hasmonean family succeeds to high
priesthood and rulership of Jewish regions. Republican
Rome extends its hegemony in the eastern Mediterranean
and in Egypt.

152 Beginnings of the community by the Dead Sea (Essenes?)
under the Teacher of Righteousness.

37 Rome designates Herod as king of Judaea and outlying
territories. Herod rules until 4 BCE, greatly enlarging and
refurbishing the Second Temple complex.

| 31 | Battle of Actium between Octavian and Mark Anthony; after years of civil war, Rome completes its transition from republic to empire under Octavian, who later assumes the titles "Augustus" (27 BCE) and "pontifex maximus" ("greatest priest"; 12 BCE). |
| 4 | Death of Herod; division of his kingdom between his three sons. |

Common Era (CE)

6	Judea becomes a province of the Roman Empire. Galilee remains a client kingdom ruled by Antipas, one of Herod's sons.
20s	Beginning of the activities of John the Baptizer; later, of Jesus of Nazareth: both prophesy the coming Kingdom of God. John is executed by Antipas circa 28; Pilate crucifies Jesus circa 30 as a messianic pretender ("King of the Jews"). Original followers, convinced of Jesus's resurrection, settle in Jerusalem. They spread his message to Jewish hearers in coastal cities and into the Diaspora.
Circa 33 (?)	Paul encounters the Jesus movement in Damascus, shifts from adversary to advocate after his experience of the Risen Christ.
40s–50s	Period of Paul's outreach to pagans; composition of his letters. Various messianic figures lead popular movements in Judea and Samaria; they are cut down by Rome.
64	Great fire in Rome under Nero.
66–73	Jewish Revolt against Rome in Judea and Galilee. Rome conquers Jerusalem, destroying the Second Temple, in 70. Perhaps the period of composition of book of Revelation.
Circa 75–100	Period of composition of various gospels: Mark, Matthew, Luke, John, Thomas. Josephus writes *Jewish War* and *Antiquities of the Jews*. Perhaps period of composition of book of Revelation, some deutero-Pauline letters.

100–120	Historical writings of Tacitus and Suetonius; the correspondence of Pliny and Trajan about treatment of Christians. Perhaps the composition of Acts of the Apostles, of the *Didachē* and of the *Apocalypse of Peter*.
132–35	Bar Kokhba revolt in Judea against Rome. Jerusalem destroyed; Hadrian builds a pagan city, Aelia Capitolina, on its ruins. Romans change the name of Jewish territories to "Palestine."
130s	Fl. Valentinus (Alexandria, then Rome).
140s	Fl. Marcion (Pontus, then Rome), who compiles a first New Testament comprising a selection of Pauline and deutero-Pauline letters and a version of the Gospel of Luke. Perhaps the composition of the Pauline "pastoral Epistles" (1 and 2 Timothy and Titus) and of the Acts of the Apostles as anti-Marcionite texts.
150s–160s	Fl. Justin (Palestine, then Rome); martyred in Rome circa 165. In his *Dialogue with Trypho*, reading the Jewish prophecies about the Babylonian exile in 586 BCE and looking through the lens of the Bar Kokhba revolt back to the destruction of the temple in 70, Justin pronounces the Jews to be in a condition of a second and permanent "exile." Sporadic and local actions against Christians. Period of great creativity among various Christian communities. Composition of the letters of Ignatius (?).
170s	Tatian composes the *Diatesseron*, a gospel harmony.
180s	Composition of *Acts of Paul and Thecla*. Melito of Sardis writes *On Passover*. Montanus, Priscilla, and Maximilla in Phrygia prophesy the imminent arrival of the Kingdom of God. Celsus writes a pagan critique of Christianity, *On True Teaching*. Irenaeus writes against "heresies." His work is the first evidence of an anti-Marcionite selection of texts collected in a "New Testament."
Circa 200	Tertullian in Carthage; Clement of Alexandria. Emperor Caracalla extends Roman citizenship to all free peoples in the empire (212). The Mishnah (Hebrew) redacted. Rome

	acknowledges the establishment of the Jewish patriarchate in Tiberias.
200–250	Origen of Alexandria writes *On First Principles* (220s?) and *Against Celsus* (248). The empire endures military and political crises in the middle decades of the third century. In 250, Emperor Decius orders the universal performance of sacrifice to the gods for the protection of the empire. Novatian protests Christian leniency in forgiving those who lapsed. Hippolytus of Rome early in the century calculates age of the world to determine the year 6000 since creation, thus the return of Christ. Dating the Incarnation to the year 5500 postcreation, he estimates that the year 6000 would occur in the modern equivalent date of 500 CE. Composition of the *Didascalia Apostolorum* (Teaching of the Apostles). Bishop Cyprian of Carthage goes into hiding (250).
257	Emperor Valerian orders universal performance of sacrifice to the gods. Martyrdom of Cyprian of Carthage (258). Further development of acts of martyrs as a literary genre.
260	Emperor Gallienus de facto legally recognizes Christianity as a Roman religion.
260s	The emperor Aurelian enforces the decision of several councils of bishops in removing Bishop Paul of Samosata from his church in Antioch. Mani conceives a new Christian revelation that has elements of Zoroastrianism and of Buddhism; he is martyred in Persia (276). Porphyry writes fifteen books of pagan critique, *Against the Christians*.
270 (?)	Anthony retires to solitary life in the Egyptian desert.
297	Emperor Diocletian orders persecution of Manichaean Christians.
303–11	Emperor Diocletian orders persecution of other Christians, and specifically the destruction of Christian books. The persecution ends in 306 in the West, in 311 in the

East. Constantine, establishing himself as an imperial usurper in the West (306), suspends this persecution there. Emperor Galerius in the East issues Edict of Toleration allowing for Christian freedom of practice (311). Donatists in North Africa and Melitians in Egypt take a hard-line stance on reintegrating the lapsed into their churches. Writings of Lactantius.

312   Constantine bests Maxentius at Rome, attributing his victory to the Christian god, to whom he owes allegiance ("conversion of Constantine"). He almost immediately becomes involved in internal Christian controversy in North Africa attempting (unsuccessfully) to settle the Donatist schism.

313   Emperors Constantine (in the West) and Licinius (in the East) issue "Edict of Milan" on tolerance for all religions within the empire.

320s   Pachomius founds a federation of monasteries (male and female) in Egypt.

324   Constantine defeats Licinius (whom he assassinates) and rules as sole emperor until 337. Bishop Alexander and the presbyter Arius in Alexandria quarrel over nature of Christ, beginning the so-called Arian controversy, which Constantine also tries to quell. To this end, the emperor convenes the Council of Nicaea in 325, insisting on the use of *homoousia* ("of the same substance") to characterize the Son's relation to the Father. Legal and social pressures brought to bear on diverse Christian churches. Aelia Capitolina reverts back to being called Jerusalem.

328   Athanasius succeeds Alexander as bishop of Alexandria. He is implacably opposed to Arius and hostile toward the Melitians. Sustaining five exiles, he remains bishop until 373. Consolidation of an "orthodox" New Testament canon, though variations will continue.

330s–340s   Constantine founds Constantinople as a "New Rome" (330). He dies in 337. The empire is divided between

Constantine's three sons, who murder ancillary branches of the family to ensure dynastic succession. Bishop Ufilas inaugurates a mission to the Goths (ca. 340).

350–61   Constantius, Constantine's son, rules as sole emperor. He is pilloried as a heretic and as a pagan murderer by prelates who think he is insufficiently hostile toward "Arian" Christians. White Monastery founded in Egypt, eventually led by Shenoute (385–465).

361–63   The brief reign of Julian, who turns from Nicene Christianity to traditional Mediterranean religion ("paganism"). Succeeded by the Christian Jovian (until 364), then by Valens and Valentinian.

360s–390s   Damasus bishop of Rome (until 384); commissions Jerome to retranslate New Testament texts (382). Jerome goes on to retranslate sections of the Old Testament from the original Hebrew into Latin (completed by ca. 405). Ambrose bishop of Milan (374–97). Emperors Valentinian II (West) and Theodosius I (East) issue Edict of Thessalonica, establishing Nicene Christianity as sole legitimate Christian church (380). Execution of Bishop Priscillian of Avila (385); various initiatives undertaken against the Manichees. Augustine converts from Manichaeism to Nicene Christianity in Milan (386). Destruction of the synagogue on the eastern border of empire (Callinicum, 388). Period of activity of the Cappadocian Fathers: Basil of Caesarea, Gregory of Nyssa, and Gregory Nazianzus. John Chrysostom is ordained priest in Antioch; he later assumes bishopric of Constantinople. Growth of Marian piety. Expansion and flourishing of cult of the saints. Era of great aristocratic Roman female ascetics. Epiphanius hunts heresies. Outbreak of controversy over Origen's theological legacy.

400–450s   Honorius in the West pronounces the Donatists to be heretics, thereby increasing their legal liabilities (405). Theodosius II becomes emperor (408–50). He orders the compilation of Roman law, the *Theodosian Code* (429–38). Rome sacked by Arian Goths under Alaric, causing a refugee wave from Italy to North Africa (410). Period of Augustine's controversy with Pelagius, and his writing of the *City of God* (ca. 413–26). Forced conversion of Jews on Minorca (418). Peeling away of the provinces of the western empire by Arian Goths (Italy, Gaul, Spain) and Vandals (North Africa). Activity of Simeon Stylites (d. 459). Period of the great Christological controversies, contested particularly between Cyril of Alexandria and Nestorius of Constantinople: these are unstably resolved at the Council of Chalcedon (451). Jewish patriarchate in Tiberias ceases. Efflorescence of stories about martyrs and of the cult of the saints.

500   The year calculated by Hippolytus of Rome (d. 235?) to be the six thousandth since the creation of the world, the date for the Second Coming of Christ, for the end-time resurrection of the saints, and for the establishment of the Kingdom of God.

GLOSSARY

adoptionism: The view that Jesus was a human being adopted as son of God at his baptism.

adversus Iudaeos (*also* contra Iudaeos): A theological rhetoric that constructs Christian identity by juxtaposing it to a negative conception of Jews and Judaism.

allegory: From the Greek "other-speak," a technique of reading that ascribes meanings to a text that are symbolic or "hidden," often associated with a "spiritual" meaning as opposed to a literal/"fleshly" one.

apocalyptic eschatology: Knowledge, often esoteric, concerning last things before the end of normal history and the establishment of the Kingdom of God. Certain themes, like the battle between good and evil or the resurrection of the dead, characterize Jewish restoration theology more generally. The difference is that apocalyptic eschatology asserts that the End is near. In its Christian iterations, it asserted the imminent Second Coming of Christ.

Arianism: A theology about the nature of Jesus's preexistence as divine Son that distinguishes him from God the Father by way of subordination: Christ derives from the father but is not equal to him. "Arianism" later functioned to label any position that differed from that asserted in the Nicene Creed.

asceticism: From the Greek *askesis* meaning "athletic training," a strict self-discipline that minimizes food, sex, sleep, or physical comfort for the purpose of spiritual advancement.

Barnabas: A mid-second-century sermon, presented as an epistle, that reads Jewish scriptures allegorically to promote the author's view of Christianity as prior and spiritually superior to Judaism.

Chalcedon: An ecumenical church council convened by the emperor in 451 to settle questions on the divine and human natures of Christ. It affirmed that Christ had two natures, both fully divine and fully human, as opposed to a single nature. The council's decision was rejected by "one-nature" (Miaphysite) Christians in Egypt and in Syria.

Christology: Theological reflection on the nature and work of Christ. Many of the categories are drawn from Greco-Roman philosophy.

confessors: Christians who were imprisoned, prepared for martyrdom, but who were subsequently released. On this merit, they claimed the authority to forgive sins.

Constitutio Antoniana: The edict pronounced by the emperor Caracalla in 212 granting all free residents of the empire the status of citizens of Rome.

cosmos: Greek "order," the term for the organization of the geocentric universe, the earth being surrounded by the spheres of the sun and moon, the five planets known to antiquity, and the sphere of the fixed stars.

cult of the saints: Celebrations and worship over the graves or relics of martyrs.

daimon (*pl.* daimones): The term for lesser gods, located in the cosmos especially in the sublunar realm.

demiurge: The go-between god of ancient cosmologies, who acted as the agent of the highest god in organizing the physical universe.

demons: Derived from *daimones*, demons were ethically demoted in Christian thought to always refer to maleficent beings, the root cause of heresies and persecutions.

Diaspora: Greek "dispersion," a Jewish term relating to all lands outside of territorial Israel.

Docetism: From the Greek *dokeo*, "to appear"; a term claiming that Christ only appeared to have a human body, but did not in fact have one. Proto-orthodox heresy hunters ascribed this position to followers of Valentinus and of Marcion.

Elvira: A church council gathered in Spain circa 303 that detailed behavioral rules for Christians interacting with heretics, pagans, and Jews. Behaviors were to be policed through withholding of sacraments.

ethnos (*pl.* ethnē): The word for people group, corresponding to the Hebrew *goyim*. In Jewish writings it usually refers to non-Jewish nations who worship non-Jewish gods. It is often translated as "gentile," but it carries a religious freight too, hence the translation "pagan."

Gnostics: Greek "knowers," from *gnōsis* ("knowledge"), a term used to designate those forms of Christianity that emphasized esoteric knowledge of a highest god and a spiritual cosmos above the cosmic god and the physical universe. The cosmic god was often associated with the divinity depicted in Genesis, while the highest god was considered the father of Christ. This way of thinking does not describe a discrete group, but rather a mood within evolving second-century Christianities.

Goths: A Germanic people on the northeastern border of the empire, divided into East (Ostrogothic) and West (Visigothic) populations. They were often federated to Rome for military purposes but became increasingly independent within the western half of the empire in the course of the fourth century. Goths observed a form of Christianity characterized by Nicene critics as "Arian." Their leader Alaric sacked the city of Rome in 410.

heresy: Derived from *hairesis*, the Greek word meaning "school" or "sect." Heresy evolved in the second century to mean those Christian groups whom a proto-orthodox writer deemed as "deviant" from apostolic tradition.

homodoxia, homonoia: Derived from the Second Sophistic, a philosophical and rhetorical movement within first- through third-century Greco-Roman culture; the terms mean "unanimity" and "concord," attributes associated with true philosophy.

homoousia: "Same essence" or "substance"; the philosophical term was applied by Christian theologians to describe the relation between God the Father and God the Son. It makes a maximal claim for the divinity of Christ, being "of the same substance" as the Father.

homoiousia: "Similar essence" or "substance," stating that Christ is "like" but not identical to God the Father.

hylē: Unformed matter, coeternal with the high god in Greek cosmologies, which formed the material substratum of the organized universe.

hypostasis: A philosophical term indicating an independently existing entity, sometimes translatable as "person" or as "substance." For classical theology, the Trinity was defined as a single ousia ("substance" or "essence") in three hypostases ("persons").

logos: "Word" or "reason" or "speech"; Logos in Jewish and Christian theological systems represents the divine aspect or agent through which the highest god creates. Christian systems identify the Logos with the preexistent Christ.

Maccabean Revolt: The war in Judea over degrees of assimilation to Greek culture fought between Syrian Greeks under the Seleucid dynasty and Judeans led by the Hasmonean family under Judah Maccabee, 167–164 BCE.

Manichaeism: A third-century form of Christianity founded by Mani; Manichaeism posited two eternally contesting cosmic realms, Light and Darkness, with the human being as a miniature instance of this struggle.

Miaphysite Christology: The view that Christ had a single, divine nature as opposed to two independent natures, divine and human. Also referred to as "Monophysite" Christology.

millenarianism: The belief that the saints will rise in a first resurrection to reign with Christ on earth for one thousand years.

millennial week: A way to calculate the arrival of the Second Coming of Christ; the millennial week stipulated that time would continue from creation in six thousand-year units ("days"), until the dawning of the thousand-year Sabbath and the terrestrial reign of the saints. In this calculus, Christ was held to have been born in the year 5500 since creation, making the appointed end-time correspond to our year 500 CE.

Milvian Bridge: The location in Rome for the battle between Constantine and Maxentius. Constantine attributed his victory there to the agency of the Christian god.

Mishnah: Hebrew "repetition," a body of orally transmitted Jewish law compiled in Hebrew circa 200 CE. This becomes a core text of rabbinic Judaism.

Montanists: A late second-century Christian movement of the "New Prophecy" formed in Phrygia and holding to a belief that the End, and God's kingdom, were imminent. Montanists believed that the Holy Spirit was the source of their continuing revelations.

Nag Hammadi library: Those second-century, often esoteric Christian texts, translated by the fourth century from Greek into Coptic, hidden at Nag Hammadi in Egypt.

Nicaea: The council convened by Constantine in 325 to decide, among other issues, on the nature of the divinity of Christ. The Nicene Creed, eventually derived from the work of the council, becomes the index of imperial orthodoxy in 380, mandated by the emperors Gratian and Theodosius I in the Edict of Thessalonica.

ousia: "Essence" or "substance," a term used to articulate the relation of God the Son to God the Father. Homousian theologians, most associated with Athanasius, held that Christ was "of the same ousia" as God; those associated with Arius held that Christ's ousia was similar to but not identical with that of God the Father.

pax deorum: "Peace of the gods," the pact between good government, thus proper religion, on earth and deities in heaven. Under Constantine, the concept will shift to the pax dei, the "peace of God."

pontifex maximus: "Greatest priest," the title adopted by Augustus that made him responsible for overseeing proper cult in the city of Rome. Eventually, the purview of this imperial position extended to the whole empire.

prosōpon (*Greek*; *pl.* prosōpa); persona (*Latin*): Originally indicating the mask worn by actors in Greek theater; the term was adopted by fourth-century Christian theologians to express ideas about the personhood of Christ.

religio: Proper cult to the gods or, after Constantine's consolidation of the empire in 324, to God. Right religio was seen as necessary for the maintenance of the pax deorum.

schism: From the Greek meaning "to tear," a division within a single church over some issue of discipline or doctrine.

Septuagint: A collection of Greek translations of Hebrew scriptures completed by the second century BCE.

spectacles: Urban feast days featuring horse races, athletic events, and gladiatorial combats that brought the city together in honor of the presiding gods.

superstitio: Originally referring to extravagant fear of the divine, and often used to characterize foreign (that is, non-Roman) cults; the term comes to mean a religious practice of questionable legitimacy.

Theodosian Code: A compendium of Roman law, compiled between 429 and 438 during the reign of Theodosius II (408–50). Book 16 famously addresses issues having to do with religion, both Christian and non-Christian, within the empire.

Theotokos: "God-bearer," a title given to Mary that emphasized the high divinity of Christ.

Vandals: A Germanic people who adopted an "Arian" form of Christianity; Vandals took over the Iberian Peninsula and Roman North Africa, ultimately besieging the city of Rome in 455.

SUPPLEMENTARY READING

1. The Idea of Israel

On Jewish apocalyptic eschatology as the matrix for the generation of Jesus and of Paul, see Paula Fredriksen, *When Christians Were Jews: The First Generation* (New Haven, CT: Yale University Press, 2018). The effects of Paul's gentile audience on his Jewish message are explored by Matthew Thiessen in *Paul and the Gentile Problem* (New York: Oxford University Press, 2016) and, by the same author, *A Jewish Paul* (Grand Rapids, MI: Baker Academic, 2023), and also in the essays collected in *Paul within Judaism*, edited by Mark D. Nanos and Magnus Zetterholm (Minneapolis: Fortress, 2015). On the intrinsic Jewishness of Paul's message, see Anders Runesson, *Judaism for Gentiles* (Tübingen: Mohr-Siebeck, 2022).

For Jewish settlement in the western diaspora, see the work of John Barclay, *Jews in the Western Mediterranean Diaspora, from Alexander to Trajan [323 BCE to 117 CE]* (Berkeley: University of California Press, 1996), and studies by Erich Gruen, *Heritage and Hellenism* (Berkeley: University of California Press, 1998) and *Diaspora: Jews amidst Greeks and Romans* (Cambridge, MA: Harvard University Press, 2002). On Jews in that premier pagan establishment, the bath (with its mixed-ethnic clientele and mixed-gendered public nudity, Yaron Z. Eliav, *A Jew in the Roman Bathhouse: Cultural Interaction in the Ancient Mediterranean* (Princeton, NJ: Princeton Univerity Press, 2023). Menachem Stern assembles and comments on classical authors' remarks in *Greek and Latin Authors on Jews and Judaism*, 3 volumes (Jerusalem: Israel Academy of Sciences and Humanities, 1974–84). On the Jews' writings as cultural capital, see Tessa Rajak, "The Mediterranean Jewish Diaspora in the Second Century," in *Christianity in the Second Century: Themes and Developments,* edited by James Carleton Paget and Judith Lieu (Cambridge: Cambridge University Press, 2017) and Timothy Michael Law, *When God Spoke Greek* (New York: Oxford University Press, 2013). For Jews in pagan places and pagans in Jewish places, see Paula Fredriksen, *Paul: The Pagans' Apostle* (New Haven, CT: Yale University Press, 2017), 32–60; see also 61–93 on "eschatological gentiles."

Paul can plausibly be placed within the webbing of synagogue communities, but he may also have networked via trade associations. John S. Kloppenborg explores the social organization of these groups in *Christ's Associations: Connecting and Belonging in the Ancient City* (New Haven, CT: Yale University Press, 2019). For the place of pagan God-fearers in the ancient synagogue, see Joyce Reynolds and Robert Tannenbaum, *Jews and God-Fearers at Aphrodisias* (Cambridge: Cambridge Philological Society, 1987). The inscription that they dated to the third century has since been redated to the fourth or fifth. See also the essays in *The Ways That Never Parted,* edited by Adam H. Becker and Annette Yoshiko Reed (Minneapolis: Fortress, 2007).

When do Christ followers become distinguished as a new group by a new term, "Christians"? When does Christ following become "Christianity"? The Acts of the Apostles (early second century) retrojects the word "Christian" back into the mid-first century ("It was in Antioch that the disciples were first called *Christianoi,*" Acts 11.26; cf. 26.28), as does the Roman historian Tacitus, early second century, when he describes the scapegoating of this group by Nero (*Annals* 15.44). Suetonius (another historian, at *Nero* 16) and Pliny (a Roman governor, in his famous *Letter* 10.96, discussed in chapter 3), both Tacitus's contemporaries, also use "Christian." The word, in short, first appears in texts that cluster in the late first / early second century, the zone of time by which these new social groups form. David Horrell investigates this construction of Christian identity in *Ethnicity and Inclusion* (Grand Rapids, MI: Eerdmans, 2020).

Rosemary Radford Ruether first drew attention to the dynamics of developing theologies and Christian anti-Judaism in *Faith and Fratricide: The Theological Roots of Anti-Semitism* (New York: Seaberry, 1976). On the ways that different forms of Christianity "thought with Jews," see John G. Gager, *The Origins of Anti-Semitism* (New York: Oxford University Press,

1983). Marcel Simon, *Verus Israel: A Study of the Relations between Christians and Jews in the Roman Empire, 135–425* (1948; New York: Oxford University Press, 1986), though dated, remains fundamental. On the entanglements of anti-Jewish and antiheretical thinking, see Mattijs den Dulk, *Between Jews and Heretics: Refiguring Justin Martyr's "Dialogue with Trypho"* (London: Routledge, 2018). Specifically on anti-Judaism and the charge of deicide, see J. Christopher Edwards, *Crucified: The Christian Invention of the Jewish Executioners of Jesus* (Minneapolis: Fortress, 2023).

Polemics against animal sacrifice, pagan piety, and Jews are all entangled as gentile Christianities develop—and compete with one another—in the second and third centuries. Two incisive examinations of this snarl of themes are offered by Daniel Ullucci, *The Christian Rejection of Animal Sacrifice* (New York: Oxford University Press, 2012), and several of the essays in *Ancient Mediterranean Sacrifice*, edited by Jennifer Wright Knust and Zsuzsanna Várhelyi (New York: Oxford University Press, 2011).

Karin Hedner Zetterholm explores Jewish configurations of Christianity in "Between Paganism and Judaism: The Law of God in the Pseudo-Clementine Homilies," in *In Search of Truth in the Pseudo-Clementine Homilies: New Approaches to a Philosophical and Rhetorical Novel of Late Antiquity*, edited by B.M.J. De Vos and D. Praet (Tübingen: Mohr Siebeck, 2022), 317–34; and "Christ Assemblies within a Jewish Context: Reconstructing a Social Setting for the Pseudo-Clementine Homilies," in *Negotiating Identities: Conflict, Conversion, and Consolidation in Early Judaism and Christianity (200 BCE–600 CE)*, edited by Karin Hedner Zetterholm, Anders Runesson, Cecilia Wassén, and Magnus Zetterholm (Lantham, MD: Lexington Books / Fortress Academic, 2022), 329–49. See further James Carleton Paget, "Jewish Christianity," in *Cambridge History of Judaism*, volume 3, *The Early Roman Period*, edited by William Horbury, W. D. Davies, and John Sturdy (Cambridge: Cambridge University Press, 1999), 731–75; and Annette Reed, *Jewish Christianity and the History of Judaism* (Tübingen: Mohr Siebeck, 2018).

Finally, for developments across this period through to the late empire, see Paula Fredriksen and Oded Irshai, "Christianity and Judaism in Late Antiquity: Polemics and Policies," in *Cambridge History of Judaism*, volume 4, *The Late Roman and Rabbinic Period*, edited by Steven T. Katz

(Cambridge: Cambridge University Press, 2006), 977–1035; many of the other essays in the volume are also pertinent. See too the essays collected in *Jews, Christians, and the Roman Empire*, edited by Natalie B. Dohrmann and Annette Yoshiko Reed (Philadelphia: University of Pennsylvania Press, 2013). Two contemporary church fathers, Chrysostom in the East and Augustine in the West, contributed importantly to Christian theologies of Judaism, on which, see especially Robert L. Wilken, *John Chrysostom and the Jews: Rhetoric and Reality in the Late 4th Century* (Berkeley: University of California Press, 1983); and Paula Fredriksen, *Augustine and the Jews: A Christian Defense of Jews and Judaism* (New Haven, CT: Yale University Press, 2010). Christian legislation on Jews and Judaism is collected in two volumes by Amnon Linder, *The Jews in the Legal Sources of the Early Middle Ages* (Detroit, MI: Wayne State University Press, 1997) and *The Jews in Roman Imperial Legislation* (Detroit, MI: Wayne State University Press, 1987).

2. The Dilemmas of Diversity

The second and third centuries witnessed a great diversity of Christianities, and the period has been likened to a laboratory. For two excellent surveys of these movements and the issues attendant on them, see especially the essays assembled in *Christianity in the Second Century: Themes and Developments*, edited by James Carleton Paget and Judith Lieu (Cambridge: Cambridge University Press, 2017), and *The Cambridge History of Christianity: Origins to Constantine*, edited by Margaret M. Mitchell and Frances M. Young (Cambridge: Cambridge University Press, 2006). In the latter collection, see especially the contributions by David Brakke (Gnosticism), Denis Minns (Irenaeus), Gerhard May (monotheism and creation) and Frances M. Young (Christian paideia). Further on paideia, see Teresa Morgan, *Literate Education in the Hellenistic and Roman Worlds* (Cambridge: Cambridge University Press, 2007). On the great diversity in the city of Rome alone, see Peter Lampe, *From Paul to Valentinus* (Minneapolis: Fortress, 2003). Finally, on constructions of the idea of "heresy," see Alain LeBoulluec, *The Notion of Heresy in Greek Literature in the Second and Third Centuries* (Oxford: Oxford University Press, 2022, an English translation of the 1985 French original).

The idea of "Gnosticism" as a discrete phenomenon has been challenged: some scholars insist that it be regarded more as a sensibility or a style of thinking than as a defined sect with a discrete body of doctrine. Key authors in this area are Michael Williams, *Rethinking "Gnosticism": An Argument for Dismantling a Dubious Category* (Princeton, NJ: Princeton University Press, 1999); David Brakke, *The Gnostics* (Cambridge, MA: Harvard University Press, 2010); Karen L. King, *What Is Gnosticism?* (Cambridge, MA: Harvard University Press, 2003); Einar Thomassen, *The Spiritual Seed: The Church of the "Valentinians"* (Leiden: Brill, 2008); and, in *A Companion to Second-Century Christian "Heretics,"* edited by Antti Marjanen and Petri Luomanen (Leiden: Brill, 2005), the essay by Ismo Dunderberg, "The School of Valentinus," 64–99. On the rhetorical advantages of the heresiologists' accusations of Docetism ("appearance" Christology), see David Wilhite, "Was Marcion a Docetist? The Body of Evidence vs. Tertullian's Argument," *Vigiliae Christianae* 70 (2016): 1–36.

The texts from Nag Hammadi in English translations are available in *The Nag Hammadi Library*, revised edition, edited James M. Robinson (San Francisco: HarperSanFrancisco, 1990), and in *The Gnostic Scriptures*, second edition, by Bentley Layton and David Brakke (New Haven, CT: Yale University Press, 2021). Pertinent texts are also available in the collection edited by Werner Foerster, *Gnosis: A Selection of Gnostic Texts*, 2 volumes (Oxford: Clarendon, 1972); see especially 1:121–61 on Ptolemy, with the text of the *Letter to Flora*, excerpted from Epiphanius, at 1:155–61.

On Marcion, see the exhaustive treatment by Judith Lieu, *Marcion and the Making of a Heretic: God and Scripture in the Second Century* (Cambridge: Cambridge University Press, 2015), with generous bibliography. Jason D. BeDuhn, *The First New Testament: Marcion's Scriptural Canon* (Salem, OR: Polebridge, 2013), situates Marcion within the swirl of mid-second-century Christianities and presents a reconstruction of Marcion's gospel and of his collection of Pauline letters. For a recent prosopography of all these various second-century Christian figures, see M. David Litwa, *Found Christianities: Remaking the World of the Second Century CE* (London: T&T Clark, 2022). Marcion's legacy lived on in the later revelations of Mani, a third-century Mesopotamian Christian visionary and also a dedicated Paulinist. Iain Gardner and Samuel N. C. Lieu provide an excellent overview in *Manichaean Texts from the Roman Empire* (Cambridge: Cambridge University Press, 2004); Jason D. BeDuhn orients his discussion around ritual practices in *The Manichaean Body in Discipline and Practice* (Baltimore: Johns Hopkins University Press, 2000). For Augustine's continuing entanglements with Manichaeism, see BeDuhn's two-volume study *Augustine's Manichaean Dilemma* (Philadelphia: University of Pennsylvania Press, 2010 and 2013).

On Paul's many afterlives, see Benjamin L. White, *Remembering Paul: Ancient and Modern Contests over the Image of the Apostle* (New York: Oxford University Press, 2014), and the texts and interpretations collected by Wayne A. Meeks and John T. Fitzgerald, in *The Writings of St. Paul*, second edition (New York: W. W. Norton, 2007). J. Albert Harrill traces the post-Pauline trajectory in the Roman world in *Paul the Apostle: His Life and Legacy in their Roman Context* (Cambridge: Cambridge University Press, 2012), 97–166.

Women and Christian Origins, a classic study edited by Ross Shephard Kraemer and Mary Rose D'Angelo (New York: Oxford University Press, 1999), investigates representations of Christian women both in ancient texts and in modern scholarship. See also by Kraemer *Unreliable Witnesses: Religion, Gender, and History in the Greco-Roman Mediterranean* (New York: Oxford University Press, 2011). For images of women and the gendered discourse of ancient religious texts, see *Images of the Feminine in Gnosticism*, edited by Karen L. King (Philadelphia: Fortress, 1988). Elizabeth A. Clark, *History, Theory, Text: Historians and the Linguistic Turn* (Cambridge, MA: Harvard University Press, 2004) both established and explored the way that "rhetorical" women do theological and political work in patristic texts. *Ordained Women in the Early Church: A Documentary History*, edited and translated by Kevin Madigan and Carolyn Osiek (Baltimore: Johns Hopkins University Press, 2005), gathers references to women as deacons, presbyters, and bishops, but the meaning of the words *presbytera* and *episcopa* is contested. For a maximalist assessment of this evidence, arguing that women indeed functioned in ordained church offices, see the essays gathered in *Patterns of Women's Leadership in Early Christianity*, edited by Joan E. Taylor and Ilaria L. E. Ramelli (Oxford:

Oxford University Press, 2021). For "pagan" women in Roman society, see two excellent essays by Ramsay MacMullen, "Women in Public in the Roman Empire" (*Historia*, 1980) and "Women's Power in the Principate" (*Klio*, 1986), now gathered in MacMullen's *Changes in the Roman Empire: Essays in the Ordinary* (Princeton, NJ: Princeton University Press, 1990), 162–68 and 169–76.

Heresiology grows to be its own literary genre. On the double helix of anti-Jewish and antiheretical polemics in Justin, see especially Mattijs den Dulk's monograph *Between Jews and Heretics: Refiguring Justin Martyr's "Dialogue with Trypho"* (London: Routledge, 2018). On the features of early heresy writing as a literary genre, see Geoffrey S. Smith, *Guilt by Association: Heresy Catalogues in Early Christianity* (New York: Oxford University Press, 2015); for heresiology's debt to classical ethnography, see Todd S. Berzon, *Classifying Christians* (Oakland: University of California Press, 2012). See too the essays collected by Eduard Iricinschi and Holger M. Zellentin in *Heresy and Identity in Late Antiquity* (Tübingen: Mohr Siebeck, 2008).

The fourth-century involvement of the Christianizing state raised the stakes in this intra-Christian argument, when forms of schism became classified as "heresies" with legal disabilities. A premier instance of this is the construction and fate of "Arianism," which will be discussed in chapter 5, "Christ and Empire." On that fourth-century heresy hunter par excellence and the haunting of imperial Christianity by heretical "others," see Andrew S. Jacobs, *Epiphanius of Cyprus: A Cultural Biography of Late Antiquity* (Berkeley: University of California Press, 2021). The impact of Christianity on Roman law, and the development of legal definitions of religious deviance, are explored in the essays collected by R. McKitterick, C. Methuen, and A. Spicer, *The Church and the Law* (Cambridge: Cambridge University Press, 2020).

3. Persecution and Martyrdom

See two collections of martyr narratives: Herbert Musurillo, *The Acts of the Christian Martyrs* (Oxford: Clarendon, 1972), and Éric Rebillard, *Greek and Latin Narratives about the Ancient Martyrs* (Oxford: Oxford University Press, 2017). For a general history, W.H.C. Frend, *Martyrdom and Persecution in the Early Church* (Oxford: Blackwell, 1965), though now dated, remains a classic. Robin Lane Fox, *Pagans and Christians* (New York: Alfred A. Knopf, 1986), 418–62, provides a brisk and insightful overview, though his analysis of the martyrdom of Pionius (462–92), like that of Frend in general, takes the embedded anti-Judaism of the tale at its word as a description of flat fact. A gold-standard treatment remains the work of G.E.M. de Ste. Croix: his important essays are collected in *Christian Persecution, Martyrdom, and Orthodoxy*, edited by Michael Whitby and Joseph Streeter (Oxford: Oxford University Press, 2006). James Corke-Webster proposes a radically revisionist reconstruction of events, based on de Ste. Croix's fundamental model, in "By Whom Were the Early Christians Persecuted?," *Past and Present* 20 (2023): 1–45 (open access). Various Christians, he argues, may have been the ones who initiated the prosecution of Christian others.

Candida Moss, *The Other Christs* (New York: Oxford University Press, 2010), and *Ancient Christian Martyrdom* (New Haven, CT: Yale University Press, 2012), has compellingly presented the case for looking at martyrdom as a type of discursive practice. As Daniel Boyarin has wryly commented, "Being killed is an event. Martyrdom is a literary form"; see *Dying for God: Martyrdom and the Making of Christianity and Judaism* (Stanford, CA: Stanford University Press, 1999), 116; for his critique of Frend, see 127–30. Further on the idea of martyrdom and Christian identity formation, see Elizabeth Castelli, *Martyrdom and Memory: Early Christian Culture Making* (New York: Columbia University Press, 2004); Lucy Grig, *Making Martyrs in Late Antiquity* (London: Duckworth, 2004); and Shelly Matthews, *Perfect Martyr: The Stoning of Stephen and the Construction of Christian Identity* (New York: Oxford University Press, 2010). On the "salience" of identity—its indeterminacy, and its situational activation—see Éric Rebillard, *Christians and Their Many Identities in Late Antiquity: North Africa, 200–450 CE* (Ithaca, NY: Cornell University Press, 2012). On pre-Constantinian Christians as town councilors—men of means who sat on city councils, maintained public works, and even funded public spectacles—see Frank R. Trombley, "Christianity in Asia Minor: Observations from Epigraphy," in *Cambridge History of Religions in the Ancient World*, vol 2, edited by William Adler (Cambridge: Cambridge University Press, 2013), 341–68.

Éric Rebillard, *The Early Martyr Narratives: Neither Authentic Accounts nor Forgeries* (Philadelphia: University of Pennsylvania Press, 2021), has drawn attention to the formal fluidity of these texts. In light of the difficulties that they bring to any reconstruction of a chronology of events, he urges that they be entirely decoupled from the history of anti-Christian persecutions. On the proliferation of martyr narratives composed in the post-Constantinian period, with texts, see Michael Lapidge, *The Roman Martyrs: Introduction, Translations, and Commentary* (Oxford: Oxford University Press, 2018). Peter Brown explores the cultic expression of martyr piety in *The Cult of the Saints: Its Rise and Function in Latin Christianity*, second edition (Chicago: University of Chicago Press, 2015). For the continuities of martyr cults with traditional Roman practices around the veneration of the dead, see Ramsay MacMullen, *The Second Church: Popular Christianity A.D. 200–400* (Atlanta: Society of Biblical Literature, 2009).

For Decius's mandate to sacrifice as a security measure for the empire, see the classic article by James B. Rives, "The Decree of Decius and the Religion of the Empire," *JRS* 89 (1999): 135–54; see also Allen Brent, *Cyprian and Roman Carthage* (Cambridge: Cambridge University Press, 2010). On the religious motivation of Diocletian's action, see Elizabeth DePalma Digeser, *A Threat to Public Piety: Christians, Platonists, and the Great Persecution* (Ithaca, NY: Cornell University Press, 2012).

On the abiding invective of classical ethnographies, readily repurposed by pagans, Jews, and Christians alike when regarding the ethnic, thus religious "other," see especially Benjamin Isaac, *The Invention of Racism in Classical Antiquity* (Princeton, NJ: Princeton University Press, 2004); see also *The Routledge Handbook of Identity and Environment in the Classical and Medieval World*, edited by Rebecca Futo Kennedy and Molly Jones-Lewis (New York: Routledge, 2020). For historical context, in the Edinburgh History of Ancient Rome series, see the volumes by Jonathan Edmundson, *Imperial Rome AD 14 to 192: The First Two Centuries*; Clifford Ando, *Imperial Rome AD 193 to 284: The Critical Century*; and Jill Harries, *Imperial Rome AD 284 to 363: The New Empire*. On the politics of religious identity in the late empire, see Stephen Mitchell, *A History of the Later Roman Empire AD 284–641* (Oxford: Blackwell, 2007), 276–300. Specifically on Roman public entertainments, the narrative setting of many of the martyr stories, see Donald G. Kyle, *Spectacles of Death in Ancient Rome* (London: Routledge, 2001). On inter-Christian violence, and the ways that this compelled and supported the Donatists' identification as the church of the martyrs, see Brent D. Shaw, *Sacred Violence: African Christians and Sectarian Hatred in the Age of Augustine* (Cambridge: Cambridge University Press, 2011). On the intra-Christian repurposing of the rhetoric of martyrdom, see *Heirs of Roman Persecution: Studies on a Christian and Para-Christian Discourse in Late Antiquity*, edited by Éric Fournier and Wendy Mayer (London: Routledge, 2021). Fournier speaks of deployments of martyr rhetoric against the Vandals in "Eternal Persecutions: Cultural Memory, Trauma and Martyrs in Vandal North Africa," in *The Making of Saints in Late Antique North Africa*, edited by Sabine Panzram and Nathalie Klinck (Stuttgart: Franz Steiner Verlag, forthcoming).

Further on intra-Christian violence, see Michael Gaddis, *There Is No Crime for Those Who Have Christ* (Berkeley: University of California Press, 2010). On Christian violence more generally, Peter Brown, "Christianization and Religious Conflict," in *Cambridge Ancient History: The Late Empire, A.D. 337–425*, edited by A. Cameron and P. Garnsey (Cambridge: Cambridge University Press, 1998), 632–64.

4. The Future of the End

Visions of the End were powerfully woven into the messianic movement that formed around Jesus: the End, after all, was when redemption would be realized. But would this end-time redemption be at the individual's end (thus, immediately after death) or corporate (thus, delayed until Christ's Second Coming)? Paul, our earliest evidence, speaks of the dead as having "fallen asleep." They will awaken at the coming of Christ. On Paul's vision of apocalyptic redemption, and its location in the heavens (Philippians 3.20), see Matthew Thiessen, *Paul and the Gentile Problem* (New York: Oxford University Press, 2016), especially 129–60. For the ways that Paul's ideas on pneumatic transformation sit within broader

Greco-Roman patterns, see M. David Litwa, *We Are Being Transformed: Deification in Paul's Soteriology* (Berlin: DeGruyter, 2012) and *Posthuman Transformation in Ancient Mediterranean Thought* (Cambridge: Cambridge University Press, 2021).

Insistence on the resurrection of the physical body, by contrast, supported terrestrial visions of God's kingdom, with corresponding hopes for effortless abundance, peace, progeny, and plenty. For an exploration of these teachings, and the ways that they are reinterpreted, see Paula Fredriksen, "Apocalypse and Redemption: From John of Patmos to Augustine of Hippo," *Vigiliae Christianae* 45.2 (1991): 151–83. See also Outi Lehtipuu, *Debates over the Resurrection of the Dead* (Oxford: Oxford University Press, 2015). On the "scientific" strategy of dating the End, see Richard Landes, "'Lest the Millennium Be Fulfilled': Apocalyptic Expectations and the Pattern of Western Chronography," in *The Use and Abuse of Eschatology in the Middle Ages*, edited by W. Verbeke, D. Verhelst, and A. Welkenhuysen (Louvain: Presses Universitaires, 1988), 137–211, with copious citations to primary materials; see also Oded Irshai, "Dating the Eschaton: Jewish and Christian Apocalyptic Calculations in Late Antiquity," in *Apocalyptic Time*, edited by Albert Baumgarten (Leiden: Brill, 2000), 113–53. On Augustine's secularization of time—his strategy for calming millenarian countdowns—the classic essay is Robert Markus's *Saeculum* (Cambridge: Cambridge University Press, 1970).

On varying visions of the afterlife—and their imbrication in the economics of piety and the impulse to asceticism—see Peter Brown, *The Ransom of the Soul. Afterlife and Wealth in Early Western Christianity* (Cambridge, MA: Harvard University Press, 2015). Ideas on the fate of the dead vary widely, but all presuppose an afterlife. Alan F. Segal, *Life After Death* (New York: Doubleday, 2004), and Richard Bauckham, *The Fate of the Dead* (Atlanta: Society of Biblical Literature, 1998), offer two rich explorations. Tours of heaven and hell became a Christian literary genre, on which most recently, see Bart D. Ehrman, *Journeys to Heaven and Hell: Tours of the Afterlife in the Early Christian Tradition* (New Haven, CT: Yale University Press, 2022). Primary texts may be found in Edgar Hennecke and Wilhelm Schneemelcher, *New Testament Apocrypha*, 2 volumes (Philadelphia: Westminster, 1963 and 1965); and in *The Apocryphal New Testament*, edited by J. K. Elliott (Oxford: Oxford University

Press, 1993). On the "invention of damned bodies," see Meghan R. Henning, *Hell Hath No Fury* (New Haven, CT: Yale University Press, 2021); on their (aestheticized) heavenly counterparts, see Candida Moss, *Divine Bodies: Resurrecting Perfection in the New Testament and Early Christianity* (New Haven, CT: Yale University Press, 2019). Henning and Moss have together explored the relation of visions of heaven and hell with Roman techniques of torture and bodily fragmentation and with ancient medical ideas about wholeness, health, and identity in "Pulling Apart and Piecing Together: Wholeness and Fragmentation in Early Christian Visions of the Afterlife," *Journal of the American Academy of Religion* 20 (2023): 1–14, https://doi.org/10.1093/jaarel/lfac069.

For a comparison of Origen and Augustine on the afterlife—thus, on salvation—see Paula Fredriksen, *Sin: The Early History of an Idea* (Princeton, NJ: Princeton University Press, 2012), chapter 3, "A Rivalry of Genius." Finally, on Augustine's construction of eschatological flesh, both of the damned and of the saved, see David G. Hunter, "Books 21 and 22: The End of the Body; Heaven and Hell in the *City of God*," in *The Cambridge Companion to Augustine's "City of God,"* edited by David Vincent Meconi (Cambridge: Cambridge University Press, 2023), 276–96.

5. Christ and Empire

In Jewish scriptures, the nation of Israel is designated as God's "son" (e.g., Exodus 4.22; Hosea 11.1). So are the kings of David's line, which is to say, "son of God" can function as a messianic title. On the Jewish backstory for this term, see especially Adela Yarbro Collins and John J. Collins, *King and Messiah as Son of God* (Grand Rapids, MI: Eerdmans, 2008); on the term's referential flexibility, see Matthew V. Novenson, *The Grammar of Messianism* (New York: Oxford University Press, 2017). On divine sons not begotten but made—that is, by adoption—see Michael Peppard, *The Son of God in the Roman World: Divine Sonship in Its Social and Political Context* (New York: Oxford University Press, 2011). On the early divinization of Jesus, see M. David Litwa, *Jesus Deus: The Early Christian Depiction of Jesus as a Mediterranean God* (Minneapolis: Fortress, 2014). James B. Rives provides an excellent orientation in the richly diverse world of traditional cults in *Religion in the Roman Empire* (Oxford: Blackwell, 2007).

John Dillon, *The Middle Platonists* (Ithaca, NY: Cornell University Press, 1977), and R. T. Wallis, *Neoplatonism* (New York: Charles Scribner's Sons, 1972), introduce the broad outlines of these two schools of thought, which were fundamental to later developments in Christian theologies. Primary texts are collected in George Boys-Stones, *Platonist Philosophy 80 BC to AD 250: An Introduction and Collection of Sources in Translation* (Cambridge: Cambridge University Press, 2018). On Philo, the essays collected in *The Cambridge Companion to Philo*, edited by Adam Kamesar (Cambridge: Cambridge University Press, 2009). The question of Paul's Christology is addressed by several of the essays in *Monotheism and Christology*, edited by Matthew V. Novenson (Leiden: Brill, 2020).

Henry Chadwick, *Early Christian Thought and the Classical Tradition* (Oxford: Oxford University Press, 1966) and *The Early Church* (London: Penguin Books, 1967, rev. ed. 1993) orient the reader in the congested world of patristic theology and the development of Christian doctrines: further bibliographies are included in both of these texts as well. Texts are collected in *A New Eusebius: Documents Illustrating the History of the Church to AD 337*, edited by J. Stevenson, revised by W.H.C. Frend (London: SPCK, 1987); in *Christianity in Late Antiquity, 300–450 C.E.*, edited by Bart D. Ehrman and Andrew S. Jacobs (New York: Oxford University Press, 2004); and—with a nice leavening of pagan materials—*Paganism and Christianity, 100–425 C.E.: A Sourcebook*, edited by Ramsay MacMullen and Eugene N. Lane (Minneapolis: Fortress, 1992). See also the texts gathered and translated in *The Cambridge Edition of Early Christian Writings*, volume 3, *Christ: Through the Nestorian Controversy*, edited by Mark DelCogliano (Cambridge: Cambridge University Press, 2022).

Mountains of scholarship have formed on the question of Constantine and his effects on evolving Christianities. On the interrelation of empire, bishops, and power politics, see especially H. A. Drake, *Constantine and the Bishops: The Politics of Intolerance* (Baltimore: Johns Hopkins University Press, 2000; with extensive bibliography); see also

T. D. Barnes, *Athanasius and Constantine: Theology and Politics in the Constantinian Empire* (Cambridge, MA: Harvard University Press, 1993). On the urban violence orchestrated by contesting bishops, see Carlos Galvão-Sobrinho, *Doctrine and Power: Theological Controversy and Christian Leadership in the Later Roman Empire* (Berkeley: University of California Press, 2013). Beginning in the fourth century, bishops were well integrated with urban elites and functioned like them: see Claudia Rapp, *Holy Bishops in Late Antiquity* (Berkeley: University of California Press, 2005), especially 208–33.

On Constantine's Roman religious context, see J.H.W.G. Liebeschuetz, *Continuity and Change in Roman Religion* (Oxford: Oxford University Press, 1979). On Constantine and civic politics, see Noel Lenski, *Constantine and the Cities* (Philadelphia: University of Pennsylvania Press, 2016). See too James Corke-Webster, *Eusebius and Empire: Constructing Church and Rome in the "Ecclesiastical History"* (Cambridge: Cambridge University Press, 2019), and Jeremy M. Schott, *Christianity, Empire, and the Making of Religion in Late Antiquity* (Philadelphia: University of Pennsylvania Press, 2008). On the theological (and political) ins and outs of the Christological debates, see Lewis Ayres, *Nicaea and Its Legacy* (Oxford: Oxford University Press, 2004); exhaustively, R.P.C. Hanson, *The Search for the Christian Doctrine of God: Arian Controversy 318–381 AD* (Edinburgh: T&T Clark, 1988); and the essays gathered in *The Cambridge History of Christianity: Origins to Constantine*, edited by Margaret M. Mitchell and Frances M. Young (Cambridge: Cambridge University Press, 2006). A still valuable survey of the period is Ramsay MacMullen, *Christianizing the Roman Empire, AD 100–400* (New Haven, CT: Yale University Press, 1984). On the ways that church councils did (and did not) work, see also by Ramsay MacMullen *Voting about God in Early Church Councils* (New Haven, CT: Yale University Press, 2006). See too Gillian Clark, *Christianity and Roman Society* (Cambridge: Cambridge University Press, 2004). Texts are available in P. R. Coleman-Norton, *Roman State and Christian Church: A Collection of Legal Documents to AD 535* (London: SPCK, 1966).

For the Roman historical context, see Jill Harries, *Imperial Rome AD 284 to 363: The New Empire* (Edinburgh: Edinburgh University Press,

2012); A. D. Lee, *From Rome to Byzantium, AD 363 to 565* (Edinburgh: Edinburgh University Press, 2013); Stephen Mitchell, *A History of the Later Roman Empire, AD 284–641* (Oxford: Blackwell, 2007). On the unanticipated shift from "pagan" to "Christian" in the fourth century, and the ways that things changed as well as stayed the same, see Edward J. Watts, *The Final Pagan Generation: Rome's Unexpected Path to Christianity* (Berkeley: University of California Press, 2015). "The story of this century," observes H. A. Drake, meaning the tale of this transition between Constantine and Theodosius, "is a story of a change in the meaning of what it meant to be a Roman. An important marker of this change is the power and leverage over public affairs that came to be exercised by Christian bishops"; see *A Century of Miracles: Christians, Pagans, Jews, and the Supernatural, 312–410* (New York: Oxford University Press, 2017), 3.

Éric Fournier speaks of the repurposing of martyr rhetoric against the Vandals in "Eternal Persecutions: Cultural Memory, Trauma and Martyrs in Vandal North Africa," in *The Making of Saints in Late Antique North Africa*, edited by Sabine Panzram and Nathalie Klinck (Stuttgart: Franz Steiner Verlag, forthcoming). Peter Brown, *Through the Eye of a Needle* (Princeton, NJ: Princeton University Press, 2012), traces the effects of the economy on the dissolution of the western empire, and the ways that this relates to "barbarian" immigrations; his earlier essay *Power and Persuasion in Late Antiquity: Towards a Christian Empire* (Madison: University of Wisconsin Press, 1992) gives a riveting tour through the political and cultural thickets of this period. Brown's *World of Late Antiquity* (New York: W. W. Norton, 1971) remains an indispensable guide to the period.

6. The Redemption of the Flesh

Peter Brown's *Body and Society: Men, Women and Sexual Renunciation in Early Christianity* (New York: Columbia University Press, 1988), gives a vivid overview of the development of ascetic ideas and behaviors in antiquity. That they were more honored in the breach than in the observance prompted his discussion of the Christian "silent majority." Robin

Lane Fox's chapter, "Living Like Angels," in *Pagans and Christians in the Mediterranean World from the Second Century to the Conversion of Constantine* (New York: Alfred A. Knopf, 1986), 336–74, provides a learned and lively review of these same issues. For an astringent assessment of ascetic spirituality, see the classic essay by E. R. Dodds, *Pagan and Christian in an Age of Anxiety* (Cambridge: Cambridge University Press, 1965).

On the development of the discourse of asceticism, see especially Elizabeth A. Clark, *Reading Renunciation: Asceticism and Scripture in Early Christianity* (Princeton, NJ: Princeton University Press, 1999). See also her study *The Origenist Controversy* (Princeton, NJ: Princeton University Press, 1992), which includes a sensitive consideration of its late Latin inflections in the arguments between Jerome, Jovinian, Augustine, and Pelagius. Kathy L. Gaca, responding to Michel Foucault's *History of Sexuality*, contextualizes the development of Christian ideologies of asceticism within a consideration of foregoing Greek traditions, in *The Making of Fornication: Eros, Ethics, and Political Reform in Greek Philosophy and Early Christianity* (Berkeley: University of California Press, 2003).

On the wild and woolly asceticism of the Desert Fathers, and the transition through different genres of practice to the organized monastery, a classic study is Derwas Chitty's *The Desert a City* (Oxford: Basil Blackwell, 1966). The argument that the flight to the desert was stimulated by the loss of the option of martyrdom—asceticism replacing martyrdom—is frustrated by chronology: Anthony precedes Diocletian. David Brakke has investigated the ways in which different styles of Egyptian asceticism reiterated contests over different models of authority—that of the school (Clement, Origen, Hieracas), which tolerated theological speculation, focused on the charismatic teacher, and welcomed the active participation of women; and that of the bishop, which focused on urban politics, control of church welfare networks, female seclusion, and doctrinal "policy" (Alexander and Athanasius)—in *Athanasius and Asceticism* (Baltimore: Johns Hopkins University Press, 1995). On the monk's participation in the cosmic struggle between angels and demons, and the ways that this distinguished charismatic Christian figures from pagan competitors, see Brakke's *Demons and the Making of the Monk* (Cambridge, MA: Harvard University Press, 2006). Further on the development of monasticism, also by Brakke, see "Holy Men and Women of the Desert," in *The Oxford Handbook of Christian Monasticism*, edited by Bernice M. Kaczynski, with Thomas Sullivan (New York: Oxford University Press, 2020), 35–50. On the surprisingly intergenerational quality of monastic life, and the experience of children in monasteries, see Carolyn Schroeder, *Children and Family in Late Antique Egyptian Monasticism* (Cambridge: Cambridge University Press, 2020).

The prominence of aristocratic women in Christian ascetic movements has commanded a huge amount of attention. Elizabeth A. Clark's contributions have remained fundamental: see her classic study *Ascetic Piety and Women's Faith: Essays on Late Ancient Christianity* (Lewiston, NY: Edwin Mellen, 1986). She has also edited a collection of important articles by various specialists in "Asceticism, Monasticism and Gender in Early Christianity," a virtual issue of *Church History* 90 (2021). See too Kate Cooper, *The Virgin and the Bride: Idealized Womanhood in Late Antiquity* (Cambridge, MA: Harvard University Press, 1996), on the social and religious changes wrought by the developing ascetic sensibility; and Susannah Elm, *Virgins of God: The Making of Asceticism in Late Antiquity* (Oxford: Clarendon, 1994), for an exhaustive examination and comparison of female asceticism in Asia Minor and in Egypt. For the ways that asceticism could tip over into accusations of heresy, see Virginia Burrus, *The Making of a Heretic: Gender, Authority, and the Priscillianist Controversy* (Berkeley: University of California Press, 1995). For women in Egyptian monasticism, see Rebecca Krawiec, *Shenoute and the Women of the White Monastery* (New York: Oxford University Press, 2002).

For an appreciation of Manichaean asceticism and its ritual expressions, see the study by Jason D. BeDuhn, *The Manichaean Body: In Discipline and Ritual* (Baltimore: Johns Hopkins University Press, 2000).

Controversies raged in the Latin West over the status of marriage vis-à-vis celibacy and virginity, on which, see David G. Hunter, *Marriage, Celibacy and Heresy in Ancient Christianity: The Jovinianist Controversy* (Oxford: Oxford University Press, 2007). Augustine's voice ultimately dominated. For Augustine's views on the resurrection of the flesh, see again David G. Hunter, "Books 21 & 22: The End of the Body; Heaven and Hell in *The City of God*," in *The Cambridge Companion to Augustine's "City of God*," edited by David Vincent Meconi (Cambridge: Cambridge University Press, 2023), 276–96. For a comparison with Origen, see Paula Fredriksen, *Sin: The Early History of an Idea* (Princeton, NJ: Princeton University Press, 2012), 97–134; for Augustine's contest both with Manichees and with Pelagians, see Paula Fredriksen, "Beyond the Body/Soul Dichotomy: Augustine on Paul against the Manichees and the Pelagians," *Recherches augustiniennes* 23 (1988): 87–114.

7. Pagan and Christian

For a consideration of the origins of the word *paganus* and its fourth-century application, see Alan Cameron, *The Last Pagans of Rome* (Oxford: Oxford University Press, 2011), 14–32. He asks, "How did Latin *paganus* come to acquire its most famous meaning?" He also challenges the older view that the late fourth century saw something like a pagan "last stand," a reconstruction that dramatizes the removal of the altar of the goddess Victory from the Senate in 382. Christians within the city at that time were consumed with (or distracted by) an internal controversy, namely the status of the married Christian versus that of the virgin or celibate, Damasus and Jerome championing asceticism against the more moderate position of Helvidius: see Robert R. Chenault, "The Controversy over the Altar of Victory," in *Pagans and Christians in Late Antique Rome*, edited by Michele Salzman, Marianne Sághy, and Rita Lizzi Testa (Cambridge: Cambridge University Press, 2016), 46–63. See also, in the same volume, the essays by Thomas Jürgash ("Christians and the Invention of Paganism in the Late Roman Empire," 115–38) and by Alan Cameron ("Were Pagans Afraid to Speak Their Minds in a Christian World? The Correspondence of Symmachus," 64–111). Cameron concludes, "Ecclesiastics might thunder against paganism in all its forms, but in the real world government turned to those with influence, whatever their religious beliefs."

On the vicissitudes of the city of Rome in late antiquity, see especially Michele Renee Salzman, *The Falls of Rome: Crises, Resilience, and Resurgence in Late Antiquity* (Cambridge: Cambridge University Press, 2021).

On the (slow) Christianization of the senatorial elite, see also by Salzman, *The Making of a Christian Aristocracy: Social and Religious Change in the Western Roman Empire* (Cambridge, MA: Harvard University Press, 2002).

Rodney Stark, *The Rise of Christianity: A Sociologist Reconsiders History* (Princeton, NJ: Princeton University Press, 1996), attempted a demographical study of the early churches based on a mathematical model of a steady rate of growth of 40 percent per decade. That rate derived from his study of modern sectarian conversions. He began with an estimate figure of one thousand as the total number of Christians in the year 40 CE and then ran the numbers to the year 350, by which time, he opined, there would have been 33,882,008 Christians out of a total population of sixty million. Unfortunately, Stark read the literature of the proto-orthodox as representative of Christianity in toto. He also uncritically took it at its word, especially about its own superior morality. This meant, Stark said, that Christian men rejected the sexual license that characterized pagan men (which would have come as news to Augustine); that Christians did not commit adultery, so that intact families guaranteed the growth rate; that Christians did not practice infant exposure as a means of reproductive control, again propelling growth rate; that martyrs evinced composure that "amazed and unsettled many pagans," inspiring conversions, which propelled growth rate; and so on. The patina of scientific thinking and the reassuring enlistment of numbers, figures, and percentages masks the degree to which Stark did not know how to read his sources. *The Rise of Christianity* is in many ways an act of demographical wistful thinking.

Bart D. Ehrman's popular treatment *The Triumph of Christianity: How a Forbidden Religion Swept the World* (New York: Simon and Schuster, 2018) adapts some of Stark's method to explain why and how Rome became Christian.

"Magic" as a contested type of ritual performance is investigated by David Frankfurter, "Christianity and Paganism: Egypt," in *The Cambridge History of Christianity: Constantine to c. 600*, edited by Augustus Casiday and Frederick W. Norris (Cambridge: Cambridge University Press, 2007), 173–88. He argues there that "syncretism is essential to

Christianization, not its by-product" (175). He also speaks there inter alia about "oracular tickets" as amulets. Frankfurter has also edited the definitive *Guide to the Study of Ancient Magic* (Leiden: Brill, 2019). The same *Cambridge History* volume investigates local paganisms in Asia Minor (Frank R. Trombley, 189–209), Italy (Michele Salzman, 210–30), and North Africa (Anna Leone, 231–47). On the ways that both "magic" and "paganism" function as discursive categories—a verbal way of "othering"—in Christian polemics and in Roman law, see Maijastina Kahlos, *Religious Dissent in Late Antiquity, 350–450* (New York: Oxford University Press, 2020). Demons figure prominently in Christian discourse on traditional cult: for the mid-second century, see e.g., Justin, *Dialogue with Trypho* and his *First Apology* and *Second Apology*; for the early third century, see Tertullian, *On Spectacles* and *On Idolatry*, and Origen, *Against Celsus*; for the fourth century, see especially books 7 through 9 of Augustine's *City of God*.

Pagan "monotheism" has been explored in three excellent anthologies: *Pagan Monotheism in Late Antiquity*, edited by Polymnia Athanassiadi and Michael Frede (Oxford: Oxford University Press, 1999); *One God: Pagan Monotheism in the Roman Empire*, edited by Stephen Mitchell and Peter van Nuffelen (Cambridge: Cambridge University Press, 2010); and, by the same editors, *Monotheism between Pagans and Christians in Late Antiquity* (Leuven: Peeters, 2010). On what I have called the neutralization of pagan civic cults in the interests of public peace, see the classic study by Robert A. Markus, *The End of Ancient Christianity* (Cambridge: Cambridge University Press, 1990).

Ramsay MacMullen has traced the seesaw of Christians and pagans for this whole period. See especially his *Christianizing the Roman Empire (A.D. 100–400)* (New Haven, CT: Yale University Press, 1984) and, on the cemetery celebrations of the cult of the saints, *The Second Church: Popular Christianity A.D. 200–400* (Atlanta: Society of Biblical Literature, 2009). The quotation about the Triune God in chapter 7, on page 194, comes from *The Second Church*, page 106. Christians of all social classes honored the martyrs: there was no split between popular and elite spirituality when it came to the cult of the saints. See *Architects of Piety: The Cappadocian Fathers and the Cult of the Martyrs* by Vasiliki M. Limberis

(New York: Oxford University Press, 2011). On the development of Christian identity as a three-way process, involving Jews as well as pagans, see Isabella Sandwell, *Religious Identity in Late Antiquity: Greeks, Jews and Christians in Antioch* (Cambridge: Cambridge University Press, 2007); also, more generally on the "indeterminancy" of Christian identity, see Éric Rebillard, *Christians and Their Many Identities in Late Antiquity: North Africa, 200–450 CE* (Ithaca, NY: Cornell University Press, 2012). Finally, on the bishops' demonizing of outsiders (heretics, pagans, and Jews) and their spaces (especially the temple and the synagogue) while developing sacramental rituals against them, see Dayna S. Kalleres, *City of Demons: Violence, Ritual and Christian Power in Late Antiquity* (Berkeley: University of California Press, 2015).

The *Theodosian Code* ultimately contained more legislation against heretics (some thirteen laws) than against pagans (only six), supporting the conclusion that heresy was considered the greatest threat to imperial well-being. Pragmatism sometimes prevailed—when fending off external threats, emperors might briefly relax internal antiheretical directives— but the restoration of stability was invariably accompanied by a return to repression. Éric Fournier investigates this dynamic in "Anticipating Disasters: Forbearance and the Limits of Religious Coercion in Late Roman North Africa," *Studies in Late Antiquity*, forthcoming. For the primary texts of imperial legislation, see Clyde Pharr, *The Theodosian Code* (Princeton, NJ: Princeton University Press, 1952). Book 16 contains the rulings on right religion.

On the effects of Christianization on other Mediterranean religious cultures, see Edward J. Watts, *The Final Pagan Generation* (Berkeley: University of California Press, 2015); see also the important essay by Jaclyn Maxwell, "Paganism and Christianization," in *The Oxford Handbook of Late Antiquity*, edited Scott Fitzgerald Johnson (New York: Oxford University Press, 2012), 849–75. Finally, on how Christianization affected a change in ways of conducting learned argument, and even a change in the concept and format of the book, see Mark Letteney, *The Christianization of Knowledge in Late Antiquity* (Cambridge: Cambridge University Press, 2023).

SOURCES INDEX

NAMES AND PLACES INDEX

CHURCH COUNCILS

SUBJECT INDEX

adoptionism, 118, 119, 219

allegory: and philosophy, 115; as technique for reading Scripture, 19, 24, 40, 45, 100

ancestral custom: as definition of "religion," 61, 62, 105; as Jewish practices, xix, 2, 5, 65; repudiated by gentile Christianities, 18; and Roman law, 29

Antichrist, 32, 94, 129 (Christian emperors); as Nero, 93, 101

apocalyptic eschatology: and the Book of Revelation, 93; calculations of, 96, 100, 104; and Christ's Second Coming, 92; continuing expectations of, 94; definition, xvi; and Essenes, 146; and ethnicity, xvi; and the fall of Rome, 101, 104; and Jerusalem, 7; and Jesus, xvi; and Jewish restoration theology, 91; and Jewish universalism, xvi, 205; and Montanism, 56; and Paul, xvi, 11, 64–65, 176; postponed due dates, 34, 48; resistance to, 99–100, 103

apostles, 8, 9, 31 34, 42; and episcopal succession, 12, 124; Junia, 49; literary afterlives of, 47, 154; Paul and Mani, 54; and Rome, 101, 187, 141

Arianism, 57, 121, 126–27, 134, 140

asceticism, 52; apocryphal acts of the apostles, 151; and Manichaeism, 53–54; and Marcion, 149–50; and marriage, 161–167; pagan and Jewish forms of, 145–48; and Priscillian, 57, 152, 159; social forms of, 156–59, 170

Bar Kokhba, 16, 20

bishops: apostles as, 124; and Arian controversy, 121, 140; at Chalcedon, 137; and Constantine, 53, 81, 123, 125, 127, 138, 139, 142, 188, 192, 202–3; and control, 52, 56, 57, 86, 87, 124–25, 129–30, 137, 152–57, 160, 170, 179, 181; and creeds, 115; and Cyprian, 78; increasing power of, 29; and Julian, 21, 131, 132, 186; at Nicaea, 126; as patrons, 124, 127, 171, 203; and Theodosius, 134–35; and urban violence, 139, 142

body: of Christ, 46, 149; of God, 114, 121, 163; of martyrs, 86–87, 192; resurrection of, xviii, 46, 87, 99, 103–4, 108, 110–112, 149; soul's relation to, xviii, 99, 105, 115, 145, 148, 162–69, 183; of spirit, 93, 99, 112, 116, 163–166, 199.

celibacy, 145, 146, 152, 162–66; and Manichees, 161; and Marcion, 43–44, 48, 148–50; radical forms of, 153–54, 159; and virginity, 160; and women, 155, 156, 189. *See also* asceticism; body

Chalcedon, council of, 88, 137–38, 141–42, 219

Christology, 116–18, 121–30, 149; and *homoousia*, 126, 129, 141, 195; and Nestorius, 136–38. *See also* Arianism

circumcision: and gentiles, 10, 24, 31–32; of Jesus, 26; and Jews, 13

conversion: of Constantine, 53, 72, 102, 122, 131, 193; of groups, 97, 139, 200; to Judaism, 202; of Roman aristocrats, 189

of Jerusalem, 14–17, 20, 65, 93; fall of in 410 CE, 55, 101, 102, 103, 167; Paul's letter to, 2, 49, 187; and political stability, 4; and religious diversity, 61, 70; and right *religio*, 58–59, 61, 62, 140, 205; and universal citizenship, 76, 197

Sabellianism, 119, 120, 121, 136
sacraments: and bishops, 78, 124, 153, 158, 180, 181, 193, 194, 203; and *mageia*, xviii, 172, 180–81, 194; and ritual expertise, 180, 181, 194; and second baptism, 82 (Donatists)
Sophia ("Wisdom"), 115; and Valentinus, 40, 52

synagogue: and Christians, 6, 18, 27, 28, 198; and God-fearers, 6, 8, 9, 64, 205; as Jewish assembly, xv, 15; and resistance to Christ-movement, 10, 13, 64; and Roman law, 29, 135, 139 (Callinicum); and spread of Christ-movement, 8, 9, 12

Theodosian Code, 29, 30, 58, 83, 134, 159, 185, 189, 198, 217, 222
Theotokos ("God-bearer"), 136
Thessalonica, Edict of (Theodosius I), 133, 216, 221
Toleration, Edict of (Galerius), 125, 215

Unity, Edict of (Honorius), 82